Paul Hattaway, a native New Zealander, has served the Church in Asia for most of his life. He is an expert on the Chinese Church, and author of *The Heavenly Man*, *An Asian Harvest*, *Operation China* and many other books. He and his wife Joy are the founders of Asia Harvest (www.asiaharvest.org), which supports thousands of indigenous missionaries and has provided millions of Bibles to Christians throughout Asia.

Also by Paul Hattaway:

The Heavenly Man

An Asian Harvest

Operation China

China's Christian Martyrs

SHANDONG

The Revival Province

Paul Hattaway

First published in Great Britain in 2018

Also published in 2018 by Asia Harvest, www.asiaharvest.org

Society for Promoting Christian Knowledge
36 Causton Street
London SW1P 4ST
www.spck.org.uk

Author's agent: The Piquant Agency, 183 Platt Lane, Manchester M14 7FB, UK

British Library Cataloguing-in-Publication Data
A catalogue record for this book is available from the British Library

ISBN 978–0–281–07888–2
eBook ISBN 978–0–281–07889–9

Typeset by Fakenham Prepress Solutions, Fakenham, Norfolk NR21 8NN
First printed in Great Britain by Jellyfish Print Solutions
Subsequently digitally reprinted in Great Britain

eBook by Fakenham Prepress Solutions, Fakenham, Norfolk NR21 8NN

Produced on paper from sustainable forests

Shandong

山东

"East of the Mountains"

Map of China showing Shandong Province

Shandong

Pronounced:	Shahn-dong
Old spelling:	Shantung
Population:	89,971,789 (2000)
	95,792,719 (2010)
	101,613,649 (2020)
Area:	60,700 sq. miles (157,100 sq. km)
Population density:	1,600 people per sq. mile (620 per sq. km)
Capital city:	Jinan 3,527,942

Largest cities (2010):		
	Qingdao	3,990,942
	Zibo	2,261,717
	Yantai	1,797,861
	Linyi	1,522,488
	Weifang	1,261,582
	Tai'an	1,123,541

Administrative divisions:		
	Prefectures:	17
	Counties:	140
	Towns:	1,941

Major ethnic groups (2000):		
	Han Chinese	89,339,046 (99.2 percent)
	Hui	497,597 (0.5 percent)
	Manchu	33,527 (0.1 percent)
	Korean	27,795 (0.1 percent)
	Mongol	23,743 (0.1 percent)

Contents

Contents

Foreword

Like the apostle Luke, the author of The China Chronicles is a faithful servant called by the Lord. This God-fearing man is a devout prayer warrior who studies the Bible carefully and walks in the ways of the Lord. Paul Hattaway was stirred by the Holy Spirit to record the testimonies of God's people since the gospel first reached China during the Tang Dynasty (AD 635) to the present time.

He has expertly woven little-known stories of both revival and persecution into the narrative, giving a blessed overview of the work of the Holy Spirit in my homeland.

The cross of Jesus Christ is able to save. His followers have always believed that the gospel will transform China into a nation filled with disciples who love the Lord, a nation that overflows with heaven's blessings. By faith, the Chinese Church has overcome fierce opposition to spread the good news with great zeal. Because of their sacrifices and willingness to lay down their lives, they have produced a fruitful harvest for the kingdom of God, for Jesus said, "unless a kernel of wheat falls to the ground and dies, it remains only a single seed. But if it dies, it produces many seeds" (John 12.24).

I remember in the early 1980s—when the Chinese house churches were undergoing severe persecution and many of our co-workers were imprisoned—our favorite songs at the time were "Be the Lord's Witness to the Ends of the Earth", and "Martyrs for the Lord." When we sang the words "To be a martyr for the Lord, to be a martyr for the Lord," everyone would cry out, "Lord, send me to preach the gospel! I am willing to follow you! I am willing to be a martyr to glorify your name." Praise the Lord! God's time has come, and China is experiencing a rich harvest that has grown out of the ground watered by the tears and blood of those martyrs.

I believe these books are not only a gift to the people of China, but that God will use them to inspire Christians everywhere to obey God's call. May we serve with a willing heart, eager to lay down our lives, so that the Great Commission might be completed and the gospel will reach everyone who has yet to know Jesus, the risen Savior. Hallelujah! I believe this gospel of salvation will be preached to the ends of the earth, even back to Jerusalem, before the blessed return of our Lord. Amen.

A servant of God,
Brother Yun ('The Heavenly Man')

Preface

Over many years and generations, the followers of Jesus in China have set their hearts to be the witnesses of Christ to the nation. Many have paid a great price for their ministry, and the brutal persecutions they have endured for the faith have often been unimaginable.

The Bible commands all believers to "Go into all the world and preach the gospel to all creation" (Mark 16.15). Many foreign missionaries responded to this command in the past, traveling to China to proclaim the word of God. They blessed the land with their message of new life in Christ, and also suffered greatly when the darkness clashed with God's light. Their faithful service in spite of great hardship was a beautiful example for Chinese believers to emulate as they served God.

China today still urgently needs more servants and laborers to take the gospel throughout the land. God is looking for people who will stand up and declare, "Lord, here am I. Please send me!"

The day of our Lord is near. May your hearts be encouraged by the testimonies of what the Lord Jesus Christ has done in China, to the praise of his glorious name!

May the Lord raise up more testimonies that would glorify his name in our generation, the next generation, and for evermore!

Lord, you are the victorious king. Blessed are those who follow you to the end!

A humble servant of Christ,
Moses Xie (1918–2011)*

---

* The late Moses Xie wrote this Preface for The China Chronicles prior to his death in 2011. He was a highly respected Chinese house church leader who spent 23 years of his life in prison for the name of Jesus Christ.

The China Chronicles overview

Many people are aware of the extraordinary explosion of Christianity throughout China in recent decades, with the Church now numbering in excess of 100 million members. Few, however, know how this miracle has occurred. The China Chronicles series is an ambitious project to document the advance of Christianity in each province of China from the time the gospel was first introduced to the present day.

The genesis for this project came at a meeting I attended in the year 2000, where leaders of the Chinese house church movements expressed the need for their members to understand how God established his kingdom throughout China.

As a result, it is planned that these books will be translated into Chinese and distributed widely among the Church, both in China and overseas. Millions of Chinese Christians know little of their spiritual legacy, and my prayer is that multitudes would be strengthened, edified and challenged to carry the torch of the Holy Spirit to their generation.

My intention is not to present readers with a dry list of names and dates but to bring alive the marvelous stories of how God has caused his kingdom to take root and flourish in the world's most populated country.

I consider it a great honor to write these books, especially as I have been entrusted, through hundreds of hours of interviews conducted throughout China, with many testimonies that have never previously been shared in public.

Another reason for compiling The China Chronicles is simply to have a record of God's mighty acts in China.

As a new believer in the 1980s, I recall reading many reports from the Soviet Union of how Christian men and women were being brutally persecuted, yet the kingdom of God grew, with many people meeting Jesus Christ. By the time the Soviet empire collapsed in the early 1990s, no one had systematically recorded the glorious deeds of the Holy Spirit during the Communist era. Tragically, the body of Christ has largely forgotten the miracles God performed in those decades behind the Iron Curtain, and we are much the poorer for it.

Consequently, I am determined to preserve a record of God's mighty acts in China, so that future generations of believers can learn about the wonderful events that have transformed tens of millions of lives there.

At the back of each volume will appear a detailed statistical analysis estimating the number of Christians living in every city and county within each province of China. This is the first comprehensive survey into the number of believers in China— in every one of its more than 2,400 cities and counties—in nearly a century.

Such a huge undertaking would be impossible without the cooperation and assistance of numerous organizations and individuals. I apologize to the many people who helped me in various ways whose names are not mentioned here, many because of security concerns. May the Lord be with you and bless you!

I appreciate the help of mission organizations such as the International Mission Board, Overseas Missionary Fellowship, Revival Chinese Ministries International and many others that graciously allowed me access to their archives, libraries, photographs, collections and personal records. I am indebted to the many believers whose generosity exemplifies Jesus' command, "Freely you have received; freely give" (Matthew 10.8).

Many Chinese believers, too numerous to list, have lovingly assisted in this endeavor. For example, I fondly recall the aged house church evangelist Elder Fu, who required two young men to assist him up the stairs to my hotel room because he was eager to be interviewed for this series. Although he had spent many years in prison for the gospel, this saint desperately wanted to testify to God's great works so that believers around the world could be inspired and encouraged to live a more consecrated life. Countless Chinese believers I met and interviewed were similarly keen to share what God has done, to glorify his name.

Finally, I would be remiss not to thank the Lord Jesus Christ. As you read these books, my prayer is that he will emerge from the pages not merely as a historical figure, but as someone ever present, longing to seek and to save the lost by displaying his power and transformative grace.

Today the Church in China is one of the strongest in the world, both spiritually and numerically. Yet little more than a century ago China was considered one of the most difficult mission fields. The great Welsh missionary Griffith John once wrote:

> The good news is moving but very slowly. The people are as hard as steel. They are eaten up both soul and body by the world, and do not seem to feel that there can be reality in anything beyond sense. To them our doctrine is foolishness, our talk jargon. We discuss and beat them in argument. We reason them into silence and shame; but the whole effort falls upon them like showers upon a sandy desert.[1]

How things have changed! When it is all said and done, no person in China will be able to take credit for the amazing revival that has occurred. It will be clear that this great accomplishment is the handiwork of none other than the Lord Jesus Christ. We will stand in awe and declare:

The LORD has done this, and it is marvelous in our eyes. This is the day the LORD has made; let us rejoice and be glad in it. (Psalm 118.23–24, NIV 1984)

Paul Hattaway

Publisher's Note: In The China Chronicles we have avoided specific information, such as individuals' names or details that could lead directly to the identification of house church workers. The exceptions to this rule are where a leader has already become so well known around the world that there is little point concealing his or her identity in these books. This same principle applies to the use of photographs.

Several different systems for writing the sounds of Chinese characters in English have been used over the years, the main ones being the Wade-Giles system (introduced in 1912) and Pinyin (literally 'spelling sounds'), which has been the accepted form in China since 1979. In The China Chronicles, all names of people and places are given in their Pinyin form, although in many instances the old spelling is also given in parentheses. This means that the places formerly spelt Chung-king, Shantung and Tien-tsin are now respectively Chongqing, Shandong and Tianjin; Mao Tse-tung becomes Mao Zedong, and so on. The only times we have retained the old spelling of names is when they are part of the title of a published book or article listed in the Notes or Bibliography.

Introduction

East of the mountains

Shandong, a crowded province containing 95.8 million people at the time of the 2010 census, is a turtle-head-shaped province sticking out into the Yellow Sea toward the Korean Peninsula. It is the second most populated province in China after Guangdong (104 million) and just ahead of Henan (94 million).

With an area of just over 60,000 square miles (157,000 sq. km), Shandong is slightly larger than the US state of Georgia but contains approximately ten times as many people. By another comparison, Shandong covers a slightly larger area

A view from the summit of the Taishan range

than England and Wales combined, but is home to almost twice the population.

Archaeological evidence shows the existence of human habitation in Shandong dating back about 3,500 years, when the Shang Dynasty rulers controlled the Yellow River plains and held power from 1554 to 1045 BC. This 500-year period encompassed approximately the same span as the biblical account of the birth of Moses in Egypt, to around the time that Saul was anointed the first king of Israel. At the time, some scholars believe Shandong was inhabited by Tai peoples who were later forced south into southern China, where they are found in large numbers today among minority groups like the Zhuang, Dai and Bouyei, and further into Southeast Asia.

Shandong means "East of the Mountains"—in reference to the Taihang range that runs down the eastern edge of the Loess Plateau spanning Shanxi, Henan and Hebei provinces. In Shandong the Jade Emperor Peak in the Taishan range is the highest point in the province at 5,069 feet (1,545 meters). Apart from other moderate mountains in the province, the rest of Shandong consists of fertile plains.

The home of Confucius

Shandong is revered throughout China as the birthplace of two great philosophers, Confucius and Mencius. Confucius (Chinese name: Kong Qiu) lived from 551 to 479 BC in the state of Lu in southern Shandong. The province is still nicknamed 'Lu' by many Chinese today.

The sixth century BC was a pivotal era in the shaping of world history. At the same time that Confucius was creating a template for all future Chinese generations, on the other side of the Himalayan range a man named Siddhartha Gautama, known later as the Buddha, was teaching his new philosophy to an

Statue of Confucius

eager group of disciples. Thousands of miles further west, the prophets Ezekiel and Daniel were pronouncing God's message to Israel. Queen Esther was used by God to bring deliverance to the Jews just a few years after the death of the Chinese sage.

Confucius was born into an impoverished family and he had a difficult youth. When he was 50 years old he held a post as a minor official, but most of his life was spent as a humble teacher. For a period of 14 years, Confucius traveled widely, finally returning home to Qufu at the age of 68. Although he hardly put pen to paper during his lifetime:

> His 3,000 devoted followers recorded his teachings and put them into a book, *The Analects of Confucius*. After his death in 479 BC, Confucius' followers mourned for three years. A follower named Zi Gong built a hut next to the tomb and stayed alongside his deceased teacher. The site became the Confucius

Cemetery, which today contains more than 100,000 graves and 20,000 trees.[1]

Mencius (Chinese name: Mengzi) was born in Shandong 107 years after Confucius' death. He is remembered in China as "the most famous Confucian after Confucius himself."

The essence of Confucian teaching is that people should respect and obey those in authority, especially parents, and that society should work for the common good. Over time the belief in a "mandate from heaven" evolved. Rulers were believed to govern only with the consent of heaven, while corrupt rulers will be overthrown and their kingdoms handed to others.

Although not strictly a religion, Confucian teachings have shaped the world view and set the ethical and moral compass of every generation of Chinese since. The renowned Shandong missionary John Nevius went so far as to say of Confucius:

> The system of ethics and morality which he taught is the purest which has ever originated in the history of the world, independent of the divine revelation in the Bible, and he has exerted a greater influence for good upon our race than any other uninspired sage of antiquity.[2]

The full impact of Confucius' teachings was not felt until later generations, although the Communists disapproved of it and launched campaigns to try to uproot many Confucian beliefs from society. The Kong clan rose to such influence in Shandong that they had the power to administer the death penalty and collect taxes, two things the new leaders of China found intolerable. In 1948, Confucius' direct heir—the 77th descendant in the Kong family line—fled the Chinese mainland for Taiwan, bringing the 2,500-year Kong family dynasty in Qufu to an abrupt end.

Today the city of Qufu is home to the imposing Confucius Temple (Kong Miao), which attracts hordes of tourists, especially during the spring and autumn fairs, and on September 28 each year to celebrate Confucius' birthday. Approximately a quarter of all people in Qufu claim to be direct descendants of Confucius, though many appear to leverage such claims in a bid to boost their ability to profit from the booming tourist industry.

Marco Polo, governor in Shandong

While most people familiar with the famous travels of Marco Polo would not be surprised to learn that he passed through Shandong during his extensive journeys, few are aware that he also dwelt in the city of Yanzhou in Jining Prefecture, where for three years in the early 1280s the famous Venetian was appointed governor of the area by the emperor of China, Kublai Khan.

After traveling north into Shandong from today's Jiangsu Province, Polo described the city of Jinan (then called Chinangli). He then noted:

> At the end of your journey you arrive at the very great and noble city of Yanjiu [Yanzhou], which has seven-and-twenty other wealthy cities under its administration; so that this is, you see, a city of great importance. It is the seat of one of the Great Kaan's Twelve Barons . . .
>
> The people are idolaters and use paper money, and are subject to the Great Kaan. And Messer Marco Polo himself, of whom this book speaks, did govern this city for three full years, by the order of the Great Kaan. The people live by trade and manufactures, for a great amount of harness for knights and men-at-arms is made there. And in this city and its neighborhood a large number of troops are stationed by the Kaan's orders.[3]

The infamous Jiang Qing

While Confucius is undoubtedly the most famous native of Shandong, the title of the most despised person probably belongs to Jiang Qing, who hailed from Zhucheng in the central part of the province. Jiang was an actress who became the fourth wife of Mao Zedong. She rose to notoriety as a political figure during the barbaric Cultural Revolution (1966–76), when tens of millions of Chinese were slaughtered throughout the country.

Jiang formed the radical "Gang of Four" alliance, but after Mao's death in 1976 she quickly plummeted from power and was held in contempt by subsequent leaders of China. Over time she received much of the blame for the excesses of the Cultural Revolution, spending many years in prison before she committed suicide in 1991.

The Christian world came to hear about Jiang Qing when a rare foreign delegation visited Beijing in 1975. One member of the delegation inquired about the state of the Church in China, to which Mao's wife replied, "Christianity in China has been confined to the history section of the museum. It is dead and buried."

As the pages of this book testify, Jiang was badly mistaken.

China's Sorrow

For most of its history, Shandong has been an impoverished rural province. Despite its location on a fertile plain, Shandong's progress was severely hindered by the Yellow River, which is aptly nicknamed "China's Sorrow." The river has changed course at least 26 times in its history and brought centuries of terrible floods to the province, resulting in the death of millions of people and the forced migration of millions more, especially to northeast China. At times the river has flooded the entire Shandong Plain.

A vibrant economy

The Chinese have a saying: "He who holds Shandong grips China by the throat." Foreign powers were attracted to the rich natural resources of the province and its strategically located ports, which offer maritime access to Korea, Japan and the east China seaboard. Shandong boasts the longest coastline of any province in China, enabling millions of residents to earn their livelihood from fishing.

Germany seized the port of Qingdao in 1898, setting up factories and transforming the city into the capital of beer production in China, while the British gained control of the coastal town of Weihai. Waves of Japanese invasions blighted the province for decades until the end of the Second World War. Today, the Qingdao area is regarded as the economic hub of the province, while the inland capital city of Jinan is considered its poorer cousin.

As most of Shandong sits on fertile soil, the province ranks first in China for cotton and wheat production, and also produces copious amounts of apples, peaches and pears. Gold and diamond mines now dot the landscape, and it is home to one of the largest sapphire deposits on earth.

The large cities of Shandong are hubs for a wide range of industry, with many chemical, electronic, textile and mechanical factories. The Shengli Oil Field on the Yellow River delta holds one of the largest oil deposits in China. Possessing an abundance of natural resources, Shandong ranks third in gross domestic product (GDP) among China's provinces, with only Guangdong and Jiangsu above it.

Shandong today

After several tumultuous decades of flood, famine and war in the first half of the twentieth century, millions of Shandong natives migrated northward to Dongbei—the three northeast China provinces of Liaoning, Jilin and Heilongjiang. Today the Shandong dialect of Mandarin is spoken in many cities of northeast China.

Shandong people are typically regarded in a positive light by other Chinese. They "enjoy a good reputation, for they are stereotyped as loyal, honest, and straightforward . . . The women of the province were considered particularly chaste."[4]

Despite its massive population of just under 100 million people, Shandong is one of China's most ethnically cohesive provinces. Remarkably, 99.2 percent of the population are Han Chinese. The only other ethnic minority groups with significant populations are the Muslim Hui people (497,000 people or 0.5 percent), with small communities of Manchu (33,500), Koreans (27,800) and Mongols (23,700).

When other Chinese consider Shandong, they often think of it as China's Holy Land, being the home of Confucius and a place of literature and philosophy. Large numbers of Buddhist and Daoist temples dot the landscape, and for centuries the Chinese emperors ascended the summit of Taishan to perform the annual Border Sacrifice.

The geography of Shandong has shaped the characteristics of its people. One scholar highlighted four factors that have greatly influenced the province. As a peninsula, its people:

> share the orientation toward the sea that is characteristic of the populations of the southern coast; this is in sharp contrast to the landlocked world of the peoples of the central plains. Second, much of the province is mountainous, as is southern China. Third, in the modern period, the Shandong people

were the only group of northern Chinese to migrate abroad in significant numbers. Fourth, because they were close to the sea, the people of Shandong were subjected to great foreign pressure . . . The province was almost carved away from China proper by European and Japanese imperialism.[5]

China's Revival Province

For thousands of years the almighty God of heaven looked down upon the people of Shandong, desiring to know them as his children. Slowly, the gospel of Jesus Christ was proclaimed throughout the province, and a small remnant of redeemed believers emerged.

Through many hardships and persecutions, the body of Christ rose from the ashes and grew greatly in size throughout the twentieth century, boosted at regular intervals by sovereign outpourings of the Holy Spirit. Although other provinces of China boast larger Christian populations and a higher percentage of converts today, in many ways Shandong deserves to be known as China's Revival Province.

As the following chapters will reveal, the living God has done a mighty work in Shandong. Today, approximately five million Shandong residents identify themselves as followers of Jesus Christ; a number more than 40 times larger than at the advent of Communism in 1949.[6]

As you learn about the powerful way the Holy Spirit has transformed entire communities in China's Revival Province over the decades, may you be encouraged, inspired and challenged, and be brought to your knees to experience personal spiritual revival.

1860s

Although the first Evangelical missionaries to settle in Shandong are usually recognized as C. J. Hall and H. Kloeckers of the English Baptist Mission in 1860, the German pioneer Karl Gutzlaff visited coastal areas of the province in 1832 and 1833, distributing gospel literature as he went. Gutzlaff wore Chinese clothing and dispensed medicine and gospel tracts wherever he traveled. When his ship docked in the Bay of Weihai in July 1832, Gutzlaff disembarked and roamed over the nearby hills among several fishing villages, only to find "an unfriendliness, which seemed depicted on every countenance."[1]

Karl Gutzlaff dressed as a Chinese sailor

Two years later in August 1835, Edwin Stevens from Connecticut and Englishman Walter Medhurst followed in Gutzlaff's steps by sailing along the coast of Shandong. They took on board with them 20,000 Chinese Bibles, books and booklets of various kinds, which they intended to distribute to people along their route. At Weihai they received a hostile welcome, however, as this was the era of the Opium Wars in China, when foreigners were generally despised. Two days later, however, they found one village where "the people were too eager to wait for the regular distribution and disposed to help themselves. Within two days they were able to distribute about 1,000 volumes of 100 pages each."[2]

James Holmes and his wife Sallie of the American Southern Baptist Mission settled in Chefoo (now Yantai) in 1860, followed the next year by Jesse and Eliza Hartwell in Tengzhou (now Penglai). Holmes' life was tragically cut short just one year after arriving in the province.

The cause of Christian work in Shandong was boosted by an appeal from Welshman Griffith John—one of the greatest of the early Evangelical missionaries to China. John traveled north from his base in Hubei Province and arrived in the coastal city of Yantai in December 1860. His stirring words were widely reported among the churches in America and Britain:

> Whilst our hearts overflow with joy at the extensive field so suddenly and marvelously opened up, we are ready to despond at the inadequacy of the means. What is one station and two missionaries for the whole of Shandong Province, with its 29 million human souls? . . . Nothing, absolutely nothing!
>
> Will the Church, unfaithful to her Head, and false to herself, as the depository of the blessings of light and life for the world, look on with indifference?[3]

Griffith John was not merely a skilled orator. He flung himself into the work, personally visiting most of the towns and villages surrounding Yantai. John was attracted to the people of Shandong, whom he described as:

> more friendly than those of the south. Idolatry has not so strong a hold upon them, and many seem to be more susceptible of religious impressions, having a distinct notion of a Supreme Spiritual Being. Their disposition to clannishness, which is a marked social feature, will also be helpful to progress the gospel. Many villages, with from 500 to 5,000 people, are composed entirely of one or two families, and to influence one person means to influence all; whilst the conversion of one of the principal men would be followed by the respectful attention of the whole clan to the truth.[4]

A trickle of Western Evangelical missionaries from various denominations settled in Shandong throughout the 1860s, only to discover their Catholic counterparts had beaten them to the province by hundreds of years. By 1663 the Catholic Church already counted 3,000 converts in Shandong.[5] This number grew to 10,750 by 1870.[6]

By comparison, Evangelicals struggled to gain a foothold in Shandong. In other parts of China, the early missionaries had used public meetings and literature distribution to great effect. The pioneers in Shandong, however, soon discovered the province was different and had to adjust their strategies accordingly. An historian wrote:

> The gentry and the populace opposed the teachings of the new religion. Open-air services and the distribution of tracts, methods used in young mission fields throughout the world, brought little response here. Thus, in order to gain a basic hearing for the gospel, many missionaries turned to the running of primary schools and small hospitals and clinics, much to the

dismay of the home boards, who charged that donations for evangelism were being misused.[7]

James Holmes and Henry Parker

One of the earliest Evangelical missionaries in Shandong was the American James Holmes, who was born in West Virginia in 1836. Holmes was ordained to the ministry at the age of 22, just a month after his marriage to Sallie. The newlyweds had already been appointed as Southern Baptist missionaries. After an arduous ocean journey of six months, they reached China in February 1859.

James and Sallie felt that God wanted them to move to Shandong, but permission was not granted for some time. China was at war with Britain and France, and only when the war ended and Yantai was made a "treaty port" were the Holmeses allowed to reside in the province. On the last day of 1860 they arrived in Yantai, along with their infant son and the Hartwell family.

In April 1861 Henry Parker and his wife began the work of the American Episcopal Church in Yantai. The Taiping Rebellion was still raging throughout China and conditions were unsafe as groups of bandits took advantage of the unrest to murder and loot. In October 1861 a band of marauders known as the *Nianfei* approached Yantai. This group had systematically destroyed towns and villages throughout the province, so Holmes and Parker went out to the rebel camp to intercede for the safety of their town. The two missionaries did not return, and "eight days later their bodies were found 15 miles [24 km] from Yantai. Holmes was only 25 years old when he was killed. Later the people erected a monument in his memory."[8]

Norman Cliff, a former missionary in Shandong and a church historian, wrote: "What exactly took place is not known, but their bodies were recovered, covered with wounds and burns. They were buried on Lighthouse Island in Yantai Bay, as foreigners could not be buried on the mainland."[9]

After Henry Parker's death, his grieving wife and son returned to the United States, but Sallie Holmes decided to continue the work God had called her to. She relocated to nearby Penglai and continued to serve in Shandong for 20 more years. Later, when the famous Southern Baptist missionary Lottie Moon arrived in the province, the two women became close friends and Moon was much influenced by Holmes' zeal and enthusiasm.

The first organized Evangelical church in Shandong was established at Penglai in November 1862. The fellowship was founded with eight members. One of the first men baptized was Liu Qingsan, who became a key Evangelical leader in

Liu Qingsan at 84 years old, surrounded by his family of four generations of Christians

Shandong for the next five decades. In 1880 Liu moved to the provincial capital Jinan, where he established the first Presbyterian congregation. Liu lived to see his children, grand-children and great-grandchildren all following Jesus Christ.

The trials of the American Presbyterians

Of all the early Evangelical mission agencies in Shandong, none suffered as many setbacks as the American Presbyterians. Two couples, the Gayleys and the Danforths, relocated north from Shanghai to Penglai in May 1861. Both couples had suffered health problems from the heat and humidity of Shanghai, and it was thought the 500-mile move to the more agreeable climate of Shandong would help.

Their arrival in Penglai coincided with an outbreak of vio-lence as the province was ravaged by bandits. Less than five months after arriving, Mrs. Danforth died from an undeter-mined cause. The sudden loss of his partner caused "Mr. Danforth's health to be shattered in body and mind and a man was employed to take him home on the long voyage."[10]

In July of the following year (1862), Charles Mills and his wife sailed into Yantai as the latest recruits to help establish Presbyterian work in the province. They arrived during "the cholera year," when every day more than 1,000 people died from the dreadful disease. Three of the Mills children perished.

Missionary Samuel Gayley had traveled to Shanghai to accompany the Mills family. On the ship Gayley was stricken and he too passed away soon after reaching home. That year approximately one-third of the population around Yantai died because of the cholera epidemic.

In 1864 two new couples, the Mateers and the Corbetts, left New York and endured the 165-day voyage to China. The steamer scheduled to take them on the last stage of their journey to Shandong ran aground off the coast. Fearing the ship would break up and sink during the night:

> Passengers and crew were brought ashore. They wandered for five hours in the snow and ice, and at the point of exhaustion found lodging in a peasant farmhouse . . . When it was light, they saw in the distance their ship still afloat on the reef. The men returned to the ship and were able to remove most of their belongings . . . Although they nearly did not make it, these two shipwrecked couples would give to China 155 combined years of service![11]

Hunter Corbett

Hunter Corbett and his family, natives of Pennsylvania, managed to rent a house in Yantai for a surprisingly inexpensive rate. They soon discovered it had a reputation for being haunted, and all the local people avoided it.

During one of his first preaching trips in 1865, Corbett met a Chinese scholar named Wang Zei, who showed a hunger for the truth. After Wang visited Corbett's home:

> He could neither sleep nor eat until he found hope in Jesus. He spent the summer with Corbett in earnest study, and in the autumn of 1865 he and two others were baptized . . . Wang became an eloquent preacher, whose labors God greatly blessed in the saving of souls . . .
>
> When he first returned home after his conversion, Wang's kind and gentle manner was so different from the stern and overbearing ways of former years that it filled his wife and son with fear . . . After a few days Mrs. Wang had an experience of her own. She argued that if the Christian religion had power to make her husband gentle and kind it must be true.[12]

As the Corbetts settled into Christian work their lives were far from easy. In the autumn of 1873 Hunter and his three children

Hunter Corbett, the "Grand Old Man" of Shandong

traveled to the town of Jimo in eastern Shandong, where they hoped to relocate and establish a church. Initially, Corbett found many people "anxious to renounce their superstition and become adherents of the Christian faith."[13]

For the first few months all went well and the friendly locals seemed to like the foreigners in their midst. The Accuser started to do his insidious work, however, and gradually rumors began to circulate against Corbett, accusing him of stealing children, of plotting an insurrection and of having weapons hidden under the floor of his house.

The people of Jimo suddenly became hostile, and stones were regularly thrown at the foreigners. Two weeks later, as Corbett and two Chinese evangelists rode into the town of Hua Yen:

He was again attacked and mercilessly stoned, escaping from a cruel death almost miraculously, being extricated by a native who was an entire stranger . . . To use Corbett's own words: "A man whom I did not know came to me and said, 'You must get out of harm's way.' I replied, 'I have no way to get out.' He answered, 'Give me your riding-whip and follow me.'

"He took the whip and opened a way with it on either side, and I followed him rapidly; he at the same time said to the crowd, 'I know you all, and I will bear testimony against you if you injure this man.'

"I tried afterwards to find who this man was, so as to make an acknowledgement of my indebtedness to him, but could not."[14]

After escaping with his life, Hunter Corbett decided to move his family back to Yantai, only to find his home had been ransacked in his absence. Corbett went on to serve in China for a total of 57 years, and was called upon to endure many storms. His first wife Lizzie died after 10 years in China, while his second wife Mary also passed away after 13 years of missionary service.

Corbett's ministry was marked by his use of unconventional methods. For example, in Yantai he found it difficult to attract locals into the chapel to hear the gospel, so he rented a theater and converted the back rooms into a museum stocked with objects of interest from around the world. Before viewing the exhibits, visitors were required to enter a room at the front of the building, where they were presented with the gospel. Only when the service concluded were the museum doors opened. In one year alone, about 72,000 people listened to his preaching and visited the museum.

Although it felt like the devil himself had thrown everything at the American Presbyterians, the men and women of the mission persevered and succeeded in establishing a beach-head for the gospel in Shandong. Over a three-decade span, commencing with the difficult start in 1865, the Shandong Mission grew to become the largest Presbyterian field in China. In 1895 they counted 63 missionaries in Shandong, with 36 organized churches, 300 "preaching points" and 3,797 baptized members.[15]

Over the course of his long service until his death in 1920 at the age of 85, Hunter Corbett came to be affectionately known as the 'Grand Old Man' of Shandong. He personally baptized more than 3,000 Chinese believers.

Calvin Mateer

Calvin and Julia Mateer, natives of Pennsylvania, settled in the seaside town of Penglai. Their lives were greatly used by God in the promotion of Christian education throughout China. Before that vision would come to fruition, however, Calvin Mateer was called to endure many years of struggle and hardship. At one time he reported:

> Every village I come to, the term "devil!", "devil!" comes ringing in my ears. Not that they always called it at me, but to one another, to come and see. Frequently, however, it was called out most spitefully for me to hear. I think that within the last two days I have heard it from at least 10,000 mouths. It is strange how such a term could have gotten such universal currency. It expresses not so much hatred for the gospel as it does the national enmity of the Chinese to foreigners.[16]

This fierce hatred inevitably spilled over into violence on a few occasions. Once at Zhangqiu, a local sorcerer stirred up great trouble against the missionary. When Mateer was surrounded by a throng of men to whom he was selling books, "in rushed this man, brandishing an ugly-looking spear; and, using the Chinese expression of rage, 'Ah! I'll kill you!' he drove the spear straight at Mateer's breast."[17]

Calvin Mateer

Mateer survived this attack and others, and went on to establish a long-lasting and fruitful work for the kingdom of God in Shandong. The first school the Mateers established at Penglai was a modest one, created after Julia discovered she and her husband were not able to have children of their own.

By 1872, Calvin Mateer decided that all instruction in his schools should be in Chinese (most other mission schools used English at the time). Determined to bring Christian education to China in a manner most helpful to the future of the Chinese Church, he wrote:

> So long as all the Christian literature of China is the work of foreigners, the Chinese Church will be weak and dependent. She needs as rapidly as possible a class of ministers with well-trained and well-furnished minds, who will be able to write books, defending and enforcing the doctrines of Christianity,

and applying them to the circumstances of the Church in China . . .

An uneducated Christianity may hold its own against an uneducated heathenism, but it cannot against an educated heathenism. We want, in a word, to do more than introduce naked Christianity into China, we want to introduce it in such a form, and with such weapons and supports, as will enable it to go forward alone, maintain its own purity, and defend itself against all foes.[18]

Mateer's persistence paid off, and by 1898 his system of teaching had spread from the small school he founded in Penglai to include college-level education. In 1904 the school relocated to the more central location of Weifang, and later moved to the provincial capital Jinan, where it became known as the Shandong Christian University.

In 1907, a year before his death, Mateer excitedly wrote to believers in America with an exhortation and challenge that rings true for the Church in China today:

Tell the young men of America for me, that China now presents to the Church the greatest opportunity of the ages. God has opened the door—opened it wide. Three hundred and fifty million people are ready to hear the gospel message. The door has not been opened without great strife and effort. In the face of steady and persistent opposition, and through much suffering and bloodshed, a large and lasting impression has already been made. The dark and discouraging days are over and the future is bright with promise . . .

Very few people in the West understand the present conditions of things in China . . . The faith of the long, old centuries is passing rapidly away, but what shall the new faith be? This is the great Christian question of the hour. The young men of China are mad to learn English, because there is money in it. With English come books and newspapers, sowing the seeds of agnosticism, skepticism, and rationalism. Who will champion the truth? Who will administer the antidote? Who will uphold the cross? Who will testify for Christ?[19]

At the time of Mateer's death in 1908, after four and a half decades of service in Shandong, graduates of the university had spread to 16 different provinces throughout China, and were serving as Christian teachers in more than 100 schools.

Wang Baogui

Despite all the trials the foreign missionaries endured in the early years, the Holy Spirit had continued to work behind the scenes, illuminating the hearts of those who sought the truth. Slowly, one brick at a time, a holy building of Chinese believers began to emerge throughout Shandong, becoming the foundation stones of a strong Church in later decades. One early Chinese pillar of the Church was Wang Baogui, who was born at Fusan, near Yantai, in 1826.

Wang came from a family of scholars with high academic attainments. After studying the teaching of Confucius and the

Wang Baogui (dressed in white) with his Bible students

Chinese classics for 12 years, Wang became a zealous advocate of ancestral worship.

One day he met a Chinese preacher, who was also named Wang. The two men enjoyed each other's company and became close friends. After many months of declining his invitations, Wang Baogui finally decided to visit the chapel with his friend. He was given a New Testament, and began to study it earnestly as soon as he reached home.

At times, deep anguish filled Wang Baogui's heart as he thought about the complete rejection he would receive from his family and community if he accepted Christ. As he continued to study God's word and seek the truth, however, a firm conviction:

> took hold of his mind that he was a wretched sinner, and there was no hope for him but to accept free salvation through Jesus Christ. As soon as he was persuaded of this, he yielded his whole heart to Jesus, made a public profession of faith, and received baptism. From that day onward his faith never wavered, and he loyally and faithfully strove to follow in his Savior's footsteps, and to win others for Christ.[20]

Elder Wang, as he came to be known, had a passion for the lost. He headed to unreached areas of Shandong to preach the gospel, often staying for six months or a year in a rented house where people daily met with him for prayer and conversation about the living God. At every place, "God's blessing bestowed his efforts, souls were saved, and believers grew in grace and more fully realized the reality of God's word."[21]

When he reached an advanced age Wang was unable to walk, so:

> he requested to be carried to church, so long as he was able to sit in a reclining chair, saying it did him much good to join with God's people in worship. He possessed a remarkably cheerful

disposition. When persecuted and wronged, he bore it patiently and harbored no malice.[22]

Elder Wang had a particular love for children and youth, and was upset that there were so few opportunities for them to grow up with the knowledge of Christ. Despite his own poverty, he was able to fund the construction of a school.

When a doctor informed him that he had contracted an incurable disease and that he should prepare to die, Wang Baogui:

> employed carpenters to bring timber and make his coffin in front of his door, so he could personally direct the work. He had a friend write in large characters, "Looking for the blessed hope and glorious appearing of the great God and Savior Jesus Christ."
>
> One Sabbath he asked to be carried into the open air so he might have another glimpse of the church and school buildings. As he gazed up at the blue sky, a peace and joy filled his soul. He said in a loud voice, "My end is near; carry me into the house and prepare me for burial. Do not delay." They were his last words, and his soul passed into his glorious inheritance.[23]

An encouraging breakthrough

Modest growth had occurred among the Evangelical churches in Shandong until 1866, when "there was a remarkable religious awakening" at Leling in the northwest of the province, after missionaries based at Tianjin ventured south to preach the gospel across the border. When W. N. Hall traveled to the area to examine the work, he declared the move of grace to be genuine. Hall and his colleagues:

> baptized 45 persons who had eagerly embraced the gospel. From this auspicious beginning there was steady growth and expansion of Christian influence, so that by December 1877,

there were in that region, 18 preaching stations, 636 church members, eight schools and 14 native preachers . . . The people truly loved and revered the Lord, and always hailed His presence among them with joy.[24]

This breakthrough at Leling encouraged the other missionaries throughout Shandong at the time, many of whom had not seen much progress in their labors. The decade of the 1860s concluded with hope that the Holy Spirit would soon water the seeds that had been scattered throughout the province and bring forth a strong and evangelizing Church.

1870s

The Evangelical churches in Shandong had an inauspicious start in the 1860s. The missionary endeavor didn't wane, however, and the following decade saw encouraging growth throughout the province. The church at Yantai (then Chefoo) had been established with just six believers in 1866, but in 1873 alone it admitted 66 new members. In the same year, the church at Jimo added 69 new believers.[1] Despite these encouraging signs, the Chinese congregations struggled to get off the ground, with many of the new believers put out of fellowship, chiefly because of sexual sins and the use of opium.

The missionary enterprise in the province was helped by the passionate appeals for new workers from early missionaries. Isabelle Williamson of Scotland emerged as a new voice as she cried out for women to give their lives for Christ in China. In 1876 she wrote:

> As I stood in the midst of that ancient city [Qingzhou in Shandong], and knew that I was the first woman of a strange race who had ever trod its streets, or walked amid all these altars which had so long smoked with incense to false gods . . . I felt I occupied a most solemn position . . .
>
> I felt my whole being roused in prayer that God would send out more women to teach these millions of immortal beings; and under the same sense of need, I would implore you, O ye Christian women of Scotland, to think of the claims of your sisters in heathen lands. Women are one-half of the human race; there ought therefore to be as many women as men in the field, especially in such countries as China, where only women can properly and powerfully teach women.

Surely God has some chosen vessels among you who will bear His name hither; women with steady zeal and firm nerve, who have already passed through the fire, and are prepared to face trials and death itself, if need be . . . women who have resolved to spend their lives in the most noble of all services under heaven, so that in that great day the Savior's crown may be adorned with jewels from among the women of this, the most ancient people on earth.[2]

Timothy Richard—the mission reject

The English Baptist Mission was one of the first Evangelical groups in Shandong, but its early attempts at establishing a base ended in failure and doctrinal squabbles between its members. One of the first English Baptists, C. J. Hall, died soon after preaching his first sermon at Yantai. His replacement, H. Kloockers, built a small chapel 30 miles (48 km) inland, and baptized 15 converts in the first several years. This promising start was cut short, however, when "owing to certain differences, his services were discontinued."[3]

Two other missionaries died soon after arriving in the province, but much hope was held in the arrival in 1871 of a missionary-doctor, Dr. Brown. Before long the petty divisions of the mission once again struck. Brown and the home committee "did not see eye to eye, and after three years his connection with it was also severed . . . When will this afflicted mission see better days?"[4]

It was into the midst of this dysfunctional and failing mission that a man emerged who was to become not only a key proponent of the gospel in Shandong but one of the most influential missionaries to ever set foot in China.

Born in Wales, Timothy Richard was converted to Christ during the great Welsh Revival of 1858 to 1860. After receiving a call to serve God in China, he applied to work with Hudson

Timothy Richard and his wife Mary

Taylor's China Inland Mission (CIM), but his application was surprisingly rejected.

Although the reason for Timothy Richard's rejection was never publicly revealed, the CIM had a strict selection policy when evaluating missionary candidates, and it's possible they had considered Richard too poorly educated for the task. The CIM turned away numerous applicants, later prompting the leaders of the mission to issue a small booklet outlining some of the reasons why. In part, the booklet said:

> While it is quite true that many who might go, and *ought* to go, prefer to stay at home, it is also the case that numbers who wish to go are *entirely unsuited* for the work and uncalled to it . . .

It is generally found that when people are of no use at home, they are of no use in the mission field. The bright, brave, earnest spirit, ready to face difficulties at home, is the right spirit for the work abroad. A patient, persevering, plodding spirit, attempting great things for God, and expecting great things from God, is absolutely essential to success in missionary efforts . . .

In the China Inland Mission high intellectual attainment is not held to be essential to success in missionary work; still, in all knowledge there is power, and men and women of education, standing, enterprise, zeal, and piety are the men and women most wanted for missionaries.

It is a mistake to suppose that any one, so long as he or she is pious, will do for this work. The China Inland Mission wants not the weakest, but the mightiest that can be found.[5]

Undeterred by the setback, Richard was convinced his call from God was genuine and attended a Bible college in Wales. After graduating, Timothy and Mary Richard set sail for the Orient, arriving in Shandong in 1870. After a time in Yantai, they moved inland and settled in the city of Qingzhou, where they soon gathered a small number of converts through preaching and medical clinics. They spearheaded the English Baptist Mission, and by the end of his decades of service in China, Richard was considered one of the greatest missionaries of not only his generation, but any generation.

As he became more proficient in the Chinese language, Richard realized China was very much a hierarchal society, and concluded that the best way to reach the masses with the gospel was to impact those in authority and have the message filter down from the top. He spent much time developing relationships with the noblemen of Chinese society, with government officials and Buddhist monks, and with Confucian scholars.

Many of his fellow missionaries, however, vehemently argued against Richard's strategy, predicting it would yield few tangible results, and pointed out that Christ had always started with the poor and downtrodden of society and worked his way upward.

By 1872 Richard was already testing a variety of strategies to reach Shandong's scholars, including posting ads in the local newspapers, offering a prize for the best essay sent in on a carefully chosen subject. He often visited the competition winners in their homes, spending countless hours getting to know the men while sharing Jesus Christ with them. In the autumn of 1873 he visited Jinan, where after a number of talks together, a military officer surrendered his life to the Lord. This man was the first known convert to be baptized in Shandong's capital city.

From his base in Qingzhou, Timothy Richard "found that there were thousands of members of secret societies who were seekers after truth. Several hundred of them came into the churches."[6] Richard's strategy of "reaching thinking men in the privacy of their own homes" was bearing good fruit, and in early 1876 a group of 15 new believers were ready for baptism. The Richards had a baptismal pool constructed in the courtyard of their home, enabling the public to observe openly the professions of faith by these new Christians.

Famine relief

A terrible famine from 1876 to 1879 caused Richard and other missionaries to focus on relief efforts. Approximately 15 million people starved to death across China, and the situation became so dire that after trying to find sustenance by eating tree bark and weeds, many people resorted to cannibalism. Desperate people tore down their houses and sold the timber at the market for just a few cents in order to buy food. One report grimly recounted: "Girls of six or seven years old were sold for a price ranging from one to two dollars; those from ten to twelve years sold from three to five dollars."[7]

The famine relief work provided a great boost to the Church in Shandong, as tens of thousands of desperate people were helped by the missionaries and their Chinese co-workers. The Presbyterians were also influential in helping thousands of starving people during the famine. They reported: "The little Church grew rapidly. In five years the membership increased from 108 to 1,000."[8]

Over time the work of the gospel in Shandong spread exponentially. Schools, orphanages, hospitals and medical clinics were opened to reach and train the people, while Timothy Richard and his co-workers strongly believed the local Chinese churches should stand on their own feet with as little foreign help as possible. This insistence on self-support caused the Shandong Church to grow in strength and commitment. From the beginning:

> The principle was adopted of doing nothing for the Church which it could and ought to do for itself . . . In fixing the salaries of the pastors the desire was not to make them rich men but respected men, and it was felt that the pay of the native schoolmaster was a very good guide. By the plan adopted the pastors live in their own homes, attend to their farms in the busy harvest season and give about nine months of their time entirely to the Church.[9]

After cancer claimed his beloved wife in 1903, Timothy Richard continued to serve his Master throughout China for many years, until poor health forced him to leave in 1916, after 46 years of sterling service. The latter years of Richard's life proved difficult, and a growing number of missionaries opposed his methods. They saw little value in ministry that focused on helping people's bodies instead of their souls, and Richard's

Timothy Richard later in life

strategy of reaching China through education rather than the direct proclamation of the gospel attracted criticism that he was a liberal who propagated a social gospel.

Timothy Richard's decades of exertion in China had drained his stamina, and the great missionary died in April 1919, having led a full and fruitful life for the kingdom of God. The esteemed church historian Kenneth Scott Latourette did not hesitate to describe him as "one of the greatest missionaries of any branch of the Church," while long before his death, China had bestowed great honor on Richard, even conferring on him the highest rank of Mandarin. A contemporary missionary, William Soothill, wrote, "Had he died in China, his funeral would have been the greatest of any foreigner who has ever lived in that land."[10]

Stunning growth in Shandong

By 1879 the total number of foreign missionaries in Shandong numbered 28, accompanied by 25 Chinese co-workers. One survey found that: "Fourteen churches have been organized, and there are 734 converts in communion. There are 26 schools, containing 534 students. The progress therefore is remarkably good considering the shortness of the time since the work commenced."[11]

As the decade had progressed, the number of Chinese believers in Shandong had steadily increased. Two missionaries, Owen and Gilmour, baptized 110 converts in November 1877, and an additional 200 people declared their desire to learn more of the Christian faith. The following March the missionary duo visited Zhanhua, where they baptized another 200 new believers in Christ Jesus. The gospel advanced so quickly that in July 1878 Owen and Gilmour reported:

> The movement has been proceeding with great rapidity. There are now 1,600 persons under instruction and of these 420 are reported as suitable for baptism. The converts belong to 20 or 30 towns and villages, and to persons of all grades in society. The movement has extended to four neighboring districts, and there is no sign of any check to its progress at present . . .
>
> One of the most prominent features of the movement is regular family worship and the use of the Lord's Prayer, even in houses where the members may not be baptized. Remarkable willingness has been shown to engage in this outward act of Christian profession.[12]

The missionaries sought out those who were interested in the gospel, and didn't waste their time trying to convince those who were hostile to their message. John Nevius remarked in 1880: "During the last four years, above 50 mission out-stations have been established in central Shandong, mostly in the district cities of Qingzhou. They have connected with them about 500 church members, and nearly as many more applicants for baptism."[13]

Meanwhile the Presbyterian missionary Hunter Corbett reported from eastern Shandong:

> In certain districts the gospel has been preached and books left in every town and village. In a few places the open opposition was such that it seemed wisest to lose no time in passing to the next village. The intense indifference to the truth in other places did not tend to cheer the heart of the laborers. In some places, however, many men and women were not only willing, but anxious to hear.
>
> Not a few who received copies of the Gospels and Christian books in the early part of the year studied them, so that they are now able to give a clear outline of the life and work of Christ. A number desire baptism. Little groups in different places meet regularly on the Sabbath for worship and the study of God's word . . .
>
> During the year [1879], 82 were received into the Church on profession of faith. There are now 613 communicants on our Church roll. There were less than 20 when the Presbytery was organized 14 years ago.[14]

1880s and 1890s

After two decades of Evangelical endeavor, missionaries in Shandong were a fractured and bruised lot as they entered the new decade of the 1880s. One magazine summarized their efforts by saying:

> During the twenty years ending with 1880, there have been in all 98 resident missionaries in Shandong. Of this number 49 were women . . . Fifteen missionaries have died, and 43 from failure of health or other causes have left the field. Twenty-five either died or left the field within one year after arrival, and 19 others did not remain beyond two years.[1]

At the dawn of the new decade, Evangelical churches in Shandong numbered a little more than 1,000 converts, whereas the Catholics boasted 72,838 adherents in 471 churches throughout the province.[2] The ratio of believers was about to draw much closer, however, as Jesus Christ established his Church among those who desired to obey his teachings.

In 1885, just five years after reporting approximately 1,000 Chinese Evangelicals in Shandong, things had improved to such an extent that *The Chinese Recorder* magazine reported: "There are 39 Protestant missionaries in the province, and nearly 5,000 native church members, which is about one-fifth of all the members in China."[3]

God's precious gems

As the decade progressed, exciting reports of conversions and healings began to flow much more regularly from the pens of Evangelical missionaries, who were eager to share news

SUICIDES, IN CONSEQUENCE OF THE FAMINE.

"*They wait for death in their houses, stript of everything. The cold winds pierce through their bones. They have no rice to cook, and the cravings of hunger are most painful. . . . To die is far better for them than to live. They hang themselves from beams or throw themselves into the rivers. Everywhere sad, heartrending scenes are to be witnessed.*"

BEGGING FOR FOOD, AND SLEEPING IN THE OPEN AIR.

SELLING THEIR FIELDS, AND TAKING THEIR HOUSES TO PIECES (TO SELL THE MATERIALS).

STRIPPING OFF THE BARK OF TREES, AND DIGGING UP THE GRASS-ROOTS FOR FOOD.

A series of sketches from the China's Millions *magazine, depicting the severe famine that blighted the people of Shandong in the 1870s and 1880s*

Mrs. Li of Penglai, who said, "I should like to wear a Christian badge on top of my hat so that all might know I am a Christian!"

of breakthroughs in their work with the rest of the Christian world.

In the mid-1880s, a CIM worker, Miss Fosbery, joyfully shared about a teenage boy who gave his life to Christ:

Soon after I arrived in Yantai a boy named Shu-nga was brought to the hospital. He had a disease in his knees and could not walk . . . Every morning I went into the hospital to bandage his poor thin legs . . . After a time we put his legs into plaster, and this seemed to do him good. He gradually got better, for we took care of him, and fed him well through the cold weather. But one day, when he was feeling better, he went outside and stayed a long time in the damp, and this brought on the inflammation in his knees again, and he became very ill. He got worse and worse, and we all thought he would die, and he could scarcely swallow anything . . .

At night we used to kneel by his bed, and ask God to make him better. By-and-by he improved, and as the warm weather came on I had him come to the house so that I might teach him to read. Every day he listened to the preaching in the chapel, and gradually understood about the Lord Jesus. One day I asked him if he believed, and he said, "Yes," and that he prayed every day to the Heavenly Father . . .

About a month ago he was baptized and received into the Church as a follower of Jesus. He has no parents, and his only brother is very poor, and has a good many children of his own to keep . . . He is a nice bright boy, with large dark eyes that sparkle as he talks. He is about fifteen years old.[4]

CIM workers shared more testimonies of Chinese coming to faith in Jesus Christ. One account said:

Recently my teacher's wife was accompanied here [Ninghai] by her brother-in-law, who remained only two days. At one evening meeting his brother, my teacher, broke down in prayer, sobbing aloud, for the conversion of his relatives. His younger brother was evidently moved. I asked him if he would like to trust Jesus and be saved. He said he would.

We knelt down together, he with tears in his eyes, and he prayed, I suppose for the first time in his life, and I believe the Lord saved him. This is the fourth from that family who has trusted the Savior since we came here, and we are expecting more of them to be saved soon.

I had a letter recently from my teacher's father, lately baptized. He says he gets persecuted, but then he opens the New Testament, and always gets joy and comfort from that.[5]

The decade concluded with another encouraging report from Shandong:

If others could see the sights that daily meet our eyes, I think their hearts would be moved to pity. Twelve persons have been baptized during the last year. One of the first three women baptized was an old lady of 84-years of age. It seems as if God had kept her alive to hear the gospel. The first time she heard she seemed to understand more than most of them do, and weak, and old, and ignorant as she was, she seemed to take in the love of Christ. One day she asked, "Do you really believe Jesus loves me?"

On another day she told me, "Ah, my life has been all bitterness and sorrow. I have never known happiness since I was eight years old, when my parents died." I said to her, "Now you know and trust Jesus, He will care for you, and soon you will go to live with Him, and then it will be happiness for evermore." Her face brightened, and she replied, "Ah yes, and when I get to heaven I shall look out for you to come." The poor old thing soon died of cholera.[6]

An estimated 15 million people starved to death during the 1876 to 1879 famine,[7] and the population had only just recovered when a second severe famine struck Shandong in 1889. Regular missionary work of the mission was again set aside as all effort focused on providing aid to the starving population. Once again the Church in Shandong grew rapidly, with the number of Evangelical Christians more than doubling from 1,020 to 2,315 in four years.[8]

As the 1880s drew to a close, the Church in Shandong looked back on a decade of steady growth. The number of Evangelical Christians in Shandong appears to have quadrupled during the 1880s. Although the body of Christ was still minuscule compared to the overall population of the province, a faithful remnant had been established in many parts of Shandong, which would prove to be the first-fruits of a great later harvest.

The opening ceremony of the Jinan Christian Hospital, attended by the governor of Shandong and dignitaries in 1889

Colonial expansion

Shandong Province was a valuable prize to foreign governments because of its rich mineral deposits and its deep-water ports. A three-way war between China, Britain and France in the early 1870s resulted in the British seizing the strategic port town of Yantai (formerly Chefoo).

The German government also had imperialistic designs on the province, and the tragic martyrdom of two young German Catholic missionaries in 1897 gave it an opportunity to plant the nation's flag in the rich Shandong soil.

Germany retaliated for the murders of Nies and Henle by invading the city of Jiaozhou with a fleet of warships. They demanded the removal of the governor of Shandong, and used the martyrdoms to seize Qingdao. In the process:

Germany obtained a 99-year lease, as well as the right to secure mining and railways concessions in Shandong. The German action precipitated a scramble for land by other countries. Russia obtained a lease on Lushun (Port Arthur) and Dalian, while Britain secured a lease on Weihai and the New Territories opposite Hong Kong . . . By the close of the nineteenth century, there was a real prospect that foreign governments would shortly control many strategic provinces and eastern ports.[9]

Partly because of the opportunities afforded them by the wave of colonial expansion, the number of foreign missionaries in Shandong Province grew markedly throughout the 1890s, although for much of the decade the missionaries appeared to have spent their time forming an effective mission philosophy among themselves. Many detailed discussions were held as the mission force tried to work out the most effective way to propagate the gospel in Shandong, and throughout China in general.

The discussions included widely disparate views on the benefits and pitfalls of supporting native evangelists; and much ink was spent arguing the pros and cons of humanitarian work in response to the regular floods and famines that blighted the people of Shandong. As today, some missionaries just wanted to proclaim the gospel and considered humanitarian assistance a compromise, while others saw it as a tremendous opportunity to display the love of Christ to the poor and oppressed, in the hope it would lift many out of bondage and into the body of Christ.

Alfred Jones, a British Baptist, was one missionary who challenged the prevailing mindset of the day with his thoughts on how to alleviate poverty among the masses of Shandong. In 1894 he wrote:

Poverty is itself a great evil, because it directly causes great actual suffering. Poverty impels to covetousness and aids vice

A group of missionaries at Yantai, 1891

and crime . . . Do not be deceived in approving of others being poor and not loving it for yourself. Moreover, to relieve poverty is not to make men rich. True, more of the poor believe the gospel than the rich, but the point is, still more would do so if not poor.

Again, some missionaries seem to look on philanthropy as if it were bait on the gospel hook. I fear missions do some things as if only to get natives to believe Christianity and enter their church. God sees such things through and through. Outwardly they look like virtue. The act is the same; inwardly there is no virtue in them.[10]

A bold prediction

Although missionaries and their Chinese converts continued to receive a rough reception in many parts of Shandong, the Spirit of God continued to move in the hearts of many people through the written word. The Chinese Religious Tract Society was founded in the late 1870s, and zealously distributed tons of Bibles, Gospels and evangelistic tracts throughout the country each year. This approach yielded much fruit, with one report detailing:

> The Chinese are a reading people, and there is every reason for operating through books on the Chinese mind. They have had an unbroken succession of writers since the days of Confucius . . .
>
> In the course of missionary journeys in Shandong I found that the practice of reading aloud exists in families, and that the women of the family sit and listen with interest. As long as the supply of oil lasts, the reading continues. The women like to be read to while working with their hands at some useful kind of needle work . . . The reader may be a youth of the family or some woman who can read. She may belong to the family or she may be hired.[11]

As the good news of Jesus Christ continued to spread throughout the towns and villages of Shandong, an increasing number of people put away their idols and dedicated their lives to the living God. The missionaries were careful to teach that the local believers must finance their own church buildings, schools and workers, lest they fall into the pit of dependency upon foreign funds. The tireless Hunter Corbett detailed some of the exciting growth in this 1890 report:

> During a journey of two months in the interior, visiting churches, stations and schools, 40 people were received into the church on profession of faith, making 92 this year. Three church buildings were dedicated. Two of them are built of stone and the other of brick. These buildings cost the Christians no small amount of self-denial. Not a few, who were unable to give money, paid their subscriptions by wheeling stone, brick, timber, attending masons, etc.

A number not connected with the church contributed labor. They said the Christians were good neighbors who helped others and consequently deserved help in return.

Our school work is extending rapidly and proving a power in dispelling darkness and extending a knowledge of Christianity. Children and grandchildren, by repeating in their homes Bible stories, hymns and truth learned in Christian schools, have awakened a desire on the part of parents and others to learn more, and have led not a few to accept Christ as their personal Savior . . .

During the year about 500 adult members have been added to the Church in Shandong. More than 1,000 others were reported as observing the Sabbath, earnestly studying the truth and desiring baptism . . .

The present outlook in this province compared with 25 years ago, when there were no converts but only prejudice and opposition on every hand, is surely encouraging. Surely there will be mighty changes all over China, and multitudes led to accept the truths before another 25 years pass.[12]

Some of the Shandong missionaries were so encouraged by progress in the 1890s that one even boldly predicted: "If the present rate of progress is maintained in Shandong, the province will be Christian in the next 50 years."[13]

Problems in the Church

Despite such optimistic forecasts, many problems continued to plague the fledgling Shandong Church throughout the 1890s. Vicious groups of bandits roamed the countryside, inflicting untold misery on the population and stunting the growth of Christianity.

With China on the verge of total lawlessness and powerful warlords holding sway over vast areas, many of the missionaries and Chinese leaders felt like the kingdom of God was struggling to survive, with each step forward being met with strong resistance.

In addition to the outward hostilities, many Shandong Christians came face to face with important moral and ethical questions as they sought how to follow Jesus Christ as devoted disciples in the midst of communities saturated with idolatrous practices and superstitions.

One of the major points of contention for Chinese Christians was the question of involvement in ancestral rites. Many generations of family lineage had created a deep-rooted sense of community and belonging among the clans and families of Shandong. Ancestors were venerated, and numerous complex rituals required the whole community to participate in festivals, funerals and other special occasions.

Shandong believers who had personally experienced the saving grace of the Lord Jesus, however, struggled to justify how a Christian could be involved with ancestor worship in any way. While they wished to remain part of their communities and sought to reach their families and relatives with the love of God, many found the rituals of ancestor worship incompatible with the teachings of the Bible.

Predictably, as soon as Chinese Christians took a stance that went against the popular grain of their communities, persecution arose. First, believers were placed under intense pressure to observe the customs, and were warned that to step out of line would bring disgrace upon their dead ancestors and calamity would afflict their communities because the spirits would be offended.

Persecution increased against Christians who refused to budge. Many believers were beaten and expelled from their villages. In various parts of the province small clusters of ostracized Christians emerged, seeking one another's help as they faced life with no family support but the family of God. Family leaders often expressed their disgust at the stance of Christians by holding funeral processions, symbolizing that the Christians were dead to them and were no longer welcome in their communities. Some churchgoers cracked under the intense peer pressure, renouncing their faith in Christ.

Disciples of Christ living in the cities tended to survive more easily as they could melt into the population and seek employment. Those in the rural areas of Shandong, however, found things more difficult and many suffered terribly because of their faith in the living God. In some cases, the village leaders grew so infuriated by the believers' refusal to venerate the dead souls of their ancestors that Christians ended up laying down their lives for the Lord Jesus Christ.

Another factor that slowed the advancement of Evangelical Christianity in Shandong was brought about by a change of strategy by the Roman Catholics in the province. For decades the Protestants and Catholics had largely left one another alone, but in the 1890s many Evangelicals found that the Catholics were attempting to steal their converts away. The problem was so acute in places that scholars Nevius and Muirhead felt compelled to write books to educate Chinese church members about the differences between the two creeds.

A new danger emerges

By God's grace, however, the body of Christ in Shandong persevered and faithfully endured many hardships. By the end of the nineteenth century—after four decades of labor—the Evangelical churches throughout the province had grown to contain 13,500 members, spread among nine different denominations and mission societies.[14] Among the teeming millions of people crammed into the province, the body of Christ was like a little flock of sheep, but little did they know that their faith was about to be tested by ferocious persecution.

In the later part of the decade a subgroup of the White Lotus Society in Shandong Province came to be known as the "Boxers." They launched the notorious Boxer Rebellion in 1900, resulting in the slaughter of thousands of Christians throughout China.

The Boxer Rebellion

In 1899 a terrible flood of the Yellow River inundated the entire Shandong Plain, drowning and misplacing millions of people. Coming on the back of years of severe drought and humiliation at the hands of foreign military powers, the flood was a turning point. The religious leaders of the day declared that the woes being heaped upon the people of Shandong were because the spiritual balance had been upset, and the only way to placate the spirits was to rid the province of foreign influence.

A postcard showing a Boxer from Shandong

For decades a secret group known as the White Lotus Society had been active throughout Shandong. A subgroup of the Society called the *Yi He Quan* (literally "righteous harmony fists") came to be known in the English-speaking world as "Boxers," because of their practice of using boxing drills for physical training.

They launched the notorious Boxer Rebellion in 1900, resulting in the slaughter of thousands of Christians throughout China. It was not until after the advent of Communism that the White Lotus Society finally subsided, although its dark legacy can still be seen today in the triads of Hong Kong, Taiwan and other overseas Chinese locations. One report claimed that an offshoot of the White Lotus Society was still operating in Shandong in the 1960s.[1]

Many missionaries in Shandong warned of the storm clouds of violence they saw gathering on the horizon. Using cautious words of restraint in keeping with the Victorian era in which she wrote, Ada Mateer described the demonic nature of the Boxer movement:

> The Boxer organization started in Shandong. Its motto, after leaving the confines of its native village, was "Uphold the Qing (the ruling dynasty) and exterminate the foreigner." Their drill consisted in burning incense before a tablet and then working themselves up by gymnastics, etc., to a state where they were no longer masters of themselves, but became unconscious. After remaining in this state for some time they would rise, declaring themselves possessed of the spirit of one of the old heroes of antiquity.
>
> In this state they could perform great feats, but the chief mark of distinction was that they were invulnerable. Swords would not hurt them, and they could knock their heads on the ground until a great lump appeared, but never feel it. This lump on the forehead became a distinguishing mark. It was enough

to make one think of the mark of the beast and to make one wonder whether, after all, these fellows were not right in their claims to be possessed. Was this not a gathering of the forces of the evil one, for one mighty struggle?[2]

The tragic death of Sidney Brooks

The British missionary Sidney Brooks is widely recognized as the first Christian martyr murdered by the Boxers. He died at Tai'an in Shandong in the last week of 1899, even though the Boxer Rebellion is generally recognized to have commenced in the summer of 1900.

Brooks arrived in China in 1897, accompanied by his sister. He settled at Pingyin in southwest Shandong, while his sister established her home at Tai'an, approximately 150 miles (243 km) away.

Sidney Brooks

Brooks saw little of his sister, as he threw himself into language study and preaching. She married a missionary, H. J. Brown, and the two newlyweds had only just returned from their wedding in England, when Brooks excitedly made the journey to Tai'an, where he enjoyed a wonderful Christmas break with his family members.

On December 28, after lovingly saying goodbye to his sister and brother-in-law, Brooks mounted his donkey for the arduous ride home to Pingyin. At ten o'clock the next morning, as he rode through Zhangjiadian, "there was a terrible commotion in the village and about thirty Chinese brandishing big knives and yelling like demons came rushing toward him."[3]

Brooks was startled, as he had no idea what he had done to deserve such a hostile reception. He found himself in the wrong place at the wrong time, and when the anti-foreign Boxers saw a white man calmly riding his donkey through their village they decided to make the Englishman the first-fruits of their blood orgy.

Brooks realized his only hope of survival was to flee, so he forced his mount into a faster speed, but the pursuing Boxers soon overtook him. Brooks leaped from the beast and ran into a temple, hoping he would be safe inside a house of religion. That hope proved futile, for the temple headman had seen the chase and refused to protect the missionary. He grabbed Brooks and tried to push him off the temple property. In self-defense Brooks struck the man to the ground. This action had the same effect as striking a beehive with a large stick, for:

> Instantly the priests of the temple became howling dervishes. They rushed upon him from all sides, and, with his back to the wall, he used both his right and left arms with telling effect. One priest, rushing in under his guard, was caught up in both his strong arms, whipped off the ground and thrown back among his countrymen, knocking them right and left.[4]

The bloodthirsty Boxers waited impatiently outside the temple for the condemned man to be brought out. Finally, by sheer weight of numbers Sidney Brooks was overwhelmed by the monks, who:

> pinioned his arms, and dragged and pushed him to the door. Then they hurled him into the arms of the Boxers. The latter set upon him, striking him on the head with their knife handles and pricking him with their blades. They kicked him, punched him, and tore his face with their nails.[5]

Brooks tried to reason with the men, offering them money for his release. They laughed and spat in his face. The only thing they wanted was his blood. The missionary was stripped to his blood-soaked underwear and made to wait, despite the temperature being below freezing. The poor man:

> shrieked aloud in his agony, but his sufferings only delighted the yellow fiends. Somehow, out of utter desperation and terror, Brooks managed to free his hands and raced away. The callous Boxers laughed at this development, focusing their attention on their meal. Three horsemen were sent in pursuit and soon overtook him. Brooks jumped into a deep gully, taking his last stand. When the Boxers came upon him, he again offered money and begged piteously for his life. Knives in hand, they stood over him and taunted him. They waved their weapons and laughed at him, and circling about him like vultures, sprung upon him until he fell dead. They then cut off his head and bore it back to their companions in triumph.[6]

It later emerged that Brooks had told his sister and brother-in-law of a premonition he had of his own martyrdom. At Christmas, they said that:

> He had just had a disturbing dream. In it, he was back in England and in passing through the college where he received his education he read again the tablet bearing the names of all

who had gone out from that school as missionaries together with the name and field and the date of departure; and that while looking through the building he saw another tablet, bearing the inscription: "To those who were martyred for the Faith." On the tablet he saw plainly his own name.[7]

Brooks was the first Christian in Shandong martyred by the Boxers, but strangely, he was to be the one and only Evangelical missionary killed in the coastal province. The governor of Shandong saw the threat the Boxers posed, and sent large numbers of troops to drive the insurgents out of the province during the winter and spring of 1900. Most of the Boxers were forced into Hebei and Shanxi, which subsequently ended up being the provinces with the highest number of slaughtered Christians during the Boxer Rebellion.

The plight of Chinese Christians

Although all remaining foreign missionaries in Shandong managed to leave safely, the local Chinese believers paid a heavy price for Christ. A British Baptist missionary, E. W. Burt, reported that in one location:

> The converts' homes and places of worship were burnt. They themselves were harmed and scattered, hiding in caves of the hills, and crouching among the tall millet, not daring to show themselves. Over 120 died a martyr's death. Others did not prove so steadfast. Some of the pastors recanted. In one single village no less than 37 men and women sealed their testimony with their blood. No doubt ultimately this severe baptism of blood purified the Church, weeding out the unworthy and the self-seeking and deterring others with mixed motives from joining it.[8]

A report in the *Missionary Herald* noted the killings in Shandong were concentrated in the Zouping area, and declared:

A sketch of Boxers inciting people to attack and kill foreigners

Zouping is now for ever memorable in the annals of Christian history in China, as the scene of the martyrdom of many scores of Christian men and women . . . who died for the sake of "the Name." One hundred and seventy six in all were cruelly done to death, slain for the Faith. For many anxious days and weeks, hundreds were hiding in the open fields from those who sought their lives. They returned to find houses burnt, property stolen and crops reaped.[9]

The church in the northwest Shandong village of Zhujia had experienced powerful revival in the years preceding the Boxer Rebellion. A missionary reported that "a whole region, hitherto closed to the gospel, suddenly and unexpectedly . . . was thrown open."[10] When the Boxers attacked Zhujia they slaughtered 28 of its church members.

A Christian woman named Zhao lived in the town of Binzhou. When the Boxers came near, she left her village and hid in a relative's home. The Boxers were informed, and immediately went and seized her. When she realized there was no chance of escape, Zhao bravely followed the Boxers to a field outside the village, where:

> They ordered her to kneel, facing the southeast, that she might worship their gods. She refused to turn her face in that direction, saying, "Since I have learned the Christian doctrine I do not worship devils, but only the true God." So she knelt in a different direction.[11]

Sister Zhao's defiant act enraged the Boxers, who immediately sliced her body to pieces with their sharp swords. Finding that the gruesome act was not enough to placate their anger, they then burned her body to ashes.

When the Boxer Rebellion erupted in the summer of 1900, the church at Pingdu was already well established. One of the most effective evangelists in the congregation was a man named Sun. He and his two sons managed to flee from the Boxers, taking refuge at an inn owned by a church member. The Boxers soon arrived and seized Sun and his two sons. They were bound with cords and roughly dragged to the magistrate's office for interrogation. When asked if he was a Christian, Sun replied with a question of his own: "I study the doctrine, worship God, and obey the laws of the empire. Why should I be killed?"[12]

Evangelist Sun

The magistrate did not want to kill the bold preacher, so in a bid to appease the bloodthirsty Boxers he ordered that Sun and his sons be beaten with 300 heavy strokes and thrown into a dungeon. The severe punishment left the three Christians struggling to breathe and badly disfigured, but it was not enough to satisfy the Boxers. The next day they went to the dungeon and dragged the three faithful men outside the city. As the sword was lifted above his head, Evangelist Sun knelt down and cried out, "Heavenly Father, receive my spirit!"

Twenty other Christians at Pingdu were seized and offered escape if they would deny their God and worship the idols. When they refused, their queues (pigtails) were "tied to the tails of horses, and they were dragged 25 miles to Laizhou where most were killed."[13]

The Boxers commanded a young Christian woman named Yu to leave her house and be killed. "Wait until I have combed my hair," she replied. She calmly combed her hair and changed her clothes, in preparation for meeting her Savior. She then asked her persecutors, "Where do you wish to kill me?" The Boxers dragged Yu outside the village to an intersection, but when they tried to force her to kneel down she refused, saying, "'I cannot worship the false gods whom you reverence.' She lifted up her soul in prayer; but the Boxers did not wait until the prayer was ended."[14]

Those Shandong Christians who did survive faced extreme hardship. Thousands of Christians' homes were burned to the ground, and all their possessions seized. Many were reduced to begging for years to come. When the missionaries returned, much of their time was spent trying to help the impoverished believers recover from their terrible ordeal. Hunter Corbett reported from Yantai:

> I found suffering in every place. Many trying to live on corn-cobs, the dried vine of the sweet potato, bark, and leaves of trees, roots, etc. I found the Christians hopeful. They feel that God had not forsaken them, but had heard and answered prayer. Wonderful grace was given to our persecuted people. They stood firm and are not giving up the Christian life.[15]

When the pain and devastation caused by the Boxers started to fade, a thorough survey of Shandong found that 245 Chinese Evangelical believers had been killed throughout the province.[16] Thousands of Christians had their homes burned to the ground, and many chapels were also destroyed. The Church in Shandong had suffered a serious setback.

1900s

The Church in Shandong suffered a setback at the hands of the Boxers, but within a few years it had recovered and grown larger than before 1900. The missionary enterprise in China also expanded, as many Christians around the world volunteered to replace those who had been slain for the gospel.

The opening of the China Inland Mission station in Yantai came about in an unexpected manner. Hudson Taylor, the founder of the mission, was ordered by doctors to recuperate in Yantai after a serious illness. The seaside environment and ocean air helped Taylor's recovery, and he asked other missionaries who needed rest to join him there. Almost every instance resulted in a satisfactory change. In due course land was purchased and a mission base was constructed in 1879, containing

Students and staff at the CIM school in Chefoo (Yantai) in 1913

a hospital and a school, which catered for the education needs of hundreds of missionary children over many decades.

The school grew rapidly, proving tremendously beneficial for the overall health of the families in the CIM. Satan, however, threw all he could muster at the school's staff members and students. In 1902, the mission's magazine reported:

> It appears that on Sunday, July 6th, all the teachers and students of the boys' school partook of chicken pie at their mid-day meal. To appearances all was satisfactory, and the teachers ate of the same pies in the evening without any bad result. The same evening Gershom Broomhall died at 8:45, after only four hours' sickness. This was attributed to cholera, which is very rife in China at present; but late on Monday poisoning was suspected. No fewer than 19 boys, who had dined together, were taken ill, and of these only six recovered.[1]

Louisa Vaughan

In 1903 a little-known single American missionary, Louisa Vaughan, held her first Bible class for women inquirers at a village called Dongjia'an in the mountains of Shandong. She soon found the task an impossible one, for most of the women were completely illiterate, "not knowing one character from another." One old woman informed the missionary that she could teach her nothing: "My mind and heart are as hard and dark as mahogany wood."[2]

Some of the women had poor eyesight, while others simply didn't believe it was possible to learn anything at all, having been told they would be ignorant their entire lives. Deeply discouraged, Vaughan went to prayer, and the Holy Spirit challenged her to have faith for a miracle, and to let her confidence rest in him and not the impossible situation confronting her. She asked the Heavenly Father to save the women and pour out his Spirit upon them, that they might return home and be shining witnesses to their families.

Vaughan records that the first day of meetings passed without any sign that God had heard her prayer. In the afternoon of the second day, however:

> One of the women began to weep out a confession of her sins. She asked that she might be forgiven and cleansed in the precious blood of Jesus and that the Holy Spirit would come into her heart and dwell there. In a few moments we rose from our knees to greet a new creature in Christ Jesus. In the course of the next few days woman followed woman in a similar experience until the entire class rejoiced in their salvation. They were marvelously transformed by the power of the Holy Spirit, and they were now so eager to learn of Christ that I could scarcely find time to satisfy them.[3]

The rain story

In 1908 the sky over Shandong again turned to brass and no rain fell for months. The crops were almost totally ravaged, and the familiar cycle of drought, famine and death began to repeat itself, when a group of Christian university students came to Louisa Vaughan and sought her advice.

The entire heathen population of the province had lost hope, and after every town had held processions beseeching the rain god to open up the heavens, the weather had become increasingly hotter and drier. The people took the idol of the rain god and threw it into a field outside Qingdao, hoping it would blister in the intense heat until the spirit granted itself respite by making it rain.

The Christian students' faith was strong enough that they knew not to participate in the idolatrous practices, but they were beginning to waver in their trust in Jesus Christ. They had prayed fervently to him but still no rain had come. After asking the missionary why their prayers were not being answered and what they should do, Vaughan replied: "There are three hindrances to God answering our prayers: sins of transgression of God's law, sin of non-conformity to His will, and the sin of unbelief." She asked them if they were willing to humble themselves before God and ask the Holy Spirit to expose any sins that were hindering their prayers for rain. "Oh yes!" they replied.

Their knees had scarcely touched the floor when these young men "were sobbing out a confession of their sins before God; sins of unforgiveness, of not trusting Him, of hating fellow students; sins of not witnessing for Jesus in their own families . . . of lying, cheating and breaking rules."[4]

After renouncing their sins they prayed together again and asked God to send the rain. The students told their classmates what had happened, and on the following day 30 people came to the prayer meeting. Again there was much confession of sin, followed by an outpouring of the Holy Spirit. On the third day, 75 students crammed into the room, with the same result. On Sunday morning the entire body of 160 students met together for prayer.

All week the students went into the suburbs and villages surrounding the city, telling the people of their prayers and that the true and living God would soon bring rain. They preached the gospel and many hard hearts softened to the truth.

Finally, after another week or two passed without a drop of rain, the believers awoke one morning to find dark clouds gathered overhead. The heavens burst open and a great deluge saturated the parched Shandong soil. It rained almost non-stop for the next week. The Christians quickly advertised a thanksgiving service, where the entire community was invited to come and give thanks to the Creator for answering the prayers of his children.

The students were so encouraged at having witnessed the hand of God during the ordeal that they organized themselves into 26 small preaching groups and went throughout the countryside proclaiming the good news of Jesus Christ. The response was overwhelming, with one report saying:

Citizens from all walks of life flocked to the church. Women hobbled on their poor bound feet for one or two miles in the country round about. Unconverted persons so crowded the church that there was scarcely any space left for the students and the Christians. Overflow meetings were held in classrooms and dormitories.

A Chinese Christian teacher with her students at Weixian, early 1900s

On the tenth day the chief official with his subordinates and their retinues came to give thanks to God for His deliverance. He said, "I believe yours is the true God, and that you preach the true gospel."[5]

Jesus and the drunkard

On one occasion Louisa Vaughan met a Chinese Christian woman who despaired for the salvation of her alcoholic husband. Vaughan asked the woman if she was able to believe God to save him, to which she replied that he had been a drunkard for their entire 31-year marriage and he was a hopeless case.

Every day for the next two weeks all the women in the prayer group presented this need before God's throne of grace, asking him to do a miracle and to make a way where there seemed to be no way. When the class ended the woman returned home and received such a severe beating from her intoxicated husband that she was unable to get out of bed for a month.

One day, however, the man came home confused after an incident had taken place that day. He asked his wife if she thought he had lost his mind, explaining that after completing his business in the town he decided to enter the wine shop. The very moment he lifted his foot across the threshold to enter the shop, the man said:

> A voice inside my body said very loudly, "Don't go in there. Go home! Don't go in there, go home!" I was so startled that I dropped my purse and spilled all my coins on the ground . . .
>
> I went across the street and searched a man's courtyard and looked carefully around the corners of his house to find the boys who had called to me, but there was not a soul in sight . . . I was very much puzzled and called myself a fool. But again as I lifted my foot over the threshold there came that voice, louder

and more insistent than ever, "Don't go in there, go home!" I came home as fast as I could. I am very much frightened. Do you think I am losing my mind, or am I already mad?[6]

The man's long-abused wife explained he had heard the voice of Jesus, and shared how the Bible class had prayed for two weeks that he might surrender his life to God. The man was struck to the core and realized the living God had intervened in his life. He repented of his sins and gave himself to the Lord Jesus Christ, vowing to never touch alcohol again.

The man was thoroughly converted, and was never again found drunk. He became a strong church member and brought the rest of his family to faith in Christ, and sent his children to the Christian school.

The woman who saw heaven

The living God performed some remarkable miracles to bless and strengthen his children in Shandong during the first decade of the twentieth century. Louisa Vaughan shared an extraordinary event that occurred at a place named Wangjiaguan in 1904.

After several days' meetings, Vaughan unflatteringly reported:

My audience consisted of the most stupid and ignorant of Chinese women. Some of them were converts, but most came to hear the gospel for the first time. Among them was a Mrs. Zhang, who seemed, if possible, a little more stupid than the rest.[7]

After four days of prayer, however, Mrs. Zhang placed her life into the hands of Jesus Christ and became a child of God. Six months later, however, she contracted tuberculosis and suffered intense pain for a year. Her family watched her distress, but were unwilling to listen when she tried to share the gospel.

Despite their opposition, Mrs. Zhang maintained a clear testimony and constantly asked God to save her family.

One day it appeared that the disease had almost completed its course and Mrs. Zhang was close to death. Vaughan visited her one last time and hugged her tightly, assuring her they would meet again in heaven. Early the next morning the father of Mrs. Zhang stopped by the missionary's home. Vaughan assumed he had come to break the bad news of her passing, and tried to console him in his grief. "Oh no, no!" he interjected. "The Lord has performed a wonderful miracle. She is alive again!"

The man explained that his daughter had died at three o'clock the previous afternoon and her body was immediately prepared for burial. At sunset they heard a noise coming from inside the death chamber, and thought that children or chickens had broken into the room. When they opened the door they could scarcely believe their eyes. Mrs. Zhang was sitting upright, and had removed her grave clothes and put back on those she had been wearing before her death!

Mrs. Zhang, who had never heard a teaching on the book of Revelation and could not read her Bible, related what had occurred:

> I remember seeing all the family around me crying. Then the Lord Jesus came into my room and took me by the hand and said, "Come with me." In a short time we were before a gate of pearl. It was the gate of heaven. Angels opened it and we went in. I saw many beautiful houses, all of many colors . . .
>
> Then we went on and I saw thousands of angels in a circle, singing and playing lovely music. In the midst was the throne of glory. The Heavenly Father sat upon it and when I saw Him I was afraid. I hardly dared to lift my eyes . . .
>
> He said, "You may go back for a while, but you must return to me here on the twelfth day of next month."[8]

When news spread of what had happened to Mrs. Zhang, people traveled from miles around to hear her testimony. When she spoke, it came with such spiritual force that nobody could reject it. Hundreds of people were converted. Many years later people in that part of Shandong still eagerly received the gospel because of Mrs. Zhang, who they said "went to heaven and came back again to tell what she saw."

The days passed until the twelfth of the following month. Mrs. Zhang lay down in her funeral clothes and prepared for her departure, without a single trace of fear or worry. Her relatives tried to convince her that she would not die, but she would hear none of it. At sunset, as her family enjoyed their evening meal, she closed her eyes and her soul returned to be with God forever.

Revival fires spread

In 1906, Weixian in north-central Shandong experienced a visitation of God's presence and power. The first signs of the coming blessing were seen during a large conference where 350 women had gathered.

The culmination was reached during the four days in which Dr. Howard Johnston, a Presbyterian minister from New York, visited the station. E. W. Burt of the English Baptist Mission reported:

> He found many of us cold and disheartened; he left us new men—with fresh zeal for our daily tasks, a new spirit of love and forbearance for one another, and an overflowing joy and freedom in prayer such as many had never known . . .
>
> On Monday the college boys spent from eight o'clock to twelve, and from two to six, and the whole evening, in prayer. I was present most of the time, and to my dying day shall not forget the scene . . . At one particular part of the afternoon I

remember that some fifty or more short, earnest prayers followed one another in rapid succession for nearly an hour. Some boys got up and said that their original purpose in coming here was to get Western learning and so make money. Now they wanted to live their lives for preaching Christ.[9]

The flames of revival spread to other parts of the province. Prayer meetings in Qingdao attracted crowds of 600 zealous believers, who often gathered at 6:30 in the morning and continued their petitions before God's throne until the afternoon. With a spirit of intercession gripping the children of God, a powerful awakening soon broke out, with meetings "marked by confessions, apologies, and reconciliations occurring in the prayer meetings that went on long after midnight."[10]

The Holy Spirit began to move powerfully among the Christians of Shandong, cleaning them up first so they could be more powerful witnesses among unbelievers. Missionary T. N. Thompson recalled his experiences when he attended a series of meetings near Qingdao:

I was impressed with the spiritual fervor of the people among whom I found myself . . . The first place where I stopped was the center of a group of 26 villages where there were Christians. At that place a church has been organized with a membership of 200 to start with. In the last three months three new churches have been added in that district, and 54 members have been admitted to the church . . . The manifest presence of the Spirit of God in these meetings, seven in all, has been remarkable.

At Daxintan, where there has been a woeful lack of harmony among the Christians and even open quarrelling, the people were greatly moved by the Spirit of God, falling to the floor and crying out to God for mercy because of their sins . . .

At the next village called Liujiaqao we also held four days of special meetings in a large tent seating about 600 people. It was full at almost every service. Our 'sunrise prayer meetings' were special features of the work. Oftentimes they lasted for three hours or more. One at this place lasted from 6:30 a.m. until 1:00 p.m. without intermission; no one feeling willing to close a meeting which was led by the Spirit Himself. The confessions of sins, prayers for forgiveness and intercessory prayers for their own friends, poured forth by the Christians, showed that they realized how shallow their Christian lives had been, and they were irresistibly led by the Spirit to seek forgiveness.[11]

The presence of God was so strong that people often just wanted to cry out for mercy in a bid to gain relief for their internal anguish. At times even the preaching of the word of God proved impossible. At a meeting in 1906:

> One old woman stood up just as the pastor was about to begin his talk on a certain subject and told him to sit down; she must speak now and confess her sins. And so it went on. There was no way to stop them. One pastor had prepared to speak on four subjects. He never had an opportunity to expound but one. Others fared worse . . .
>
> This had mostly been a work of grace among the church members themselves. There were many hypocrites and cold ones among them while many were living in open and secret sin. These meetings brought home to them their sins with tremendous conviction.
>
> The work goes on in the countryside. Women have contributed hundreds of finger rings, bracelets, large hair-pins, earrings, and other ornaments of silver, giving them to the native pastors and asking them to open schools in the country where they might learn of this new doctrine which cares for women and teaches them to read.[12]

Jonathan Goforth in Shandong

Canadian Presbyterian missionaries Jonathan and Rosalind Goforth first arrived in China in 1888, basing themselves in the

Jonathan and Rosalind Goforth

eastern Shandong port city of Yantai. The Goforths' ministry was revolutionized after they read reports of the Welsh Revival and the Azusa Street Revival in California in the early twentieth century. News of these awakenings caused the Goforths to seek God more fervently, and they felt their work had lacked the kind of power and fruitfulness God desired.

After participating in the great revival that swept the Korean Peninsula, the Goforths returned to Shandong in 1908, from where Jonathan reported:

> A movement began and steadily increased in intensity until it finally reached a climax on the sixth day. I have been present at movements which have been more powerful, more far-reaching, perhaps, but none where I have felt so completely conscious of the Spirit's controlling power over a large body of people. It did seem that day as if every last vestige of opposition had been swept away and that Christ alone was exalted . . .

A wonderful testimony meeting was held on the last evening. Spontaneous resolutions to new obedience were heard from many. One remarkable thing about these testimonies was the great number who claimed that . . . when the Spirit's fire had swept so irresistibly through the audience, they had been healed of their bodily ailments. In my address I had made no special mention of divine healing. Yet here was the testimony of these people that suddenly, at some crucial moment, the illness which ailed them passed away.[13]

The Goforths spent the following years traveling widely throughout China, and saw the fire of the Holy Spirit fall in many locations, expanding and strengthening the body of Christ wherever they visited. In February 1914 the revivalist returned to Shandong, where he held a series of meetings at Qingzhou.

Goforth's reputation as a man of God preceded him, and more than 1,000 expectant believers crammed into the church building, expecting great things from God. A report on the meetings noted:

Towards the close of the nine days' meetings, it became quite impossible for Mr. Goforth to give the addresses he had prepared. No sooner had we had the opening hymn and reading of Scripture than one after another rose—either in their seat or coming to the platform—and confessed sin and asked for prayer to live a better Christian life. This was not confined to any class or sex or nation—all were constrained to make public confession—pastors and evangelists, missionaries and professors, men and women, students and schoolgirls, old deacons in their 70s and little girls in their teens . . .

That the movement is of God and not of man is seen from nothing more than the fact that the greatest manifestations took place when Goforth was most in the background—when he was in fact compelled to remain silent.[14]

Revival at Weixian College

At the Union College in Weixian in 1909, 196 out of 200 students made public confessions of faith in Jesus Christ, and believers who had been in conflict with each other fell on their faces and cried out for God's mercy. In one place, a prayer meeting that continued for six hours resulted in Christians abandoning lawsuits they had lodged against one another.

The catalyst for the Weixian revival was the Shandong preacher Ding Limei, who quietly slipped into the town at the end of March 1909. The next morning he spoke at the chapel, and the Holy Spirit moved powerfully among the students, convicting them of their sins and of coming judgment. Ding's personality was low-key and self-effacing, and the revivals God brought about through his ministry often shared the same characteristics. Even the conservative *Chinese Recorder* magazine was moved to report:

> The most noticeable feature was the quietness which characterized the revival from beginning to end. Recently in China many revivals have been remarkable for the intense emotion manifested and unwonted public confession of sin. However necessary these things may be elsewhere, and on other occasions, here, for the most part, God spoke through the still, small voice, in the quietness of men's hearts, producing very deep but well-controlled conviction.[15]

Rebellious students

At Zhuocun, the missionaries had been struggling to deal with unruly students at the Christian high school. The boys had smashed all the school furniture and even burned an effigy of their principal. While Goforth gave his address, a group of boys were seated in the choir loft behind him. While he was speaking, he noticed amusement on the faces of some of the audience. When he asked a missionary if the boys were playing up behind his back and distracting the crowd during the preaching of God's word, Goforth's suspicions were confirmed.

On the third morning Goforth ordered all the boys to leave the choir loft and sit in the front row directly in front of him. The rebellious teens took this as a great insult and refused to sing. The principal asked the missionary if it might be better to command the boys to sing. "Not on my account," Goforth replied. "The Spirit of God is going to make these boys yield and glorify their Master, and He will do it without either of us needing to lift a finger to help Him."[16]

Throughout the fourth day the boys continued their silent protest, and it appeared they were a long way from yielding their hearts to Jesus. On the fifth morning, however, many of the boys were in tears as the Spirit of God convicted them. They sang heartily when called upon, and as soon as the service was opened for prayer:

> Boy after boy came running up to the front to make confession of sin. Among other things they confessed to drinking, gambling and to visiting houses of ill fame. Some of the boys were so overcome that they had scarcely begun to pray when they fell to the floor in agony. After the meetings, the boys went in bands on Sundays and preached in the surrounding villages.[17]

At Qingzhou, in central Shandong, the students of the local mission school also strongly opposed Goforth's message and tried to obstruct the move of the Holy Spirit. Between 500 and 600 students were ordered to attend the revival meetings, and while many adults and most of the girls were broken and touched by the Holy Spirit, the boys remained completely unmoved.

As Goforth preached, he noticed that many of the boys had their heads down, reading from books in their laps. He pleaded with them to lay whatever they were reading aside and concentrate on the message, but they ignored his instructions.

On the sixth evening, one of the missionaries came up to the platform and publicly confessed his sin of smoking cigars. His contrite and tear-filled admission touched the hearts of all present, and the next morning one of the boys approached the platform carrying a pile of books. He flung them to the ground in disgust, and then he turned to face the congregation and said:

> "These are 'devil books.' Some of us boys picked them up in the city. They are written with the express purpose of polluting the mind with vile thoughts. Through them I have been led to commit adultery. While these meetings have been going on the devil has prompted us boys to keep reading these books so that we wouldn't hear God's truth and be convicted of our sin" . . .
>
> One after another came forward and in great brokenness told how they had been led astray by the vile literature. Hour after hour scores kept pressing toward the platform. Finally, after the meeting had lasted five and a half hours, with dozens still waiting for an opportunity to confess, the missionaries practically compelled Goforth to take a rest.[18]

In many other parts of Shandong the Lord Jesus visited his Church with great cleansing power. Missionaries and Chinese church leaders alike confessed gross sins, and many relationships were restored as wrongs were made right and years of offense were canceled and left at the foot of the cross of Christ. One man came to a meeting pushing a cart full of items he had stolen from people in the town. After asking forgiveness he proceeded to return the goods to their rightful owners.

Pingdu

Beginning in 1906 God also moved mightily at Pingdu, where more than 20 Christians had been slaughtered during the Boxer Rebellion just six years earlier. The principal of the Christian school stood up to publicly confess his sins, but when Goforth invited him to the stage, the man proceeded to make a speech that attacked others while not touching on any of his own faults.

Jonathan Goforth placed his hand on the man's shoulder and said:

> Brother, you know perfectly well that there is not one atom of truth in what you are saying. Furthermore, you are not confessing sin. You are not being prompted by the Holy Spirit. You are merely taking advantage of this opportunity to vent your spite upon other people.[19]

After hearing what Goforth said, the schoolboys rose in great anger, furious that their principal's integrity had been questioned. Goforth noted that they stormed out of the church, "shouting and yelling as they left . . . I thought they would kick the door off its hinges as they went out. Yet, strangely enough, a mighty conviction seemed to fall upon all who remained."[20]

Some of the other missionaries present expressed their concern that the evangelist had overstepped the mark by publicly rebuking the principal in front of his students. Goforth was unconcerned, believing he had spoken under the authority of the Holy Spirit and God would bring the truth to the surface.

The boys went through a time of terrible conviction after they walked out of the meeting, and many were unable to sleep as God searched their hearts. On the eighth morning:

they stood up before the church and acknowledged their fault. And, to crown the devil's defeat, the principal himself came up to the front, weeping, and confessed his sin . . .

Three years after these meetings were held it was reported that about 3,000 had been added to the churches in that region.[21]

Lottie Moon

The Southern Baptists were the first to work in the Pingdu and Tengzhou (now Penglai) areas of Shandong Province in the early 1870s. The most famous of their missionaries was the diminutive American Charlotte ("Lottie") Moon, who served in Shandong from 1873 to the time of her death by starvation in 1912.

Born into a wealthy Virginia family in 1840, Moon met Jesus Christ at the age of 18 after she was unable to sleep due to a

Lottie Moon in 1873, aged 33

barking dog. Wide awake with nothing to do, she decided to honestly examine the claims of Christ. A short time later she dropped to her knees in prayer and dedicated her life to the living God.

Moon's desire to serve God in China was delayed by the final years of the American Civil War, but her vision was ultimately fulfilled and she became one of the first unmarried women ever sent to the mission field by the Southern Baptists. After arriving at Yantai, the new recruit headed overland to Penglai—a trip of two days.

Lottie's entire 40-year missionary career was spent in Shandong, first at Penglai and later in Pingdu. She spent countless hours traveling around the province in a *shentze*—a contraption that was described as:

> like a covered wagon slung on poles instead of wheels. It was a sort of basket turned on its side with mouth pointed forward. It was covered by a thick cloth which more or less weather-proofed the inside. The shentze poles were fastened on mules in front and behind. One or more drivers walked beside to guide the beasts through narrow, rutted trails. Inside the housing, the passenger lay back on mountains of bedding to cushion the jolts. The ride was violent and often sickening.[1]

Soon after settling into her work, Moon's contribution to the cause of the gospel in China began to emerge through her writings and passionate challenges to church members in her homeland. Despite standing just four feet, three inches (1.3 meters) tall, Lottie's words packed a powerful punch. Not content just to send letters to private individuals, she wrote directly to magazines and newspapers, which were glad to publish her unique and politically incorrect views. Numerous memorable quotes flowed from her pen.

Lottie Moon often traveled around the Shandong countryside in this shentze

One of Lottie's first blunt rebukes of the Southern Baptist churches came just months after her arrival in China, when she wrote:

> It is odd that a million Baptists of the South can furnish only three men for all China. Odd that with 500 preachers in the state of Virginia, we must rely on a Presbyterian to fill a Baptist pulpit here. I wonder how these things look in heaven. They certainly look very queer in China.[2]

As Moon matured as a believer her challenges became even more piercing. She even rebuked her own mission board for sending missionaries to Africa, while many Baptist church members in the southern states continued to oppress black people.

The hard-hitting nature of her challenges shocked many American churchgoers, causing consternation among the status quo. She was accused of being a radical feminist, and subtle pressure was brought to bear to try to remove her from the mission field.

In Shandong, Lottie was admired for her sharp sense of humor and ability to make her points for God. Deeply troubled by the daily barrage of spiteful calls of "Foreign devil!" everywhere she went, she adopted a unique response to the taunts. Whenever a child called her a foreign devil:

> She took the boy or girl to his or her mother and asked that the child be taught good manners. If a woman goaded her, she would turn and retort, "Do not call me a devil. We are both women, and we both come from a common ancestor. If I am a devil, what does that make you?" With this approach, slowly the attitude of the taunters began to change.[3]

Loneliness

At one stage Lottie Moon was engaged to a highly educated young man, Crawford Toy, who claimed to have a call to missions. She broke off the engagement, however, when she learned that he had embraced Darwin's theory of evolution. Toy went on to become a professor at Harvard University, while Moon was left in China to, in her words, "plod along in the same old way."

Years later when asked if she had ever fallen in love, Lottie replied, "Yes, but God had first claim on my life, and since the two conflicted, there could be no question about the result."[4]

Lottie Moon often found missionary life excruciatingly lonely, and she struggled with depression. Four years after arriving in China she wrote to her mission board:

> I am bored to death living alone. I don't find my own society either agreeable or edifying . . . I really think a few more winters like the one just past would put an end to me. This is no joke, but dead earnest.[5]

Conflict on the field

From the time of her arrival in China, Lottie had struggled to get along with other missionaries, and she frequently clashed with her supervisor, Tarleton Crawford. A man who mixed business pursuits with his missionary work, Crawford constructed a tower in which he planned for Lottie to live with her sister, Edmonia, who had preceded her to Shandong by a few years. The local Chinese, who lived in walled compounds, rioted in protest against the missionary's tower. The only reason they could imagine why someone would build a high tower was to look down on them and spy on their wives and daughters.

To quell the rioters, who were armed with sticks and stones, Crawford pulled out a gun and aimed it at the crowd, causing

Tarleton and Martha Crawford

the people to flee for their lives. Lottie was shocked and confused at how a servant of Jesus Christ could threaten to use a weapon against those he was supposed to serve.

To make matters worse, one day her sister Edmonia lowered her voice and whispered:

> People in America might think it's proper for single women like you and I to live with a married couple, but do you know how the Chinese view it? They think I am Tarleton Crawford's second wife, and I am sure they will think you are his third.[6]

After serving in China for several years under such trying circumstances, Edmonia's physical and mental health reached breaking point, and she was sent home to Virginia to recuperate. She never set foot in China again, and Lottie deeply mourned the loss of her sister.

By 1885, after a dozen years in China, Lottie found herself at her wits' end. She had grown tired of Crawford's "ever-repeated annoying demands and constant humiliation, as he tried to make all around him stultify themselves by absolute submission."[7] Crawford, from a Kentucky farming family, was a notoriously difficult person to get along with. A historian wrote:

> Forty of his 50 preaching years were spent in Shandong Province, mostly at Penglai . . . He never liked the Chinese very much, and sometimes one feels that there were not many people whom he did like. Fortunately, perhaps, Crawford was so intemperate in urging his personal enthusiasms on other Southern Baptists that he finally "threatened the very existence of the Convention," not to mention its China missions, and his church had—as he termed it—to "refrigerate" him.[8]

A breath of fresh air

Desiring to flee the toxic atmosphere in Penglai, Lottie decided to relocate inland to Pingdu, where she planned to preach the gospel to anyone willing to listen—male or female. In Chinese society at the time it wasn't considered proper for a woman to address a man directly. Lottie directed her messages to the women, but their husbands invariably found a way to listen too, out of sight but not out of sound.

Moon seemed to be on the verge of resigning her post and returning home in frustration when, in 1887, three Chinese men from the small village of Shaling knocked on her door and begged her to come to their village and teach the "new doctrine."

Although she had long clashed with Tarleton Crawford's leadership, Lottie was good friends with his long-suffering wife, Martha, who hailed from Alabama. Martha was a zealous evangelist, having presented the gospel to the women and children of 315 different villages in a single year.[9]

Lottie sent a message asking Martha to meet her in Shaling. On the journey she prayed fervently, hoping the trip would not be in vain and that they would meet some people with hearts open to the claims of the gospel. Moon was soon shocked by the reception that greeted her.

As she entered the village of about 50 households, "Many people rushed out to meet Lottie. 'It is the lady with the heavenly book!' exclaimed one man. 'Yes, and she will tell us how our sins may be evaporated!' shouted another man, waving wildly at Lottie."[10]

For days the two female missionaries answered questions about Jesus Christ from the spiritually hungry people of Shaling. The first evening flew by:

> but no one wanted to go home. Long into the night the men and women shouted out questions, which Lottie did her best

to answer. The crowd left the house only when Lottie was too hoarse to speak anymore. The crowd the next night was even larger, and larger still the night after that.[11]

The duo left Shaling greatly encouraged, having experienced a breath of fresh air. Lottie wrote that she had found "something I had never seen before in China. Such eagerness to learn! Such spiritual desire!"[12]

Buoyed by this success, she excitedly wrote home:

I have never gotten so near the people in my life as during this visit. I have never had so many opportunities to press home upon their conscience their duty to God and the claims of the Savior to their love and devotion. I feel more and more that this work is of God.[13]

A thriving church gradually formed in Shaling. The new believers were distraught, however, when they discovered Lottie would be taking a summer break and her mission board hadn't appointed anyone to replace her. Several letters from China were received at the Southern Baptist headquarters in Virginia. One letter said:

For more than ten years I have known of this doctrine but did not inquire into it. On having an opportunity to inquire, immediately I truly believed. I am deeply in earnest in learning, but there is no pastor here to teach. I earnestly look to the Venerable Board to send out more teachers . . . The light of this mercy will shine everywhere, and gratitude will be without limit. I am longing for it as if, when the earth is dry, rain is longed for.[14]

An elderly man listened to the preaching at Shaling village and was presented with a New Testament by Lottie Moon. He was unable to read, so he asked his cousin, a Confucian scholar named Li Shouding, to read it to him. Li set out to mock the teachings of Jesus, but was struck by the words of life as he read. Li Shouding believed and was baptized in 1890, going on to become the most outstanding evangelist in north China. He was greatly used by God and personally baptized more than 10,000 converts, including over 1,000 in the Pingdu area alone.

The experience at Shaling was a turning point in Lottie Moon's life. For the next two decades she spent part of the year traveling through the villages of Shandong doing evangelism, and part of the year at her home in Penglai, where she trained new missionaries and continued to write provocative letters to mission magazines back in America. Many responded to her call to missionary service, and her influence was so far-reaching that the Southern Baptists established an annual Christmas offering to enable them to recruit more workers. It was later renamed the Lottie Moon Offering in her honor.

Lottie Moon's home in Penglai

"You will have to kill me first"

The gospel expanded quickly throughout Shandong, bringing with it an increase in persecution. The Christians refused to participate in ancestor worship rituals, infuriating their families and communities. In 1890, at the height of the persecution, a bloodthirsty mob surrounded an elderly Chinese Christian named Tan Huopang and were on the verge of beating him to death. The diminutive missionary rushed to the scene and refused to bow to the mob's intimidation. Instead:

> Lottie fought her way to the center of the crowd. She gasped when she saw Tan Huopang kneeling with his head in his hands. Blood streamed from his face and he was being kicked and spat upon. Lottie shoved several men with sticks out of the way and ran to his side.

Lottie Moon in 1901, aged 61

A gasp rose from the mob, and then the people fell silent. Lottie did not know how long the silence would last, so she began to yell out . . . "If you try to destroy the church here, and the Christians who worship in it, you will have to kill me first. Our Master, Jesus, gave His life for us Christians, and now I am ready to die for Him" . . .

One of Tan Huopang's nephews yelled back, "Then you will die, foreign devil!" With that he lifted a huge sword over his head and aimed it at Lottie. Then, inexplicably, his hand dropped to his side and the sword clattered onto the cobble-stone road. With that, the mob's energy appeared to drain, and slowly the people wandered away.[15]

"Oh, how she loved us"

As the years progressed, frequent plagues of cholera and smallpox blighted the Shandong population, and the continual cycle of floods and famines taxed the missionaries' energy and resources. The overthrow of the Qing Dynasty in 1911 brought chaos to the whole country, resulting in mass starvation and misery.

Lottie and other Christians quickly established a relief service to help as many people as possible. Her sensitive heart was torn by the suffering of those around her, especially the Christians she had played such a crucial role in bringing to the faith. She pleaded for funds from the United States, but the economy back home was struggling and the Southern Baptist mission board was heavily in debt.

Deeply upset by the lack of assistance, Moon decided to set an example of personal sacrifice. If those back home were too preoccupied with their own problems to care, she would leave no stone unturned in her efforts to help the afflicted people of Shandong. She emptied her bank account and gave away as much of her food as possible, feeding hundreds of starving people. She wrote a note in her bankbook: "I pray that no missionary will ever be as lonely as I have been."

With no help arriving from home, Lottie was plunged into depression. She stopped eating regularly and her physical and mental health rapidly deteriorated. Other missionaries grew deeply concerned and summoned a doctor. Although she now weighed a mere 50 pounds (23 kg), the missionaries were shocked when the doctor announced Moon was starving to death and that little could be done to arrest her condition.

Colleagues immediately bought the ailing missionary a ticket for the long journey home, accompanied by a nurse, Cynthia Miller. After several days at sea, Lottie's mind seemed to clear. She smiled at her helper and said: "He has come. Jesus is here, now. You can pray that He will fill my heart and stay with me. For when Jesus comes in, He drives out all evil, you know."[16]

Alas it was too late, and when the ship docked at Kobe, Japan, on Christmas Eve 1912, the nurse at her bedside said:

> For a long time that morning she had lain very quietly, unconscious. Then she stirred, and seemed to be looking for someone . . . The frail, thin hands were clasped together in the Chinese fashion of greeting, and gently unclasped. Over and over there came that look, and the greeting to Chinese friends long since gone on before her—her Chinese women of Penglai and Pingdu, of the villages round about, who she had told of the heavenly home . . .
>
> And it was thus, with the Chinese handclasp, a smile of greeting and the whisper of a friend's name that Lottie Moon went home.[17]

Lottie, who had turned 72 the previous week, had completed her service for God. She would never be lonely again.

Both Christians and unbelievers in Shandong grieved deeply when they heard that their special friend had died. The church leaders at Pingdu simply wrote: "Oh, how she loved us." Stirred by Lottie Moon's example, the believers in Shandong added extra determination to their preaching of the gospel. In the year following her death, 2,358 new converts were baptized in Baptist churches alone.

When news reached America that the veteran missionary had starved to death, there was widespread shock and dismay. Many Christians felt ashamed of their inability or unwillingness to respond to Lottie's appeals for famine relief, and thereafter the annual mission offering in her name was significantly higher.

Lottie Moon's sacrificial life for God helped sow the seeds of revival throughout Pingdu and other parts of Shandong. Although she did not live to see the full fruit of her labors before her death in 1912, by the end of the following decade a tremendous revival was sweeping parts of the province, with the Baptist work at the forefront of the outpouring of the Holy Spirit. A Southern Baptist annual report from the early 1930s said: "In the densely populated Pingdu County, there are now villages in which every family has one or more saved persons, and in some villages nearly everyone has accepted the Lord."[18]

Today, Pingdu City continues to have a strong and godly Christian presence, and is home to approximately 70,000 Chinese believers.

More than a century after her death, Lottie Moon is still highly regarded as the "patron saint of Southern Baptist missions." Generations of church members have grown up knowing her testimony, and a total of $1.5 billion has been raised during the annual offerings, which have typically funded half of the mission budget of the entire denomination.

1910s

The Church in Shandong in the decade from 1910 to 1919 experienced strong growth, as the Holy Spirit transformed the lives of many people who consecrated their lives to him.

The decade also brought terrible hardship to the people of Shandong, mostly due to the invasion of the Japanese military, who coveted the province because of its abundant natural resources and string of seaports. The invaders were

Lottie Moon's co-worker Li Shouding baptizing new believers at Pingdu in 1910

undisciplined and brutal. They looted the towns and villages they passed through, and countless women and girls were raped by the treacherous soldiers. As the Japanese inflicted untold misery on the people of Shandong and elsewhere in China, they created a deep anti-Japanese resentment that lingers to the present day.

The key city of Qingdao had been a German colony since 1897 (the only German colony anywhere in Asia), but in August 1914 the Japanese demanded the unconditional surrender of the city. When the Germans refused to oblige, the Japanese moved tens of thousands of soldiers and heavy artillery into areas surrounding the city. Some accounts say the Germans were outnumbered fifteen to one (60,000 Japanese troops to 4,000 Germans).

A great missionary goes home

In 1861 the Southern Baptist missionary Jesse Hartwell was one of the first foreigners to reside in Shandong Province. At a time when a large percentage of his fellow workers died or left the field within their first year of service, Hartwell battled on faithfully, enduring numerous hardships and heartaches along the way.

Hartwell was born in South Carolina in 1835, after his father had prayed fervently for a son he could dedicate to the Lord as a missionary. On the very first Sunday he spent in Shandong, after Hartwell preached on the streets of Penglai, "the Holy Spirit sent the arrow of conviction into a man's heart. He afterwards gave his heart to the Lord."[1]

Because of a family illness, Hartwell returned to the United States in 1875, where he spent the next 14 years working among the Chinese in San Francisco. He led many of them to Christ, establishing the first Chinese Baptist church in America.

Jesse Hartwell, who served for more than 50 years in Shandong

After returning to China, Hartwell led the mission and church in Penglai, and was a close associate of Lottie Moon for many years. He later became a beloved seminary teacher, and lecturing occupied him until his homeward call to heaven.

In 1897 Hartwell fell gravely ill, and his life was in the balance for months. Doctors said his days were numbered and that it was unlikely he would survive. The missionary felt his time had not yet come to depart, however, and set himself to pray earnestly. One afternoon he sat up in bed and told his family and fellow missionaries that God had revealed to him that he would live another 15 years.

He later fell sick again, but from the time God spoke to him, Hartwell never wavered in his conviction that he would live until 1912, and he didn't hesitate to tell physicians and any other interested person what God had shown him.

The end of 1911 arrived with Jesse Hartwell seemingly on his deathbed, but the Lord intervened. When his life finally expired at Yantai on January 3, 1912, Hartwell had spent 53 years of his life in the Lord's service among the Chinese. One memorial summarized some of the ways God had used this humble man:

> It was he who baptized the first man in Shandong Province, which now numbers its native Christians by the thousands.
>
> It was he who baptized the first woman in Shandong.
>
> It was he who organized the first Protestant church in China, north of Shanghai.
>
> It was he who organized the first Chinese Baptist church in America.[2]

God heals Old Liu

In the spring of 1915, an 80-year-old Christian man named Liu received an unexpected blessing from God. Liu, from Gaomi City in eastern Shandong, became blind at the age of 70 when he learned that his wife and only son had suddenly died. As Liu mourned their deaths, his grief was so deep that the blood vessels in his eyes burst, causing him to lose his sight.

Despite his blindness, the old man didn't give up his faith and regularly attended church meetings despite his handicap. One Sunday, as he felt his way along the road toward the church, a heathen neighbor, seeing the old man stumble among the mounds of a graveyard on the side of the road, derided him:

> How come your God is unable to make a blind man to see? Can He not see you? Is He not strong? Why don't you call on your

forcign Jcsus for help? Go and die, old man! Go and die like a dog![3]

The severe mocking failed to shake Liu's faith, and he boldly told his tormentor:

The true and living God can help me, and from now on I shall trust Him, and in faith I am going to ask Him to heal my eyes![4]

That day Old Liu surrendered himself fully to the grace and power of God. He meditated on the promises of the Bible and claimed them by faith. Just a few days later his eyes were supernaturally healed! He did not even need to use glasses, and the mockery of his wicked neighbor was rebuked.

When a blind evangelist heard about Liu's healing, he was struck with conviction that he should not accept his own condition as a natural consequence of growing old. The evangelist gathered a small group of intercessors around him, and they regularly prayed together for the restoration of the man's sight. After a year the evangelist's sight was restored, and he also had no need for glasses.

A demon-possessed grandmother

When the gospel was first declared to villagers in eastern Shandong, a teenage boy named Li was converted to Christ, and soon began attending the mission school at Qingdao. Li proved to be a tremendous witness for the Lord, and he won many of his friends and family members to the faith. In all, 12 people had surrendered their lives to Jesus through the young man's ministry.

One family member who steadfastly refused to believe, however, was Li's aged grandmother. She was the matriarch of the clan, and had grown very upset that the ancestral spirits were being disturbed by the conversion of so many of her family members to Christianity.

One day during the school holidays, Li returned to his home village. While he was leading family worship, his grandmother suddenly became violently ill. As the old woman trembled uncontrollably:

> She clutched the air, striking at unseen beings, and gnashed her teeth . . . Her fingers were so firmly clenched together that one of her grandsons, who was called in to force her hands apart, was unable to do so . . . For some time she talked, though not understandingly, breaking out at the close in this clear sentence: "I am a herd of swine demons."[5]

Li had been accompanied home by a classmate named Wan, who was a mature Christian. The duo watched as the grandmother's body became as stiff as a board and horrific sounds emanated from her mouth, as though hell itself had laid claim to her body.

Wan led the other startled Christians in prayer, and he read aloud from the Gospel accounts of Jesus casting demons out of tormented people. The believers then knelt together and prayed for half an hour, before calling on the unclean spirits to come out of the woman in Jesus' name.

As a result of their prayer, the grandmother was thrown back onto her bed, and the life appeared to have drained from her limbs. After considerable time, she finally declared:

> "I am so relieved! The dirty herd has left me. The true God has driven out the demons and my heart now has peace!" Without effort she opened her hands. Previously the grandson had tried so hard to release her grip that he had rubbed skin off her fingers in his exertions to set her free.
>
> The old woman smiled as she looked at the sweat-covered Christians in her room, and said, "Oh, I have seen Him."

"Who?" they asked.

"Jesus the Savior!" she answered. "He came to me when they were tearing me. He gave me release."[6]

The experience was so dramatic that all the members of the Li family became Christians. Some weeks later three generations of the family were baptized together, including the grandmother who had been delivered and transformed by the blood of Jesus Christ.

Little Lingzi

As the name of Jesus continued to spread throughout Shandong, hungry people from all walks of life found their way into the kingdom of God. In 1914 a China Inland Missionary, Mrs. Botham, told how a little girl named Lingzi had touched her heart. Botham wrote:

Thirteen miles away lived a little girl with a round laughing face, big bright eyes, and quick memory. Poor Lingzi had no Christian parents to lead her to Jesus and teach her to pray; no Sunday school at which to learn hymns and Golden Texts. Until she was about eleven she had never heard the gospel, but when she did hear, how eagerly she learned! She only needed to be told a Bible story once, and she could repeat it in graphic language to others. Last winter I spent ten days in the village where Lingzi lived, and during that time several little girls, of whom she was one, learned many Bible truths.

After we had gone, and there was no one to hold the women's meetings, she, with one or two others, would stand outside the window listening to the men's service, and when even this had to stop—the preachers having gone on to other places, she worked away at her reading herself, and taught other little girls what she knew.

Sad news has recently reached me. Dear little Lingzi is gone! She was bitten by a mad dog, and died after a short illness. It

Girls graduating from the mission school at Weixian in 1908

is a great sorrow. I had bright dreams of her becoming such a useful worker for the Lord. But He has willed it otherwise. It is too late now for us to do more for her, but oh, the many, many more still wandering in darkness![7]

Ding Limei—morning star of revival

Of all the Christian leaders in Shandong during the first half of the twentieth century, few were as influential as Ding Limei (1871–1936).

Named Limei ("Established Beauty") by his parents, Ding grew up in the rural village of Da Xintan near Qingdao, and as a teenager he attended the Presbyterian school at Penglai. When the Boxer Rebellion broke out, Deng was 29 years old and was already a well-known preacher. His life was spared, but he was arrested and thrown into prison for 40 days, during which time he was severely beaten and received 40 lashes on five different occasions.

Ding emerged from prison with a renewed vision to preach the gospel throughout China, and he believed the key to securing a Christian future for his nation was to reach students

Ding Limei

for Christ. From 1908 to 1923 he served as an itinerant evangelist affiliated with the YMCA's China Student Volunteers for Evangelism. He traveled extensively throughout the 18 provinces in China at the time, and thousands of people were saved at his meetings. In 1919 he fulfilled his vision of preaching in every province when he led a team to work among the Miao minority group in distant Yunnan Province.

By the early 1920s, Ding believed God was refocusing his efforts from evangelistic crusades to theological education. He was burdened with the realization that although he had led thousands of people to faith in Christ, many had perished because they lacked a basic knowledge of the Scriptures.

Ding taught for eight years at the North China Theological Seminary, and in 1932 he became the professor at a newly established seminary in Tianjin. Ding Limei was held in such high regard by the foreign missionary community that they conferred on him the nickname "The Moody of China," in reference to the great American revivalist D. L. Moody.

The blessed village

Although Ding Limei traveled far from his home village and was away for long stretches of time, many testimonies emerged of how God protected the little village from natural and man-made disasters. Many people believed the divine protection on that community was due to the hand of God on Ding's family.

One year was particularly bad for floods, and the river that flowed near Da Xintan broke its banks in 18 different places within a six-mile distance from the village. Dozens of villages and thousands of homes were completely destroyed by the torrents, and a larger village across the river from Da Xintan was demolished by the floodwaters even though it was situated at a much higher elevation. Da Xintan was somehow spared, even though it sat lower than the surface of the raging river. The community at the time was home to four generations of Christians, with one report noting:

> Ding is one of the most able and consecrated preachers in the land, and is used more largely in leading Chinese students to decide for the ministry than any other person. And in the midst of flood conditions exceeding in duration and virulence anything for fifty years, his village had deliverance little short of miraculous . . .
>
> The Ding clan has conspicuously and signally stood for the Lord in the face of great opposition, even loss and persecution. They realize that all their hopes are bound up in the one true and living God and they are committed to his service. They had marked deliverances before, which had bulwarked their faith,

and which were now to them earnests of God's grace in these days of flood, famine, pestilence and civil war.[8]

For the last few years of his life, Ding battled serious illness. He remained home with his wife and three children, and devoted his time to prayer and writing. He kept three notebooks with the names of those for whom he was praying, and at one stage more than 5,000 names were recorded in his books.

1920s

Most of the 1920s was a difficult time for the Church in Shandong. Society was in a state of upheaval, with the civil war raging, violent warlords dominating large areas, and the ever-present twin plagues of famines and floods afflicting millions of people.

Despite these severe trials, the Christians of Shandong continued to grow in grace and in number in the early part of the decade. Whereas a survey in 1904 found there were only

Buddhist pilgrims fascinated by a gospel presentation at Tai'an in the 1920s

14,226 Evangelical Christians in the entire province,[1] by 1922 the number had nearly quadrupled to 53,480.[2]

Only the provinces of Fujian (86,094), Guangdong (78,519) and Jiangsu (70,084) contained more Evangelical Christians in China at the time.

By comparison, however, the Catholics had mushroomed in Shandong, reporting 149,730 members in 807 churches in the same year.[3]

By the late 1920s, however, the Church in Shandong had fallen away alarmingly and was in dire need of an infusion of spiritual life. The 1929 *China Christian Year Book* summarized the state of the Shandong churches with this grim assessment:

> Not a few of our Christian people feel utterly depressed and exhausted; a kind of flatness seems to reign in the hearts of many—a lack of spirit and energy to make any forward move. The bitter experiences of the past and the uncertainty of the future have made many shy of attempting great things for God and expecting great things from God.[4]

The 50-year-old baby

The spiritual backsliding of churches throughout Shandong impacted a vast number of congregations. In one county, 18 churches had been established over the decades, but their reliance on foreign funds to keep them going had eroded the vitality of local believers and held back their spiritual growth, to the point that some people called the head church, "The 50-year-old baby."

At the end of one year, the finance committee of the 18 churches visited the village where the main congregation was located and scolded the believers for their lack of giving to God's work. Only a fraction of the pledges the local Christians had made the previous year had been honored, and as a result the Christian school could not afford to reopen in the new year. Parents had enjoyed the benefits of sending their children there without contributing to the teacher's salary or the upkeep of the school.

Although many of the church members in that village were relatively wealthy landowners, the church building had fallen into a state of disrepair. Like in the time of the prophet Hosea, the people had diligently taken care of their own homes while neglecting the building where they met to commune with God.

An urgent meeting was arranged, and all the believers were summoned to hear of the dire situation. At the very moment the preacher referred to the need to repair the church building before it became unusable:

> a chunk of the wall under a beam supporting one section of the roof fell down on the audience. It was a most pointed intima-tion of the need of the Christians getting together and adopting some effective plans before the whole side of the building should cave in on them.[5]

A revival conference was arranged for the Christians in the area, and many prayers were sent heavenward as concerned believers cried out to God to break the stubborn selfishness of their backslidden churches.

On the first night of the meetings the preacher spoke from the third chapter of Malachi. As the text was presented to the people:

> Their minds under the Spirit's guidance began to grasp the heinousness of their sinfulness in God's sight—the sins of luke-warmness, of indifference to Christ, and to the propagating of His gospel; and that sinfulness became very real to them in its actual hatefulness . . . It became plain to them as the meetings progressed that the source of all their troubles was in the little word "disobey" . . .

On the last morning the Holy Spirit was present in special power . . . At once the people began to be care-lightened and resolute in faith to face with confidence the problems of the church . . . No longer did they look on these things in shame and confusion; for, though their money was not nearly enough to put the church building in shape, they now had the spirit to attack the problem. They opened two new schools in nearby villages . . .

At the close of the meeting the Christians looked at each other in amazement. Families that had not spoken were inviting each other to the season's feasts. Many volunteered to go out into the surrounding villages and preach. The spirit of hopefulness and the gentle warmth of mutual love were diffused; everybody's face was beaming.[6]

A fresh wind starts to blow

Although the Evangelical churches in many parts of the province were at a low spiritual ebb during the 1920s, there were encouraging signs that God was about to do something special. Meetings by a number of revivalists such as Marie Monsen prepared the soil for what was to come. Missionary Leslie Lyall stated that in 1927:

The pioneer of the spiritual "new life movement", the handmaiden upon whom the Spirit was first poured out, was Marie Monsen of Norway. Her surgical skill in exposing the sins hidden within the Church and lurking behind the smiling exterior of many a trusted Christian—even many a trusted Christian leader—and her quiet insistence on a clear-cut experience of the new birth, set the pattern for others to follow.[7]

Before God poured his Spirit out upon the Chinese churches, however, he did a deep work in the lives of the missionary community, bringing many to their knees in repentance. When a group of American Southern Baptist missionaries gathered together at Yantai in 1927, they found that one of the women, Ola Culpepper, was suffering in extreme pain because of a degenerative eye disease. She had visited numerous doctors but they could not help her, except to prescribe ever-thickening lenses for her glasses.

The missionaries discussed the promises in the fifth chapter of James, where believers are exhorted to confess their sins to one another and anoint the sick with oil. Such practices were unheard of in Southern Baptist circles at the time, but the group decided to obey the Scriptures. When Bertha Smith went to lay hands on Ola Culpepper's head in prayer, however, she was convicted of her negative attitude toward another missionary, Miss Hartwell. As she confessed her sin, two Chinese cooks who hated one another broke down in tears and reconciled in an adjacent room. During the prayer, Culpepper took off her glasses and set them aside. The Lord Jesus healed her, and her eyes never again bothered her.[8]

The awakening of the Shandong churches was characterized by deep confessions of sin as the Spirit of God moved on people and exposed parts of their lives that displeased the Lord Jesus. These public confessions of sin were completely contrary to typical reserved Chinese behavior, but God used them to break people and to do a deep work in their lives. American missionary R. W. Frame explained how this practice confronted normal Chinese culture:

> The Chinese are a most proud and self-righteous people. They strive above all else to hold up a good face for the world to see— whatever they do in the dark. There is only one way whereby a person may sin and yet appear innocent and respectable . . . and that is to keep his sin covered up. "Nothing is sin unless it is found out" seems to be the principle on which life is run in China; so woe betides the person who exposes his neighbor's sin.[9]

In the last few years of the decade, new indigenous movements emerged from the Shandong churches. The Pentecostal Ling En (Spiritual Gifts) movement began at Feixian in 1928 and spread northward. This group received strong criticism from some of the more conservative church leaders, although a Presbyterian minister conceded: "There has been some excesses manifest, but on the whole the movement demonstrated marvelous evidence of the Holy Spirit."[10]

Even today there is disagreement regarding the legacy of the Ling En churches. Seven decades later, at the end of the twentieth century, historian Norman Cliff observed:

> These meetings produced a revival that brought renewal to the churches as well as deep division on account of excessive emotionalism and extravagant behavior. The response of the missionaries was to give systematic teaching on the work of the Holy Spirit as a corrective to this branch of the revival and to invite some of China's best Bible teachers to hold conventions in the main centers. Thus John Sung, Watchman Nee, and Wang Mingdao addressed large congregations, seeking to consolidate the fruits of the revival and warning against emotional forms of worship. In spite of these addresses, an unstructured Spiritual Gifts Movement outside the mission churches developed, the influence of which can still be felt in Shandong today after fifty years of Communist rule.[11]

Back from the dead

Although the Shandong Church of the 1920s was just a foreshadow of the one to emerge in the 1930s, extraordinary reports of God's power occasionally surfaced. At Tai'an, an American Pentecostal missionary named Paul Dykstra had only labored in the city for seven months when he fell ill with typhoid and double pneumonia. In his agony he suffered seven hemorrhages of the bowels. Medically speaking, there was no hope for his recovery. The missionary himself felt his end was drawing near and he would soon be departing this world to join the Lord.

At 6:30 in the evening, Dykstra passed away and two doctors pronounced him dead. In his own words, the missionary later told how after he had been dead for 15 minutes one of the doctors, a Christian named Mrs. Lawler:

> felt a mighty spirit of rebuke over death, and rebuked death in the name of Jesus. Shortly afterwards my eyes opened, and they heard me say, "Oh, the music. Oh, the glory." I looked around and when I saw I was back in this old world, a feeling of great disappointment came over me, and I said, "Why did you call me back? I don't want to be in this old sinful world."
>
> I had left this dark and gloomy world and entered into a glorious place of celestial beauty and brightness. I had heard the heavenly music and the heavenly songs, and was in God's very glory and ready to enter into my everlasting habitation. Oh, the glory and the music were so beautiful, sacred, and holy that words cannot describe . . .
>
> For over a week I lingered between life and death, resisting to continue in this world. But my work was not finished and He called me back to life to complete my unfinished work . . . He gave me a new vision of the work He had for me to do in Shandong. I surrendered my life afresh to Him.[12]

Dykstra threw himself into the ministry of the gospel. The people knew his story and how the living God had brought the missionary back from the grave, and they flocked to hear him speak. He later wrote:

> The hearts of the people were stirred upon seeing the miracle God had wrought in my life. They saw the mighty power of God and realized it was the Lord, who is the Resurrection and the Life, who had raised me up . . . The Tai'an active membership was

between 40 and 50, but within a year, the membership increased to about 275. The Spirit of the Lord was poured out in our midst in a most wonderful way . . . Unto our Christ be all the glory![13]

Paul Dykstra summarized some of the results that occurred from his ministry after being raised from the dead:

In the villages of Luotie and Gongli, the Lord did a most marvelous work. In three or four months, 300 souls came from raw heathenism to the Lord. There were wonderful conversions. The courts of heaven were made to rejoice. Drug addicts were set free by the power of God, and the sick were healed. From surrounding villages people heard that the True God was in our midst, and they walked many miles to the mission stations to listen to the gospel message.[14]

An elderly Buddhist couple

As the Spirit of God continued to move in people's lives throughout Shandong, many testimonies emerged of his power to save and deliver people from sin and bondage.

One Sunday a missionary was preaching in a rural church when the pastor told him of an ill 65-year-old woman who needed to go to hospital. Both the woman and her husband were Buddhists. The missionaries transported her to the Christian hospital, and while she was there the doctors and nurses led her to faith in Jesus Christ.

The old woman's life was transformed, and although she wasn't able to read, she memorized many Scripture verses and placed bookmarks in her Bible so she could find them and share them with others. When she had recovered from her illness the missionary drove her back home. When she got out of the car she bowed to her family members and proclaimed: "Look at me; I am a new person! The doctors cured my body but Jesus has cured my soul. Now I am saved!"[15]

Her husband was less than impressed to learn of his wife's new faith. When she knelt to pray at night he pushed her over and threw his shoes at her. Once as she was communing with God, her husband kicked her until she fell off the bed onto the floor. After that, she determined to pray outside the house. One night the husband woke from a deep sleep to hear his wife crying out in prayer for his salvation, begging God to have mercy on his soul.

The Buddhist man was puzzled at what had come over his wife. The next day he visited the pastor of the church and asked:

> What have you Christians done to my wife? She went to your hospital and came back completely changed. I have lived with her for 35 years and we fought all the time. I used to curse her and she cursed me back. I used to hit her and she hit me back. Now when I curse her, she just smiles. When I hit her, she just walks away. She does better work than ever. Last night I woke up and heard her crying and praying for me. What have you Christians done to her?[16]

Not only did that sin-hardened man repent of his sins and believe, but their entire family bowed before the Lord Jesus and received his salvation.

Simeon the storyteller

In a time long before television and other electronic media, storytellers were influential figures in Chinese society, earning their living by entertaining crowds with their musical instruments and stories. These men were usually very bright and clever individuals who could hold the attention of an audience for hours with their oratory skills.

After a storyteller named Simeon submitted his life to Jesus Christ, he became a diligent student of God's word and a powerful witness for the gospel. It was said of this man:

Simeon makes his Chinese instrument almost speak in his fervent manner of playing it and telling what the Lord has done for them all. When he recites the Scriptures, each word stands out as a living Word, under the power and anointing of the Spirit, for it is the living Word to him. He is wonderfully used of the Lord in this ministry, and the people are moved to tears as he explains in his singing fashion, how Christ was crucified for their sins, and the redemptive work of Christ Jesus. It is most impressive to see the crowds listening to him with tears running down their cheeks.[17]

Marie Monsen

One of the most beloved foreign missionaries ever to serve in China was Marie Monsen, a single woman from Norway whose unassuming appearance belied a spiritual giant within. Although most of her ministry occurred further south in Henan Province, where many Christians still fondly refer to her as "The mother of the house churches," Monsen also spent considerable time in Shandong, where she was a catalyst for revival.

Marie Monsen

Having arrived in China in 1901, aged 23, Monsen led a relatively quiet life as a Lutheran missionary until the 1920s, when her bold and uncompromising messages began to stir the body of Christ and cleanse it in preparation for an outpouring of God's power. The genesis of the Shandong revival that swept a great multitude of people into God's kingdom in the 1930s is often believed to have started with a series of preparatory meetings Monsen held throughout the province in 1927. One historian recounted the impact those meetings had on the Church in Shandong:

> She visited mission stations and churches giving her testimony. After each service she greeted the Chinese and missionaries alike with the probing question, "Have you been born again?" The question insulted some and angered others. But she spared no one, asking preachers, deacons, missionaries and others the same question. When their anger subsided, the Holy Spirit began to search hearts. People discovered and admitted they had not been born again.[1]

One missionary, who was wary of the "sensationalism" that often accompanied revival meetings, carefully studied Monsen and the fruit of her meetings. He wrote:

> Miss Monsen herself is one of the quietest speakers I ever heard. There was very poor singing and no invitation for public decisions, only the quiet question, "Have you been born again?" Were it not for a wonderful spirit of prayer and an occasional testimony, no unknowing visitor would believe we were in the midst of a revival.[2]

Marie Monsen came from a conservative church background, and was averse to allowing what today would be described as "hype" in the meetings. She was careful not to place pressure or manipulate people with her words, and she:

constantly warned others against "picking unripe fruit". That could only produce spurious results, which were not the work of the Holy Spirit. But when people became aware of their sins, their responses would inevitably be accompanied by emotion, and sometimes by tears for what they had done. Then, as they appreciated God's love, mercy and forgiveness, and His welcome for those who trusted in what Jesus had done for them, many also experienced overwhelming relief and joy. In the old Chinese religions many people spent years obsessively fasting, making long pilgrimages and doing penances. They had lived their lives in bondage trying to earn forgiveness, and now the good news of Jesus had set them free. They had something to rejoice about.[3]

As the Spirit of God moved in Marie Monsen's meetings throughout Shandong, demonstrations of his matchless power emerged. In one service a Chinese Christian worker:

tried to deceive himself and others by insisting he was saved. However, he could not deceive the Holy Spirit. One night this healthy young man was suddenly struck down in the courtyard and had to be carried in. He was stiff, blue, and cold. Concerned friends knelt at his side, praying. The missionary urged him to confess his sins quickly. As soon as he could open his mouth, he confessed and stood upon his feet again, forgiven.[4]

Captive at sea

One of the most famous stories involving Marie Monsen occurred in July 1929, when the ship she boarded en route to a conference in Shandong was hijacked by pirates. Monsen told the events of her 23-day captivity in a book entitled *We Are Escaped*, which was published two years later.[5]

Monsen's life was characterized by her dependence on the Holy Spirit and her determination to obey his leading. In the providence of God, she was impressed to take a boat that sailed one day earlier than she had planned. She was also led to buy several boxes of apples before departure, for no apparent reason. Furthermore, in the months leading up to the incident she had unexpectedly received several boxes of chocolate in the mail from supporters back home. Each time she thought of giving the chocolate away, Monsen heard the still, small voice of the Holy Spirit tell her, "Keep it for an emergency."

The morning after the ship left Tianjin, as it neared the Shandong coast, a band of about 20 armed robbers boarded the vessel and took control. Monsen remained in her cabin as she heard shots ring out all over the ship. She later wrote:

> I was immediately reminded of the word that I had been using much in years gone by, based on Isaiah 41:10: "Fear not, Marie, for I am with thee. Be not dismayed, Marie, for I am thy God. I will strengthen thee, Marie, with the right hand of my righteousness. Fear not, Marie."[6]

When all the passengers were ordered to leave their cabins and assemble on the deck, Monsen refused to do so under the prompting of God's Spirit. She remained on her bed, singing hymns and quoting Scripture out loud.

When a young pirate entered her cabin and demanded she hand over her watch, the bold missionary refused to oblige. When he pointed a gun at her and threatened to shoot, Marie told the man:

> Oh no, you cannot shoot me. You cannot shoot me whenever you like. My God says that no weapon formed against me shall prosper. You cannot use your pistol whenever you like and shoot me. You must have special permission from the living God to do that.[7]

Several times the agitated man threatened to shoot, and each time Monsen calmly quoted the Bible to him. Over the course of the next three weeks she often heard the man repeating those words to himself.

On another occasion a different ruffian pushed his way into her cabin. Monsen said that it felt like:

> The devil himself was there. The man's face and neck and hands were all covered with hideous open sores. He sat down on my suitcase, almost breathing in my face . . . I claimed the promise that God would be like a wall of fire round about me, and that vile man sitting there was up against the wall before he could touch me.[8]

The missionary talked to the man for an hour, sharing the gospel with him and ministering to him. He said he knew some real Christians in his home area, and when he left her cabin he had tears in his eyes.

For the next week the pirates looted every boat they came across at sea, until they had a dozen vessels under their command. Another ship with 50 or 60 more robbers joined them in their merciless plunder.

The whole time, Monsen refused to come to the dining room to eat any of the stolen food offered to her by the gang. They thought she was staging a hunger strike and were concerned for her well-being, not knowing she was enjoying the apples and boxes of chocolate the Lord had unexpectedly provided for his servant.

Every day as they were eating their meals, Monsen handed out gospel tracts to the pirates. One would read aloud while the others listened intently. She frequently saw tears welling up in the men's eyes.

Finally, after more than three weeks at sea, the pirates decided to part with their loot the following morning, after learning the Chinese navy was on its way to confront them. Monsen overheard the men discuss how to carry her off the ship, as they desired to hold her hostage to aid their escape. One of the leaders then said: "What's the use of carrying the foreigner with us? She hasn't eaten anything for 23 days. She won't be able to run or walk. You see the circumstances we are in. Leave her behind!"[9]

After the pirates left the ship, the other passengers crowded around Marie and asked for gospel tracts. They said: "We have seen that your God is the true God, and we want to believe in him too."

A few years after her experience as a captive at sea, Monsen returned to Shandong to conduct revival meetings. After ministering at Jinan, a local missionary reported:

> People were broken up and wept for their sins. There were then special manifestations of the Spirit's power and great rejoicing . . . Missionaries, pastors and others, willing formerly to work only as average Christians, became dissatisfied, placed themselves on the altar anew, were filled with the Spirit, and now see the Lord in a different way.[10]

Partly due to the godly influence of Marie Monsen and other servants of the gospel, Jinan to this day remains the part of Shandong with the highest percentage of Christians.

In 1932 Monsen surprised many when she decided to leave China and return to Norway to take care of her elderly mother. She was 54 years old at the time and had lived the last 31 years of her life in China. While some were shocked that her missionary career came to an abrupt end at a time when her ministry was bearing much fruit, no one who knew her doubted that this maidservant of the Lord had sought and obeyed the voice of the Holy Spirit.

Marie Monsen's long and fruitful ministry in China was later summarized with this glowing tribute:

> Blessing came to large numbers of Christian leaders, both Chinese and missionaries. Those who had seen little response to

the Christian message had been discouraged by apathy, feeling God had abandoned them. Some had lapsed into doubt; others had tolerated sin in their attitudes and relationships. Now they had a new experience of the power of God. The message was as old as the New Testament, but as Marie talked to individuals, she found that many "Christians" had failed to have a real understanding of the work of Jesus.

For over twenty years, large numbers had been entering the churches, but too often the preaching had been vague, calling people to "believe" without explaining what and why. One missionary had assumed that she became a Christian as a child when she raised her hand at a meeting, without understanding what it signified. Others had become Christians without an inward understanding of what God had done for them.

Marie Monsen's memorial stone, erected in 1999

When people realized in their hearts what they had believed theoretically with their heads, their love for God deepened and led to great joy.[11]

In Marie Monsen's place, God surprised many by raising up another Scandinavian woman, the younger Anna Christensen of Denmark, who took over much of the ministry Monsen had left behind. Christensen had a remarkable ministry of evangelism in all of China's provinces, until she was forced to leave China at the advent of Communism.

Marie Monsen passed away in 1962 at the age of 84, and is buried in a cemetery in the Norwegian city of Bergen.

1930s

———•◦•———

The encouraging signs of spiritual life that emerged among many Shandong churches in the late 1920s proved to be adequate fuel for the Spirit of God, who blew on the embers and fanned them into flame, as a powerful revival broke out among the churches of Shandong for much of the 1930s.

The outbreak of revival seemed to take many Christian leaders by surprise. The conditions could scarcely have been worse. With the Great Depression ravaging the world economy at the start of the decade, many missionaries wondered if there would be any financial support available to keep them on the field. The Lord Jesus Christ was ready to display his glory, however, and the results were thrilling and far-reaching. One witness of the Shandong revival wrote:

> One of the most amazing results of the revival was that it did what the word 'revival' implies. It revived spiritually-dead churches. Many of the churches had stopped holding worship services, and others met only when the missionaries had time to visit them. Following the revival they began meeting regularly, and when no preacher was available, laymen led the services . . .
>
> Church attendance increased many times within a few months. Those who attended were serious workers for Christ. Many churches began to disciple their members. After an attempt was made to interest those who never attended, the church withdrew fellowship from them.[1]

In 1932, the Southern Baptists in the province reported:

> In the revival here at Huangxian last spring, the Bible school came in for a great blessing. Every one of the faculty got a

distinct blessing, and nearly every one of them was filled with the Holy Spirit. It has become a new school . . .

At Jining our people have become of one heart and mind in the Lord Jesus as never before—we feel that the year has led us on to new spiritual heights . . . At Laizhou and Laiyang it is absolutely beyond the power of human tongue to express the sheer joy and rapture of this new, marvelous, intimate fellowship into which we were brought with the glorified Redeemer Himself.

At Pingdu, God has been adding daily to his church. The general estimate is that 3,000 souls have been saved this year. There have been about 900 baptisms, with others waiting . . .

The evidence of changed lives includes: opium given up, idols torn down, quarrels of years' standing made up, village hoodlums turned into humble men of prayer and soul-winners. Many have given up home and land and gone out to the lost around them.[2]

The Holy Spirit fell in great power upon the Southern Baptist missionaries and Chinese believers at Huangxian, and they cried out in prayer for four days and four nights. Everyone present came under conviction and confessed their sins. Toward the end of the meeting, the Chinese Christians told the missionaries: "We thought you considered yourselves above us. Now we are all one."[3]

The church in Jinan experienced more conversions to Christ in 1932 alone than during the previous six decades combined. The churches reportedly "reached a new spiritual high plane. Nearly every one of the preachers, teachers, Bible women and missionaries had an experience of the deeper life, and each one began to have genuine victory and power in his life."[4]

Signs and wonders

Like in the book of Acts, miracles took place throughout Shandong as God confirmed his word with signs and wonders. One missionary reported:

I saw a man who had crawled around like a worm because his legs had grown together. God responded immediately to the prayer of faith. As these simple believers waited upon Him, the flesh was separated, the man rose and walked, and he is now preaching the gospel.[5]

An old man in another town was dying of tuberculosis. His coffin and grave clothes were prepared, and his family and neighbors awaited his death. After an evangelist visited and prayed for him, the man suddenly jumped up and shouted: "I am well!" He sold his coffin and contributed the money to the construction of a new meeting hall.

In a small village a woman had laid out her burial garments and her family members gathered around her bed to mourn. Just as the woman's eyes closed, a lady who had only been saved for a few days entered the room. She exhorted: "You must pray to the living God. He hears prayers!"

She walked over to the bed and started to pray for the sick woman. As she prayed:

the dying woman opened her eyes and immediately became better. The believing woman witnessed to the power of the gospel . . . The whole family and a large number of other people were saved. About twenty in the village were also filled with the Holy Spirit.[6]

Visions lead to repentance

As the Spirit of God was poured out on people with hungry hearts throughout Shandong, many insights were provided into the supernatural realm that caused people to repent of their sins and get right with Jesus Christ. Some saw visions of heaven, others of hell. In a meeting in one town, a Christian was praying when he saw a clear vision of a pitchfork. He didn't know what it meant or what to do about it, but he got to his feet in the church meeting and simply shared what he had seen.

At the sunrise prayer meeting the next morning another Christian arose and confessed:

> "Brethren, I am the guilty party; I stole a pitchfork twenty years ago. It had left my mind until the brother saw it in a vision last night" . . . After breakfast he took money to his neighbor to pay for the tool, begged him to forgive him, and brought his neighbor to church to hear of the Jesus who can change people's hearts.[7]

The living God also gave a vision to a group of four schoolboys as they prayed together. The vision was deeply troubling to them. In it, they saw the Lamb's Book of Life being opened in heaven. They were thrilled to see the names of so many of their classmates and relatives whose lives had been impacted by the revival, but the name of their Christian teacher, Mr. Hou, was listed in a different book, the Book of Sin, which included a note that he had stolen $400 from the Christian school he worked for.

The boys were afraid to confront their teacher with the details of their vision, but were so overcome with dread for his lost soul that they visited his home. With tears in their eyes they knelt before him and said God had shown them something to share with him. Hou encouraged them to tell what they had seen, and when they did the teacher broke out in a cold sweat and said: "I am guilty. I thought no one would ever know." He made restitution and became a wonderful witness for Jesus Christ.[8]

A mighty wind blows on the Southern Baptists

At Laiyang in eastern Shandong, church members had back-slidden to a desperate state throughout the 1920s, and by

1930 many fellowships were described as "dead." A revival meeting was held in December 1930, and from the start the Holy Spirit powerfully manifested his presence in their midst. On December 3 a prayer service was held. The meeting began normally with singing and prayer, before a Southern Baptist missionary reported:

> A complete hush possessed the room. There were several of us kneeling in the front of the church. Mr. Li, our evangelist, had been suffering with hoarseness and could hardly speak. After quite a period of stillness, he began to sing a song. His voice had absolutely no huskiness in it. I realized that it was something extraordinary, and I suddenly cried out, "The Holy Spirit has come!"
>
> The next moment both he and I were hurled down on the floor and could not get up for about two hours. Oh! The rapture and the ecstasy of it! It seemed that I was so full I would burst, and the fire of the Holy Spirit seemed to be burning away everything . . .
>
> Twenty people were really and truly converted. Born-again, in the truest sense of the word. At times I did not even get to preach, as we took up the whole preaching time dealing with souls who were crying out to God for mercy . . . Man's feeble efforts were thrust aside, and we had the privilege of standing to the side and seeing the Spirit work. Praise His Holy Name.[9]

When reports of the Shandong revival began filtering back to the Southern Baptist churches across America, many concerns were raised that the movement was merely based on hype and human excitement. The board back in Virginia expressed concern that the missionaries had "indulged in Pentecostal excess." Dr. M. E. Dodd, then president of the Southern Baptist Convention, decided to visit China to evaluate the movement for himself. Dodd summarized his findings with these words:

The so-called Shandong Revival is a spiritual movement of tremendous force which has been going on in northeast China for more than three years. It corresponds quite markedly to the Welsh Revival of the past few decades and to other historic revivals of both Biblical and post-Biblical times.

I had heard something of this Shandong Revival before leaving America. I had facetiously said to my church, which so generously voted me a six-month leave of absence, that if I found the Shandong Revival to be anything like the reports I had heard of it, I might never come back. When I got there and observed and also experienced some of its power, I felt like Peter on the Mount of Transfiguration . . . I also felt the more practical and useful thing would be to bring back with me to America as much of the revival spirit as I could.[10]

Miracles at Pingdu

Although the missionaries involved in the Shandong revival preferred to focus on testimonies of repentance and salvation, numerous supernatural healings and deliverances of demons also occurred throughout the province.

A Chinese doctor who worked at the Pingdu Christian Hospital was not yet a believer in Christ. He belittled reports of the revival, and commented that only if two of his paralyzed patients were healed would he believe the gospel. Both women were described as "hopeless cases."

His first patient, a woman named Jiao who had been paralyzed for 28 years, was completely healed, by the power of the Holy Spirit, and a great number of people were saved as a result.

The second woman, Mrs. Luo, had been unable to walk for 18 years. Her "lower limbs were drawn up, large at the joints, but small as little sticks with no muscles at all."[11]

After both patients were healed by the supernatural power of

Mrs. Luo, who was healed of paralysis after 18 years

God, the doctor, "trembling with fear and conviction, repented and accepted Christ."[12]

When a missionary traveled to Pingdu to investigate the healing of Mrs. Jiao, the local pastor told him:

Mrs. Jiao has been a faithful Christian and a church member and is well-known throughout the community . . . The 72-year-old woman came walking into the church. She bowed to me and said, "Pastor, look at me. I am a new person from the top of my head to the bottom of my feet. Do you see these shoes? This is the first pair of shoes I have had in 28 years" . . .

None of the congregation had much faith; but Mrs. Jiao was so sure, and we began to have deep confidence in her. We put her in a big armchair, brought her to church, and placed her in front of the Communion table. I then asked all the members to kneel and pray, and I knelt beside the pulpit. In a few minutes I heard a noise and looked up to see Mrs. Jiao walking across the front of the church and down the aisle . . . It was like an electric shock to the whole congregation. We all knew her condition, but there she was walking in our midst! We began praising the Lord and telling the story of what He had done.[13]

The Chinese pastor bubbled with excitement as he testified of the transformation that came into his life after witnessing this great healing and the mighty revival that followed. He said:

I have been preaching for 30 years and have not been worth my salt. I was so lazy I could not walk a mile and a half to tell people about Jesus. Since the revival I go to prayer meetings at five o'clock in the morning, go home and eat breakfast, take a little bread for lunch and walk 25 miles witnessing in villages, then come home and go to prayer meetings at night. The next morning I am ready to go again.

When this revival began, we had about fifty members in our little church. Now we have at least one Christian in each of the 1,000 homes in this town. Dozens of villages surround us, and we have witnessed in all of them. There are hundreds of Christians in them.[14]

A large tent was used by missionaries and Chinese evangelists to preach the gospel in the Pingdu area, and thousands were exposed to the message of eternal life for the first time. A band of robbers decided to steal the tent, but the authorities were made aware of the plan and advised the Christians to end the meetings and take the tent to a safe place. The believers, however, decided to continue the meetings, and began to earnestly pray for the salvation of the thieves. A short time later:

The young bandit leader was stricken blind and a swelling came upon his face. This frightened him greatly. He realized it was from the Lord, and came to the tent confessing his sins and asking for prayer. Converted, his sight was restored and the swelling left. Later he joined a Bible class. His life has been wonderfully transformed, and those who know him believe that now he will give the remainder of his life to preaching.

There have been between 2,000 and 3,000 conversions in Pingdu County this year (1932). Not less than 1,000 have been baptized![15]

More than eight decades later, evidence of the impact from the revival in Pingdu still lingers. Today, the city contains approximately 80,000 Christians of various denominations, more than half of whom attend Evangelical house church meetings. The percentage of believers in Pingdu is among the highest of any city in Shandong.

Revival in the schools

Before the revival, missionaries had already established dozens of schools, orphanages, hospitals and other Christian facilities throughout Shandong. Those institutions were transformed into key hubs of blessing as the fire of God swept through the province.

In one town the revival began when two Christian students were filled with the Holy Spirit. The next day was the start of the new school year, and the students returned to class. At the girls' school, which had a roll of 600 students, a teacher reported:

When we arrived at the school we found the girls in groups of two or three in a room, all in deep conviction of cheating on examinations, stealing peaches from the school orchard, lying to their parents and to others, and stealing pencils, pens, and money . . . The next morning even more were under conviction.[16]

The boys' school experienced a similar outpouring of conviction of sin. The church leaders in the town wisely stood back and allowed the Spirit of God to perform a deep cleansing work. They threw open the doors of the chapel for the male and female students to use twice a day. The capacity of the chapel was 1,500 seats, but the two schools filled it to overflowing for each service.

To commence each meeting, a preacher read a passage of Scripture and gave a simple message of salvation. Dozens rushed forward, eager to surrender their lives to Jesus Christ and experience his salvation. The desperate students:

> filled the front and the aisles, kneeling, praying, and confessing sin. The conviction was so deep that tears flowed as they prayed. You could count the number who came forward by the tear-stained spots on the wooden floor.
>
> The series of meetings lasted ten days. By the end of that time: "all 600 girls had made professions of faith. Nine hundred of the 1,000 boys also made professions. Most of the boys who weren't converted left school because they could no longer endure the warm spiritual atmosphere without receiving Christ."[17]

A Communist cell is destroyed

During a meeting in Huangxian in 1932, one schoolboy was so convicted of sin that his body became rigid and he fell against one of the teachers. He was instructed to pray to God, but the boy was sure he was about to die, so great was the weight of guilt upon him, for he had given himself over to terrible sin. After half an hour of great agony, with his body still as rigid as a board:

> He cried aloud, "O God, if you will not kill me, I will confess my sins!" And then for an hour he poured out his heart to God. He confessed the deepest and blackest sins, such as had never been heard in that school . . .

He hated and wanted to take the life of a classmate who had kindly loaned him money, simply because his friend was better off than he. His hatred of the rich had become so great that he wanted to destroy them and seize what they possessed, for he had become a real Communist at heart.[18]

In another service a Chinese boy was moaning in agony as he lay under a bench at the back of the chapel. A missionary went to investigate and found the boy in an agitated state of mind. He told the missionary:

You don't know me. I am a Communist. We have a secret Communist cell here in the school. I've threatened to kill you and all the missionaries, and I've sworn to wipe out Christianity and burn your churches. When I heard about this revival, I thought the missionaries were just hypnotizing the students and that the concept of God was foolishness . . . I started to stand up and challenge you, but something struck me and knocked me under this bench. I know it was God. I know that you Christians are right, but I can't believe. I have gone too far. I can't believe![19]

After the meeting was dismissed, several teachers stayed behind and pleaded with the boy to give his heart to God. He kept insisting he had gone too far. The next morning he left the school, and a week later the school leaders heard he was dead.

Another schoolboy was so full of demonic hate against the people of God that he screamed out: "Oh God! You know I have said that when I have destroyed all the Christians I would like to climb up to heaven and kill You!"[20]

When this boy had finished his rant he became completely limp. Lifting him up by the arms, the believers were able to stand him up on his feet. After a while he was able to return to his room. For several days he was in a dazed condition, but:

he finally accepted Christ and was saved. We discovered the Communist cell in the school consisted of eight or ten members, including these two boys. About half of the members were saved during the meeting, and the others left the school. The cell was destroyed.[21]

Struck to the core

The revival in Shandong touched thousands of lives, as the Holy Spirit moved without regard to reputation or position. Countless church leaders and missionaries were struck to the core and repented of their sins. Many who presumed they had experienced God's saving grace were brought under deep conviction and had to face the reality that the quality of their lives was inconsistent with the Scriptures. A Chinese pastor in Feixian testified:

> I have been a preacher for 22 years, but for the last 17 years my ministry has been as it were in a dry and thirsty land, without fruit and without flavor, and my work has been by constraint rather than by inner inclination.
>
> In the summer of 1930 the Lord made me feel an especially deep conviction of sin, and His judgments fell heavily upon me. I confessed my sins, and Jesus revealed Himself to me on two occasions. The most difficult of all to bear was to see the nail-prints in His hands. From this time on there was a change in my spiritual condition . . .
>
> During the past four years I have led revival meetings. Many church members have been revived. Many have been changed from coldness to warm-heartedness, and their lives are different. Miracles of healing and driving out of evil spirits have followed my ministry.[22]

At Huangxian a missionary with an outstanding reputation throughout the church was convicted of sin and pride by the Holy Spirit. Under the searching finger of God, the man's conscience was pricked to the core, and he realized he was a hypocrite. He went to the church and asked to make a statement. The believers were used to him speaking so nobody expected what was to come. The missionary confessed that he was proud and loved the acclaim of others, and that his heart was so burdened by the realization of his sin that he didn't believe he could live any longer. He later wrote:

> While I was speaking, the Holy Spirit so deeply convicted those present of their own sins it seemed they could not bear it. I watched their faces grow pale. Then they began to cry and drop on their knees or fall prostrate on the floor. One missionary, sitting on the front seat, dropped to his knees and began to weep. When he got up, he went across the chapel to a Chinese preacher and said to him, "Mr. Jiang, I have hated you." The Chinese gentleman answered, "Yes, and I have hated you too."
>
> Missionaries went to missionaries confessing unpleasant feelings toward one another. Chinese preachers, guilty of envy, jealousy and hatred, confessed their sins one to each other.
>
> No one had said a word about public confession of sin, but the Holy Spirit brought such conviction upon the group that none could keep from it. It was so unexpected and unplanned that no one realized what was happening. The time scheduled for ending the meeting passed, but all wished to continue. When we would try to close, someone would say, "Please don't go! Pray for me! I am in desperate need!" As soon as we would pray for that one, another would confess his bitter inner feelings.
>
> One could sense that the Holy Spirit controlled the confessions because no one accused or implicated others. There were no unwholesome confessions, only broken and contrite hearts making things right with God and each other.[23]

Anointed for burial

The results of the 1930s Shandong revival went deep and were long-lasting. Before the outpouring of God's grace, churches had generally become fragmented and were struggling. The gospel was advancing but slowly and inconsistently. The visitation of Jesus to the midst of his people totally transformed the body of Christ. One observer wrote:

> I saw missionaries and Chinese Christians embrace each other as God removed pride, envy, jealousy and criticism from all of us and molded us together in Christian love. I saw Chinese preachers put their arms around each other and weep and laugh together in the renewed joy of Christian love . . . We sang one song after another for two or three hours. No one wanted to go home because it seemed that heaven had come down, and we wanted to praise God and rejoice.[24]

Although most reports from Shandong focused on the extraordinary salvations and miracles taking place, Satan was enraged by the revival, and persecution was commonplace. Much of the strongest opposition came from within the local communities, where unregenerate individuals lashed out in anger at the joy and peace experienced by those who had submitted to the Lord.

A Chinese evangelist named Li was preaching the gospel to a crowd of people on the street when a soldier approached and asked: "If I become a Christian, can I have two wives?" Li told him the Scriptures forbade such arrangements. The soldier was incensed, "beat Evangelist Li severely, and hung him on his thumbs for over an hour, when some foreign missionaries came to his rescue."[25]

Before the revivals of the 1930s, the churches of Shandong had become lukewarm and many were falling away from the faith. After being transformed by the Holy Spirit, they were characterized as a praying Church, with one report noting:

> The spirit of prayer was an outstanding result of the revival. People loved to pray. Many times prayer meetings lasted two

or three hours. The prayers were not long and monotonous but fervent, sometimes tearful, always as if those praying were simply talking to the Father with the confidence that He was listening. It was beautiful to hear them pray for each other. Many parents came to know the Lord through the prayers of their children.[26]

As seems the case with many revivals throughout history, the mighty outpouring of the Holy Spirit in Shandong in the 1930s appears to have been part of God's plan to strengthen his children before coming persecution. For the next two decades war and political unrest was rampant in Shandong and elsewhere in China, before a long and brutal persecution commenced at the hands of the Communist government beginning in the early 1950s.

When the Japanese launched a full-scale war in China in 1937, Shandong was a major piece of their imperialist goals. A large group of Japanese pastors accompanied the invading soldiers. These men, most of whom were government stooges with little or no understanding of the Bible, wreaked havoc among the churches of Shandong, spoiling some of the fruit of the mighty revival. The Japanese "pastors" were said to have:

> functioned primarily as agents of their country with instructions to put pressure on the churches to form a union and to influence the churches to support their program for "a New Order in East Asia" . . . These pastors infiltrated local churches and mission schools, disseminating their propaganda. One student complained that in his school class a Japanese pastor spoke of the Godhead as consisting of four persons—Father, Son, Holy Spirit and the Emperor of Japan.[27]

The Japanese occupation ended at the conclusion of the Second World War, and a time of civil war and widespread calamity ensued, followed by decades of brutal suppression of the

膠東各公會曁佈道團假煙臺文會中西信徒會誼攝影紀念

Shandong church leaders at a meeting in Yantai, 1934

Church under Communist rule. Before Satan could do his worst, however, God had set aside a remnant for his glory in Shandong, one that had been divinely fortified to withstand the approaching storms.

The Evangelistic Bands

As the flame of the gospel burned throughout the cities and villages of Shandong Province, thousands of redeemed believers naturally desired to share their faith with those who didn't yet know Jesus Christ. Not only did Christians share their testimonies with relatives and acquaintances, but groups were organized to travel together to proclaim the good news, in keeping with the example of the New Testament when Jesus' disciples were sent out in small groups.

Ranging in size from two or three people to sometimes dozens, Christians formed into what came to be known as

An Evangelistic Band made up of retired businessmen in Shandong, 1930s

"Evangelistic Bands." Some bands headed deep into the rural areas of the province for weeks at a time, trusting the Lord to provide as they went, while other bands would gather together after church on Sundays and visit nearby villages with the message of eternal life. This spontaneous initiative of the Holy Spirit gave an additional boost to the advance of the gospel. Lost people heard the gospel in their home villages or while working in the fields, and were not required to travel into a city to hear preachers in large meetings.

The Evangelistic Bands usually carried bags of gospel literature with them to aid in the sharing of their message. A custom emerged where small flags were produced, usually triangular in shape, which each band carried with them wherever they traveled. The flags often displayed information about the location of the local church, or a key Scripture verse.

God powerfully used the Evangelistic Bands in Shandong, and many thousands of people heard the message and believed in Jesus Christ. The emergence of the bands caused a shift in the body of Christ, where normal men, women, boys and girls became preachers of the gospel, and the churches no longer relied so heavily on ordained ministers to do the work of evangelism. This shift caused the gospel to spread more quickly to the unreached masses.

No willing Christian was barred from participating in an Evangelistic Band. In 1932, the girls from the Jinan Christian School organized themselves into a preaching group and shared the gospel in surrounding villages on Sunday afternoons. One day the girls walked five miles (8 km) in the searing summer heat. Later that evening they:

> came home beaming because they had experienced the joy of witnessing for their Savior. The road was dusty, and the day uncomfortably hot, but this little group of schoolgirls sang

A girls' Evangelistic Band

praises to their God as they walked and spent their rest time by the roadside praying for the souls of those to whom they were taking the gospel.

When they returned at twilight with shining eyes, and voices still joyous with praise, we found that during the whole long, hot afternoon the girls had not bothered about the comfort of a single drink of water, but exclaimed, "It was the best trip we ever took!"[1]

Three famous Chinese preachers

Although the gospel was primarily spread throughout Shandong during the revival by multitudes of normal Chinese believers, some of the more famous names in Chinese church history were also involved. The list of anointed preachers who ministered in the province included Marcus Cheng, the

138

former naval officer Leland Wang, John Li, Charles Li and Wang Mingdao, who is still fondly remembered by many Christians in China today as "The father of the Chinese house churches."

Three other famous Chinese revivalists spent considerable time in Shandong. They were connected to one another through their shared vision to evangelize all of China, and together they encouraged the formation of hundreds of Evangelistic Bands that took the gospel by bicycle, on foot or by whatever means necessary to reach the lost. The English names of these three famous Chinese preachers are Andrew Gih, Watchman Nee and John Sung.

Andrew Gih

Andrew Gih (Chinese name: Ji Zhiwen), was formerly employed as a post office official in Shanghai, before 1931, when God led him to establish the largest and most effective Evangelistic Band in China, called the Bethel Worldwide Evangelistic Band. The Bethel bands went on to lead hundreds of thousands of Chinese to Jesus Christ in China and among the Chinese diaspora throughout Southeast Asia.

The Bethel Band preachers did not spend much time specifically in Shandong, but when they stopped in the province en route from Henan to Inner Mongolia, their meetings in the provincial capital Jinan had a long-lasting impact. Gih reported: "The Holy Spirit did a great work. Within three days more than 200 soldiers were brought to Christ. One day 44 individuals came for personal prayer support and help. Very hard cases were settled before the Lord."[2]

The following letter was sent by a church leader in another part of Shandong after the Bethel Band's meetings there:

We sat for eight days under some of the most powerful preaching I have ever heard. These young Chinese evangelists have stirred us to the depths of our souls by their singing and preaching . . .

What did they preach? Nothing new at all. Just the same old gospel; no sob-stuff and no working on the emotions. Just the plain facts that the blood of Jesus Christ cleanses and saves from all sin, and that He puts a new song in our mouths and a new purpose in our hearts. These preachers are men whose inner life shines in their faces and whose prayers for the lost fairly shake the rafters. An audience of over 800 people listened to every message.[3]

Andrew Gih

An American Presbyterian chairman, Dr. Paul Abbott, closely observed the work of the Bethel Evangelistic Band in Shandong, and offered a favorable comparison with some of the other Chinese movements of the time:

> Their work impresses one as sane and constructive with emotion released in laughter and song, under control and with no excesses or results to undo or live down. Their follow-up work with correspondence, prayer lists and printed material is skillfully carried on as part of their service to the churches.[4]

No part was left untouched when the preachers of the Bethel Band visited a community. Although many Chinese were resentful of Christians and there were many instances of persecution, most of the time the Bethel bands received a warm reception as they sowed God's word and found fertile soil in the hearts of thousands of people. As a result:

> Bloodthirsty bandits, rapacious officials, overbearing soldiers, anarchist students, dishonest servants, polygamists, sedate scholars, businessmen, rickshaw coolies, beggars, men and women, young and old, city-dwellers and country folks, were moved to confess and forsake sin and to make reparation and restitution.[5]

Watchman Nee

Watchman Nee (Chinese name: Ni Tuosheng) was another to make a mark on the Church in Shandong Province. Already famous in China and around the world for books he had written, Nee came to Jinan in 1932 for a short series of meetings at the medical college, which were attended by large crowds. A report said:

> The longed-for revival spread as more and more of the students found the Savior. Among many of them the experience was to become a legend, for heaven itself seemed to open up their

Watchman Nee

hearts. Afterwards a group of more than 100 students gathered at a mountain beauty spot in the Taishan Range above the city of Tai'an, traditional site of Confucius' grave. They studied the Bible and prayed; and before the end, a large group of them were baptized in the cold pool of a mountain torrent, publicly confessing Jesus as Lord.[6]

John Sung

The third of the trio of great preachers to impact Shandong in the 1930s was perhaps the most effective Chinese evangelist of all, John Sung (Chinese name: Song Shangjie). Sung visited Tai'an City in 1931 for a series of meetings. Although Tai'an had previously been a beacon for spiritual life, the light of the gospel had dimmed, and Satan was wreaking havoc among the local believers. Missionary Leslie Lyall observed:

> A wave of anti-Christian animosity had swept over the community. Churches had been wrecked, mission schools forced to close and some of the pastors compelled to flee with their

John Sung

families . . . Here, in this center where the Christians were greatly discouraged after their terrible experiences, Dr. Sung was greatly used by God. There were 103 new converts. One of them was a youth of only 19 who had broken every one of the Ten Commandments. He heard the sermon on the Prodigal Son and he came back to God in true repentance. And there were many others like him.[7]

When Sung and his team visited Penglai, a group of trouble-makers attended the meetings intent on stirring up dissent, but the Spirit of God continued to move in the hearts of the eager crowd. One night:

There were more than 300 people seeking to get right with God and with one another, amid scenes of deep distress and tearful repentance. The news of this revival spread and many more came in from the country to attend the meetings. The largest building in the city was filled to overflowing. As sin was confessed and put away, waves of joy seemed to sweep through the congregation. Praises mingled loudly with the prayers. The girls of the high school rose from their knees and stood in groups with their arms around one another singing praises to the Lord.

The sermons were sometimes cut short by someone who could not wait to make restitution or confession to someone else present. One aged pastor confessed a sin of 37 years previously which had been weakening his power as an evangelist. The Registrar at the hospital had for years been misappropriating funds and he now reckoned up the total amount of his thefts and made full restitution to the hospital there and then.[8]

John Sung returned to the province in March 1935 for a series of meetings in Jinan and Penglai. Martin Hopkins described the meetings:

> Seminary and high school students and Christians from far and near filled the shed three times daily for eight days. Dr. Sung is a preacher of the true gospel of grace . . . There were 500 professions of faith and re-consecration. Much stress was laid on personal evangelism and at the close of the meetings 130 evangelistic bands were organized . . . Our students received a great spiritual uplift and as a result are most earnest in carrying on the work of teaching the unsaved.[9]

Revival reaches the villages

Although the revival was centered in the main population hubs of Shandong in the early years, it soon spread to countless rural villages throughout the province. For the most part, the gospel was spread by faith-filled Chinese evangelists who

A bicycle preaching band at Yantai in 1938

were propelled forward by the Spirit of God throughout the thousands of unreached villages in the interior of the province. An intrepid missionary wrote:

> The native workers and I go into the interior places some 300 miles [486 km], where we travel by bicycle and on foot. We cross rivers, some a mile wide, with the water coming above our waists, in order to reach those villages where the gospel has not been brought.
>
> Our hearts are made to rejoice as we see the multitudes of heathen gather about us with their hearts eager for the gospel message, to hear of Him who died for the whole world that all men everywhere might be saved. We rejoice that it is our privilege to be in such street meetings.[10]

Many Chinese preachers were raised up by God during the revival. The results were often spectacular. After severe flooding in 1936 one evangelist, David Lu, reported: "During the past three months, 950 souls have accepted the Lord as their personal Savior, the large majority of whom are refugees driven from their own villages because of the flood."[11]

Although in later decades the triangular flags may have been discarded and their methods adjusted to suit the day, the Evangelistic Bands proved to be a forerunner of how the house church movements have sent teams of zealous evangelists all over China to spread the gospel in recent decades. Whereas in the 1930s and 1940s the Chinese Christians were overjoyed to see thousands of people come into the kingdom of God, the house churches of a later era were mightily empowered to lead millions of people out of the kingdom of darkness and into the kingdom of light.

1940s

The revival in Shandong throughout the late 1920s and 1930s had far-reaching effects and attracted numerous new mission groups to the province. Almost every Western denomination was represented in Shandong during the 1940s, up until the time missionaries were expelled from China by the new Communist regime in the 1950s.

Until the end of the Second World War the Christians in rural areas of Shandong experienced an intensely difficult time because of the Japanese occupation. The province was invaded

Chinese evangelists preaching outside the home of Confucius at Qufu

from the north and east in December 1937, and many cities and towns were heavily bombed. Troops on the ground murdered, looted, and raped defenseless women and girls. In the rural areas of Shandong:

> Utmost confusion prevailed. Chinese guerrilla bands raided enemy outposts, and Japanese soldiers retaliated by attacking villages and small towns. Regular church and evangelistic work became impracticable. But Chinese pastors and local Christian leaders did their utmost to carry on . . . Missionaries found it practically impossible between 1938 and December 1941 to undertake country journeys.[1]

The Church of the Nazarene

During a severe famine in 1920–1, the Church of the Nazarene Mission had constructed a large school and other facilities to bring relief to the desperate population. The location chosen for their base was the town of Chaocheng in western Shandong. This strategic location sits just north of the Yellow River, near the juncture of the three provinces of Shandong, Hebei and Henan. A new church building, built on the spot where a Chinese prison had long stood, was described as a place where:

> Men and women could be set free from the bondage of sin, where they could be fed on the Bread from heaven and drink to their heart's content from the wells of salvation; a place where a real liberty of soul might be found, and where the matchless love of God through the forgiveness of their sins and the sanctification of their hearts might be realized. It was in this building that the working of the Spirit was so manifested during the revival in 1927 . . . Many will be found in heaven as a result of those revivals.
>
> Here we saw a great many people, both young and old, getting right with God and with each other. We saw demons cast out and unhappy souls made happy indeed. People with

penitent tears confessed their sins and many sought holiness of the heart. Families were reunited around the altar. We were living night and day where the glory came down.[2]

When the Japanese launched war in Shandong, tens of thousands of troops arrived on ships across the Sea of Japan, and the entire province soon fell into the hands of the cruel Japanese forces. One day Japanese bombers flew low over the Nazarene church and reduced it to rubble.

The buildings may have been destroyed but the wickedness of men could not snuff out the fire of the Holy Spirit that had transformed the lives of many people in Chaocheng. The revival spread from the little-known town to many outlying areas. Hundreds of people had been deeply touched by their experiences after visiting the Nazarene church, and had taken the revival fires home with them. As a result:

> Evangelistic parties were sent out to other sections of that territory with outstanding results. One village came to be called "The Christian Village." There were professing Christians in almost every home. Where formerly there were many beggars in the village, now, having destroyed their idols, and having established a Christian school for their children, only two beggars remained in the whole village . . .
>
> So many people came for personal prayer between meetings that there was little time to rest or to eat meals . . . Within a few years in this village, people were wearing better clothing, eating better food, dwelling in better homes, and buying more land than they had ever owned before.[3]

Eric Liddell

Perhaps the most celebrated Christian martyr ever called to lay down his life in China is the Scottish-born Olympic champion and world-record holder, Eric Liddell. Born to missionary

Eric Liddell

parents in Tianjin in 1902, Liddell returned to his homeland as a teenager. Even as a young man his life was marked by a deep faith and consecration to Christ, and he considered all worldly achievements nothing compared to the joy of walking with God.

Liddell was already an outstanding athlete at the age of 16. He captained his school cricket team, and possessed an exceptional turn of speed. After entering Edinburgh University in 1920 his sporting career blossomed. He excelled in running events, especially the 100-meter sprint, and his speed enabled him to play international rugby for Scotland. Many athletic victories came Liddell's way, including a winning run for the British Empire team against the United States.

With the 1924 Olympic Games in Paris looming, Great Britain placed its hope in "the flying Scot" to bring home multiple gold medals. Sport was not the priority of Liddell's life, however. In 1923 he joined the Glasgow Students' Evangelistic Union, and gave himself wholeheartedly to the service of God. He continually asked himself: "Does this path I tread follow the Lord's will?"

Eric Liddell's devotion to Christ was complete, and he viewed his athletic ability as a God-given gift by which he could glorify Jesus. This opportunity came in a unique way during the Olympics.

A short time before the Games commenced, Liddell discovered that the heats for the 100-meter sprint were scheduled to be run on a Sunday. The prospect of running on the Lord's Day was abhorrent to him and he withdrew, thus giving up the almost certain prospect of winning a gold medal in his strongest event.

The Olympic 100-meter competition went on without him, and a world that idolizes its sports stars was left reflecting on Liddell's radical obedience to Jesus Christ. For weeks his decision not to run was vehemently criticized by the press in Britain and other parts of the world. Much pressure was brought to bear on him, but nothing would alter his convictions. He later explained his decision:

> Ask yourself, if I know something to be true, am I prepared to follow it, even though it is contrary to what I want, or to what I have personally held to be true? Will I follow it if it means being laughed at, if it means personal financial loss, or some kind of hardship?[4]

Liddell did compete in the 400-meters, which was not held on a Sunday. He won a gold medal and set a new world record for the event, and also won a bronze in the 200-meters. The deep admiration Scotland held for Liddell was later seen at his university graduation. One account said:

Scotland loved this young man. He demonstrated on the field just the sort of determination, stamina, and honest excellence that—though perhaps not flashy—the Scots love to see in a native son . . . He was literally paraded around the streets of Edinburgh to the adulation of its inhabitants.[5]

For the next few years people flocked to see the Olympic champion. This opened many doors for Liddell to share his faith. Although he had returned to his homeland for education, his plan was always to return to China after he had graduated. Despite his success and popularity, Liddell shocked Scotland by returning to China to engage in missionary work in 1925.

Liddell fell in love and married Florence Mackenzie at Tianjin in 1934, and their union produced three beautiful daughters. For years he faithfully worked at the Anglo-Chinese College in Tianjin, where countless missionaries passed through from far-flung fields, sharing their victories and struggles.

Liddell inwardly longed to experience pioneer work for himself, and in 1936 he sensed the Holy Spirit was leading him to a new ministry. A vacancy opened at Xiaochang in Shandong Province, but the opportunity coincided with the arrival of the Japanese army. It was considered too dangerous for a family to live in the war zone, so to accept the appointment Liddell would have to spend periods of time away from his beloved wife and daughters. After wrestling with the decision for a year, he was convinced that God was calling him to accept the position.

Shandong was in a state of chaos due to the war. Liddell spent much of his energy rescuing wounded soldiers, knowing that if caught he would be sentenced to death by the Japanese. With the outbreak of the Second World War in 1939, the danger for missionaries intensified. Florence and the three girls traveled to safety in Canada, but Eric decided to remain in China. In 1943 he and all his missionary colleagues were arrested and held in a Japanese internment camp at Weifang in Shandong.

For Eric Liddell, being imprisoned with more than 2,000 other foreigners—including 327 children—meant an opportunity to teach and encourage the downcast, and he threw all his energy into his activities. One account of life in the internment camp said:

> Of the missionaries in Weifang, none aroused more admiration and affection than Eric Liddell of the London Missionary Society, and former Olympic hero. On arrival at the camp, the Employment Committee appointed him teacher of Mathematics and Science, and organizer of Athletics. Later he also became the Warden of Blocks 23 and 24. As sports activities decreased with the diminishing vigor of the inmates, Liddell gave more and more of his time to keeping the restless youth in the camp entertained with chess, square dancing and other pastimes.[6]

After nearly two years of incarceration and separation from his family, Liddell's health began to break down. He battled depression, and interpreted the symptoms to mean he was wavering in his faith. He didn't realize he was suffering from a malignant brain tumor. The end came quickly, and on February 21, 1945, the missionary and Olympic champion went to be with Jesus Christ, just months before the end of the war.

The story of Eric Liddell was celebrated in the award-winning 1981 movie, *Chariots of Fire*. In 1991 a memorial stone was sent from Scotland to be placed on Liddell's unmarked grave in Shandong. After much research the grave was located within the grounds of a school in Weifang. A service was held at which:

> Communist cadres, Asian missionaries, Scottish businessmen, British diplomats, and family and former friends of Liddell gathered for the ceremony, which included a number by the

school band and Scottish bagpipes as well as fond remembrances from Liddell's friends. At the end of the ceremony a small group of Christians bowed their heads in prayer in front of the memorial stone but were sent away by authorities.[7]

Although he was just 42 when he died, millions of people have been touched by Eric Liddell's self-sacrificial life and death.

Pang Zhiyi—Korean missionary to China

After a phenomenal revival swept millions of Koreans into the kingdom of God during the first two decades of the twentieth century, the Holy Spirit raised up many servants with a passion to preach the gospel wherever he would send them.

Pang Zhiyi, back row, center, with some of his Chinese co-workers

One such servant was Pang Zhiyi, who became one of the first Korean Evangelical missionaries to China. Pang was born in Korea in 1911, and although details are scarce, it's believed he first crossed the Chinese border to commence work in Shandong in the mid-1930s.

To earn money, for years Pang's wife worked as a piano teacher. Her job was considered a novelty as few people owned a piano at the time, and crowds regularly flocked to their home to hear the strange new instrument. This afforded the Pangs a tremendous opportunity to share the gospel with people.

Although they arrived in Shandong toward the end of the revival in the 1930s, God mightily used the Pangs, and hundreds of Chinese placed their trust in the Lord Jesus Christ because of their ministry. They continued to serve

Pang Zhiyi (back row, second from left) with his Chinese co-workers in Shandong. Pang's wife is in the front row on the right

faithfully during the tumult of the 1940s and remained in Shandong until the early 1950s, when the Communist government expelled them. After carefully watching Pang for years, one day members of the Public Security Bureau called him into their offices and showed him a huge file of evidence they had collected against him, detailing his key involvement in the churches of Shandong.

Pang and his wife were expelled from China, but before returning to Korea they stopped in Hong Kong. At the time, the

Eager students at missionary Leslie Lyall's home listening to God's word in 1948. Two of the men on the wall later entered full-time Christian service

Christian world was divided over whether the new Communist regime in China was a positive development for the Church or whether it was a ravenous wolf dressed in sheep's clothing that was waiting to pounce on the body of Christ.

Pang had firsthand experience of the true nature of the Communists and the brutal persecution they were already conducting throughout Shandong. Feeling a responsibility to warn Christians around the world of the truth, in Hong Kong he wrote a long article exposing the reality of life under Mao's regime.

After publishing the article, Pang and his wife traveled to South Korea, where they spent decades in the service of the Lord. Pang finally died in 2015, at the ripe old age of 104. He had been a faithful weapon in the hands of God his entire life, and many people both in Shandong and on the Korean Peninsula will rise up and call Pang blessed at the Judgment.

The Jesus Family

Jing Dianying was born in Shandong in 1890 and grew up in a Buddhist family with strong Confucian traditions. It was not until he entered middle school at Tai'an in 1911 (when he was aged 20) that he heard the gospel for the first time.

Although he first believed in Christ around 1913, it appears Jing was not serious in his Christian faith until he came into contact with Pentecostals in the early 1920s.

After he was born-again, Jing read in the Bible: "Husbands, love your wives" (Ephesians 5.25). This command immediately placed him in a dilemma, as he had divorced his wife and sent

Jing Dianying, founder of the Jesus Family

her back to her mother several years earlier. He later said: "She had bound feet, and was not my equal, and I didn't love her."[1]

A few days later, out of obedience to the Scriptures, Jing walked to his wife's village and brought her back home. As she couldn't easily walk because of her feet, Jing borrowed a wheelbarrow and pushed her the 15 miles (24 km) home. A missionary-doctor, Vaughan Rees, later wrote:

> As soon as they entered the door of his home together the Holy Spirit descended on them both. This was in 1920. In 1940 I received a broken-hearted letter from him. His beloved wife was dead. She had proved his equal and beloved companion for twenty years. Contrary to his former opinion, she was the backbone of the work which had started in 1921.[2]

Jing and his wife knelt together and dedicated themselves unreservedly to obey the Bible. One of the first things they did was sell all their possessions and give the money to the poor.

In the beginning, Jing's church movement was called the Fellowship of the Saints, but there were few members. As the movement grew, the name was changed to the Jesus Family. Together, believers pooled their resources and purchased 43 acres of land in the village of Mazhuang, near Tai'an in central Shandong. The property came to serve both as headquarters for the church and as home to a flourishing community of believers. The group's five-word slogan encapsulated their commitment to Christ and their pattern of frugal living: "Sacrifice, abandonment, poverty, suffering, death."

The radical vision of the Jesus Family was for members to be a unified body where everyone shared all possessions regardless of their background. In each Family, a respected married couple was appointed to be the "parents" of the group. The men were responsible for leading evangelism and Bible teaching, while the women took responsibility for home and family life. People were given work to perform, thus benefiting the entire community. Work projects included the farming of livestock, carpentry, boot-making, electrical work, and baking and cooking.

Each day in Mazhuang village began with communal prayer at 4:00 a.m., when:

> There would be fervent simultaneous praying. Likewise the day ended with prayer and testimonies. In their worship the community liked to sing whole psalms or chapters of the Bible.
>
> Five hundred people shared the area of 43 acres, or less than one-tenth of an acre per person; while the Communists worked on one person requiring one acre for food . . . The Jesus Family won the amazed admiration of many Communists; for its honest and thrifty members, marked by their love for one another and by unselfish service to others, were practicing some of the ideals preached by Communists, but much better.[3]

To outsiders the main distinguishing feature of the Jesus Family was the tremendous love the members had for one another. The elderly were treated with the utmost respect and children raised in a loving environment. Each day began and ended with a group Bible study. On Sundays, all members of the Family came together for worship.

In 1930 the Jesus Family began to tithe one-tenth of the harvest of its land to the poor. God blessed the crops to such a degree that in 1942, when a severe famine blighted north China, the members decided to give away 20 percent of their harvest. One of the leaders, Heng Shin, later testified: "The Lord blessed us. We felt we should add a tenth each year. This year we are giving away nine-tenths."[4] Incredibly, on 43 acres of land the Jesus Family was able to support 500 people and still give away 90 percent of its harvest to the poor.

As the movement grew, Jesus Family members visited many towns and villages, preaching the gospel as they walked from one place to another. Their example of communal living and

The entrance to the Jesus Family property at Mazhuang

deep Christian love attracted those searching for life's answers, especially the homeless, destitute and despised. Many blind people and beggars joined the Family and found eternal life in Christ. Life was far from easy, however, and often when the believers entered a new town the entire population would come out to beat, scorn and humiliate them.

The chicken and the egg

The moral transformation of members of the Jesus Family was far-reaching, and one incident of brazen honesty resulted in God receiving glory. During the civil war that was raging throughout China, the Jesus Family decided not to take sides in the conflict but to demonstrate the love of God and preach the gospel to all who would listen.

One of the Jesus Family leaders was arrested and thrown into jail for sheltering a Nationalist soldier. One day his wife was deep in prayer when a chicken wandered in from the street and laid an egg. The woman's conscience wouldn't allow her to take the egg laid by someone else's chicken for free, but she didn't know who the owner was. She caught the chicken and tied a note to its leg along with a banknote to pay for the egg, and released it back into the street.

The owner of the chicken was astounded when he received the note and payment, and soon news of the deed reached the Communist judge in the area. He investigated the matter and was amazed to discover the existence of such honesty. The judge dismissed the case against the pastor and immediately released him from jail.

The Jesus Family was the first Christian group in China to have a vision to take the gospel, by foot, from China all the way back to Jerusalem. Its workers carried baskets of food and essentials as they walked across the country. The movement grew rapidly, and by 1941 there were 141 different Jesus Family communities in eight provinces, the majority of whom lived in Shandong, with approximately 6,000 members.

Criticism

It appears that after a time the Jesus Family lost its direction. What began as a wholesome ideal of communal living ended up going too far and the movement appeared to be on the verge of becoming a cult. One report lamented:

Except for the youngest married couples, men and women lived in separate buildings. Engagements and weddings were arranged by Jing, the Family head. It happened that young teenagers were made to marry old men, the pretty were matched with the crippled, and educated ones with the illiterate.

Husbands and wives seldom had a chance to live together, for there were just a few rooms allotted to married couples which had to be shared by them in turn. Nurseries took care of the young children. Quite often, children of three to four years old did not know who their parents were.[5]

One of the main points of alarm regarding the Jesus Family among other parts of the body of Christ was its extreme positions on certain teachings. One observer wrote:

In doctrine the movement stresses the filling of the Spirit to the neglect or exclusion of the doctrine of redemption through the cross of Christ. There is a tendency to elevate personal experience above the word of God as a criterion in spiritual matters. Often the word of God is not used as a basis for sermons, and when it is used, it is interpreted in a highly allegorical way, without regard for the common-sense meaning or the principles of true exegesis.[6]

Persecution

In October 1949, when Mao Zedong established the People's Republic of China, there were 20,000 people enlisted in more than 100 different Jesus Families throughout the country. The movement had spread to Manchuria, Inner Mongolia, and across south and central China.

At the start, the government seemed to view the Jesus Family with both admiration and fear. The authorities knew the movement was different from all other Christian groups in China, and that its members practiced many of the ideals of Communism. On the other hand they feared the Jesus Family because they could not control the group. It was a completely indigenous movement, receiving no money from overseas and having minimal contact with foreign Christians.

Jing Dianying later told a friend:

> Little did I think . . . how the Lord would lead, or what He had in store for me. How foolish and ignorant I was. Now I see what He has done. He has raised us up for this purpose, that the Communists might see what Christianity is.[7]

Even the official Three-Self Church magazine, *Tianfeng*, published complimentary articles about the Jesus Family in 1951. One reporter was moved to say:

> It is really touching to see their earnest and down-to-earth spirit of life. Solid and hard-working, from childhood they are taught to bear hardships for the Lord. I have seen the most holy and beautiful faces in the world among these elders and the brothers and sisters in the Family. They love the Lord, love people, love poverty, love production, and love labor.[8]

In 1952 the government decided it could no longer tolerate the Jesus Family. The headquarters at Mazhuang were seized and the buildings torn down, and the 500 Christians there were forced to disperse back into society. Other fellowships of the Jesus Family throughout China continued to meet discreetly, but they too were heavily persecuted.

Just two years after the glowing report in *Tianfeng*, the same publication published a new article with a completely different tone. In February 1953 the magazine launched a series of politically motivated diatribes against the Family, led by Jing's nephew, Jing Zhendong. The increasingly aggressive denunciations included:

In the past few decades, the Jesus Family has insulted the holy name of Jesus and endangered the Chinese people. From now on, this shameful name should not be heard again in New China. Jing Dianying colluded with Japanese invaders and the reactionary officers and officials of the puppet regime in the past 30 years; he also collaborated with the British and American imperialists, collecting information and engaging in anti-Soviet and anti-Communist propaganda.[9]

After initially experiencing a "honeymoon period" with the Communist authorities, the Jesus Family now found itself outlawed and being severely persecuted. The characteristics of the movement:

which were acceptable to the Communists were that it was indigenous and free from western influence, and initially at least it was communal. It was unacceptable to them in that it emphasized miracles, healing, the Second Coming and Sabbath; and

Part of the Jesus Family compound at Mazhuang demolished by the Communists in 1952

these distinctive tenets more than outweighed any advantages which the Communist authorities might have found in it.[10]

Jing was arrested and imprisoned in 1953, and his second wife, Chen Bixi, was assigned to work in a government hospital in Shaanxi Province. By 1955, "their communities had been liquidated, and their members scattered or killed."[11] For several years there was no information about the fate of Jing Dianying. Then, in the spring of 1957, the founder of the Jesus Family contracted liver cancer, brought about by the filthy, unhygienic conditions in prison.

Knowing that he would soon die, the prison authorities released Jing on medical parole. He traveled to Xi'an, where his wife worked, and was immediately visited by Jesus Family leaders. According to some who visited him: "Jing's faith was still strong and his voice clear."[12] His condition worsened, however, and he passed away on August 31, 1957.

Jing Dianying's body was wrapped in a white cloth and buried with neither a coffin nor a tombstone in a cemetery in the suburbs of Xi'an. Four days before his death he had written: "I am going home to see my Father, you wait here for the return of the Lord."[13]

The Jesus Family rises from the ashes

Many China-watchers believed the Jesus Family had been completely obliterated during the excesses of the Cultural Revolution from 1966 to 1976, but in the early 1980s the group surprisingly re-emerged. The strong faith of the Family members had not deserted them during the decades of persecution. Dozens of the movement's leaders had spent years in prison, and more than a few had received a martyr's crown.

Although they are not allowed to form into Christian communes like they did before 1952, there are still hundreds of

Jesus Family congregations today in provinces like Shandong, Hebei, Shaanxi, Henan and Fujian. Some of the Jesus Family fellowships have joined the registered Three-Self Patriotic Movement, while others meet as independent house churches.

Occasional reports emerged throughout the 1980s and 1990s, telling of hardships the Jesus Family was called to endure. In 1983, six believers from the group were "suspended from branches and beaten."[14]

In 1992 the police crushed one of the Jesus Family fellowships at Duoyigou village near Weixian in western Shandong. The believers there led peaceful lives, supporting themselves by breeding long-haired rabbits and making shoes.

The church at Duoyigou attracted the attention of the authorities when it exploded in size to 3,000 members, and on one occasion more than 1,000 believers flocked to the village to

Members of the Jesus Family eating together in 1989

be baptized. There were so many people that the baptisms took ten days to complete!

Revealing how much the Chinese authorities still feared the love and self-sacrifice of these Christians, the police called in a helicopter to circle the normally peaceful village for hours. The 60-year-old leader of the community, Zheng Yunsu, was arrested and sentenced to 12 years in prison, while each of his four sons was sent to a coalmine labor camp for between two and four years.

Before being taken away to begin their sentences, Mr. Zheng and his sons were paraded through the streets, each with a sign around his neck that read: "Member of the Jesus Family."[15] Although the authorities intended the parade to be a humiliation and disgrace, the Zhengs rejoiced greatly that they had been counted worthy to suffer for the name of Jesus.

More trouble came in late 1993, when a group of 60 Jesus Family members in Shandong were arrested as they celebrated

A gathering of the Jesus Family in 1992

Communion on the first day of the month. Thirty of the leaders were charged with "holding illegal religious meetings, resisting arrest, and disturbing social order. [The authorities] destroyed the church hall with a bulldozer and took any belongings of value they could find."[16]

Despite decades of severe and brutal persecution, the Chinese authorities have been unable to eradicate the Jesus Family. Left confused and red-faced, the government repeated the experience of Pharaoh many centuries ago, who found himself unable to subdue God's people. The Bible said of the Israelites, "The more they were oppressed, the more they multiplied and spread" (Exodus 1.12). The same dynamic happened to the Jesus Family in twentieth-century China.

One of the last public communications from the Jesus Family came in 2001, when three imprisoned members were able to smuggle out a stirring letter addressed to Christians around the world. It is fitting to finish this section on the Jesus Family by reprinting their letter:

To the Elders, brothers, and sisters of the worldwide Church. Peace.

As you read this letter, please know that we miss you very much. We are undeserving of your love and all your tears which we can never repay. May God remember your tears.

Today, for the sake of our loving God, we are in prison. We know that this is God's will for us. We present our bodies as a living sacrifice. In this matter we do not follow our own wishes or choices, for this is the road of the cross along which God helps us to walk and of which we are unworthy to walk by ourselves. We have experienced the difficulties and hardships of walking along this narrow path, but we have also experienced the sweetness and comfort of it. By walking on this road we are continually filled with the life of the heavenly kingdom. Our outer nature is wasting away, but our inner nature is being renewed daily.

Dear ones, we wish that you too will exert yourselves on this road. The time is short, and the Lord is coming soon! We know that you also have encountered difficulties, but you must not be disheartened or disappointed. Lay down your heavy burdens and walk! Our hope is in our heavenly home.

Watch and pray continually that you may not be left behind. If we do not see one another again in this world, we will meet again in our heavenly home when the Lord comes. Dear ones, wait patiently!

Now, another eighteen sisters and eight brothers are waiting to be sentenced. We do not know how many years they will get for re-education. Brothers and sisters, don't forget to pray for your dear ones in prison.

Although the road is often very narrow, it will lead into the presence of the Lord. Even though our homes have been demolished, our minds will not change. We will faithfully march forward, our clothes stained with blood, as we go to see the Father.

Because of the situation we cannot write more.

Emmanuel!

Your brothers: Xiuling, Jingxiu, Fuqin.[17]

The enduring legacy of the Jesus Family

After decades of severe suffering, the Jesus Family continues to live on today in the consecrated lives of believers throughout Shandong and other provinces of China. Although most Family members don't identify themselves as part of that movement anymore, tens of thousands of Christians in both the house

Members of the Jesus Family earnestly praying together

church and Three-Self church systems trace their spiritual heritage back to the impact of the Jesus Family.

An incident in Guizhou Province in 2006 offers a glimpse into the hardships and blessings of this unique church movement. A group of believers had gathered together in Liupanshui to hear a house church preacher share about the Back to Jerusalem mission vision that God first gave the Chinese Church in the 1920s and 1930s. After three hours an elderly lady in the back of the meeting stood up and said:

> You don't know who I am, but I am the granddaughter of Jing Dianying, the founder of the Jesus Family. When I was a little girl I saw my father and grandfather arrested for preaching the gospel. I saw my family members sent to concentration camps by the Communists. I saw my mother abandoned by the Chinese community with no way of getting a job or feeding us children. I was not allowed to go to school. I was treated

like a leper. Because of what my family did I was punished by society.[18]

For many years the granddaughter of Jing Dianying had strug-gled with bitterness. She was bitter against the government and bitter against her grandfather and father. Worst of all, she had become bitter against God and had vowed to never become a follower of Jesus Christ.

Years earlier she had moved away from Shandong and married a government official. They had children but she was determined to make sure they never became Christians either. Decades passed, and the gospel seed that had been lodged in her heart as a little girl sat dormant. She exclaimed to everyone in attendance:

> I am hearing the same exact words that I remember my father and grandfather saying so many years ago. The government may have killed my father and grandfather, and tortured their families, but they couldn't kill the vision! . . . The vision of the Church in China still burns deep and even though I have denied it for most of my life, it still runs through my veins . . .
>
> Though I may be old and have already wasted so many years, I promise from this day forth that I will not remain silent any longer. Another day will not pass without me sharing the Good News of Jesus Christ with everyone I can![19]

1950s

The pastor who took down a picture of Mao

Many Christians around the world had welcomed the arrival of the new Communist regime in 1949. Chinese society under the Nationalist government was riddled with corruption, and it was reckoned the new rulers of China couldn't be any worse. Throughout China, however, Christians saw signs that the approaching Communist storm would be dark and destructive.

A typical house church Bible study

The true nature of the Communist plans was revealed when Mao Zedong issued this dire threat:

> Whoever wishes to oppose Communism must be prepared to be mauled and torn to pieces by the people. If you have not yet made up your mind about being mauled and torn to pieces, it would be wise for you not to oppose Communism.[1]

The suppression of the Church in Shandong was gradual. For much of 1950 there was little trouble, as the new government gathered "evidence" to be used against the body of Christ. Then the noose of restrictions began to tighten around Christians' necks. Services could only be held at certain times, and home fellowships were banned. Pastors were forbidden to visit church members, and all children were required to attend Communist meetings on Sunday mornings.

In December 1950 in the seaside city of Qingdao, Pastor Wang Deyun (David Wang) was visited by officials who demanded the use of the church building for a Communist conference a few days before Christmas. The pastor agreed on two conditions: that no political portraits or flags be displayed and that no smoking would be permitted on the premises.

As soon as the conference began both conditions had been broken. A portrait of Chairman Mao was hung at the front of the sanctuary with flags on either side of it, while many in the audience were smoking. Wang, who was known as a gentle and non-confrontational person, realized a stand had to be taken. He:

> summoned his family into his study and asked them to concentrate in prayer for him. With shaky steps he walked to the door of the church on the first floor of the building. He went up the aisle of the crowded church, removed the portrait of Mao as well as the flags, and walked out.[2]

Wang's brazen act of defiance immediately made him a marked man. He fled south before the authorities could sentence him, so the Communists vented their anger on his sons and wife instead. They too managed to evade capture and ultimately, after many stressful months, the whole family reunited in Hong Kong, where Wang Deyun worked for the Christian and Missionary Alliance until 1968. Wang and his wife later migrated to Europe, where they continued to serve the Lord among Chinese churches until their deaths.

The wind blows where it pleases

Although the 1950s was marked with much brutal persecution of Christians in Shandong, the life and power of the Holy Spirit could not be extinguished from the hearts of those who loved God. As the government unleashed waves of dire persecution against the Church, all Christians were ordered to register and face a public trial. One elderly brother lived a simple, consecrated life in a remote village. His pastor had tried to train him what to say under questioning, but the old man replied he would only say what the Spirit of God told him to say at the time.

The Communist official began the interrogation by asking: "What has Christianity done for you?"

"It's made me a better man," the elderly farmer replied.

The official turned to the assembled villagers and asked if this was true. "Yes!" they emphatically replied. "His farm used to be the dirtiest and worst in the village but now it is the best." When he was pressed to explain how these changes had occurred, the farmer spoke with great power and authority:

> I was a drunkard and an opium smoker. Nothing could rid me of those two vices, and my farm had been brought to ruin. But I accepted Jesus as my Savior, and He changed me. He enabled me to break with both opium and drink. My fellow villagers can now testify to these things and my farm is now the best. Ask them.[3]

As the Communists tried to transform the country in the 1950s, they struggled to deal with the true testimonies of simple-hearted believers like the elderly Shandong farmer.

On another occasion a house church leader had a dream in which he saw himself visiting Miao village about 15 miles (24 km) from his home. He saw a man and his wife preparing breakfast, but all they had to put into their pot was grass and leaves. The leader declared: "Miao village has turned to the Lord and some of its people have started a fellowship. We must take them some grain."

A man immediately set out in a cart loaded with food, and arrived at Miao village a few hours later. On arrival:

> he found things just as in the dream. The Holy Spirit had fallen on the man and his wife, and they had given all they had to the poor . . . They held a joyous feast which the neighbors joined in. Many immediately turned to the Lord when they saw the grace that was given.[4]

When the Holy Spirit swept through the villages of Shandong in great power, the revival touched every community in one district except one isolated village. The young people of that village were mystified as to why God had bypassed them alone, and they sought the advice of house church leaders. "Much prayer has been prayed," the young men explained. "Idols have been torn down and burned, and many of the villagers have apparently been converted, but things remain as before. There is no revival and no manifestation of the work of the Holy Spirit."

The leaders prayed earnestly, seeking to put aside their human wisdom to gain the mind of Christ on the matter. The Spirit of God revealed that there was hidden sin in the village and that his blessings were being withheld as a result. It was revealed to them that certain idols of earth gods had been buried in the ground by the older men of the village.

Shovels were used to dig up the pots containing the idols, and "when the last had been removed, destroyed and burned, revival began. The rejoicing in that village was mingled with awe and the fear of God."[5]

Zhang Tangwu

Shandong is a province where many old men and women of God died for the gospel in the 1950s and subsequent decades. One such brother was Zhang Tangwu from Weifang.[6] Zhang, who had never married, was thrown into prison in the 1950s, where he contracted a strange skin disease on his upper back.

Even when he was taken to court and questioned by judges, Zhang smiled and told them about Jesus' love. In prison his witness was so strong that the other inmates gave him the nickname "Living Jesus." He always shared his meager portions of food with the other prisoners.

Zhang was sentenced to death, and as he awaited the day of his execution his disease grew so bad that pus openly oozed from his back. The prison doctors were convinced he would soon die. For many years this man of God had prayed that he would not die in prison, but that he might die on the mission field spreading the gospel with sinners.

The other prisoners were terrified of Zhang's disease, and believing he would soon die anyway, they threw him out of their cell and made him sleep in the disgusting latrine, covered in human excrement and urine. The officials began to make arrangements for Zhang's burial the next day. Since his body was covered in open sores, they knew the unhygienic surrounds of the latrine would quickly cause infection. Throughout the day, despite death knocking at his door, Zhang continued to preach the gospel to every prisoner and guard who came to use the toilet.

With tears in his eyes and in great anguish of soul, Zhang Tangwu cried out in a loud voice that could be heard throughout the entire prison:

> I am not crying because of my sick body or because of my impending death! I am crying because of the death of the gospel among you all! Your souls are precious to God. He loves you and longs to call you His children.

He then sang from the depths of his heart, "My thoughts are not clean . . . My love is not pure."

Zhang knelt down in the excrement and wept bitterly for the opportunities he had wasted in his life. He decided he must share the gospel with everyone in the prison while he had the chance. Painfully, he dragged his half-dead body out of the latrine. With the Lord's help he inched his way to the prison courtyard, which had a mound of stones in the center. He climbed to the top of the mound and held on to the top stone. With a loud voice he proclaimed: "Everyone listen to me! You must receive Jesus Christ as Lord!" All the prisoners could clearly hear him because the cells faced toward the courtyard.

Right at that moment the ground shook. An earthquake came from nowhere and the prisoners were terrified. They were afraid because of the earthquake, but also because they couldn't understand how Zhang had been able to drag himself back from death's doorstep to preach to them in such a loud and authoritative voice.

Because of the exertion of dragging himself from the latrine to the courtyard, Zhang Tangwu's infected back had split into two. The skin between his two shoulder blades was no longer joined together and pus flowed down and covered his waist and legs.

The prison guards finally came and carried him back to the latrine. They decided not to shoot him because they expected him to die within hours anyway.

The next day when they came to inspect Zhang they were amazed to find that somehow his back had become better and was healed! Within three months he recovered completely! Terrorized by the supernatural events that had displayed the glory of God, the prison authorities were too afraid to deal with Zhang, and they released him from prison.

Zhang Guquan

Zhang Guquan was the leader of an indigenous Chinese mission known as the Northwest Spiritual Movement.[7] In many ways they were an offshoot of the Jesus Family, which was the first group to receive the Back to Jerusalem vision to preach the gospel throughout the Muslim world, all the way back to the birthplace of the Great Commission, Jerusalem.

Most of the original leaders of the Northwest Spiritual Movement hailed from Shandong, including Zhang Guquan. After graduating from Bible school, he sought the Lord as to what direction his life should take. On one hand:

> He was very much impressed by the communal life-style of the Jesus Family where the members contributed all their individual possessions and held all things in common. On the other hand, he admired the Little Flock for their study of the Bible and their way of penetrating the depth of the Word. During his time of indecision, he seemed to hear a voice speaking directly to him: "My child, neither of these is the road you should take. I have something special in mind for you."[8]

This new direction led to the emergence of the Northwest Spiritual Movement. The leaders of this new mission said:

> Let's rise to our feet and carry the cross to the nations where God is not known. Let's go forth in Jesus' name, giving up

everything we have, even our very lives if necessary, so that the name of Jesus will be glorified among all the Gentiles.[9]

The strategy of the Northwest Spiritual Movement was simply to proclaim the gospel, believing that Jesus would soon return. God blessed their efforts, and they established many new groups of believers, fruit that remains to this day. The first team of workers was sent to Xinjiang in 1947, where they won people to Christ among many ethnic groups, including Muslim Uygurs, Hui and Kazakhs. One hymn composed by the movement typifies their dedication:

> Brothers and sisters, work hard for the Lord, for the Lord,
>   for the Lord.
> Bring the Gospel back to Jerusalem, tramping over hill and
>   dale, on foot and by boat,
> Making a way in the wilderness and the desert.
> Selling and giving up possessions to do the will of God;
> Shedding tears and sweat, following where the Lord
>   leads . . .
> Men and women, young and old, foolish and wise,
> Make up your mind to sacrifice and be willing to shed
>   blood to repay the deep love of the Lord.[10]

Zhang Guquan moved to the town of Hami, which became the movement's base of operations to reach into other parts of northwest China. A chapel and nursery were established, and a small Bible school was opened. The work progressed until persecution struck in 1951. In the early part of the year the believers in Kashgar were arrested. The following year Zhang and his colleagues were thrown into prison at Hami. For years nothing was heard of Zhang, but it was later reported:

> Zhang died in prison in 1956 when he was in his early 30s. Other leaders also died for the Lord. Quite a few who survived the long trek from Shandong to Xinjiang could not stand the

test and wavered from the faith, speaking out against Zhang and the Movement. Later they were sent back to Shandong. Those who kept their faith and stayed behind faced a very bitter life . . . They had become the refuse of the world, "the scourge of all things" (1 Cor. 4.13). They were willfully wronged, suppressed, persecuted, insulted, beaten . . . For the sake of the Lord they were publicly exposed to abuse and affliction.[11]

The last missionary to leave Shandong

After the Communist Party assumed control of China in October 1949, the hundreds of foreign missionaries stationed in Shandong knew their remaining time on Chinese soil would be short. Many left voluntarily before the approaching storm, while others remained to the bitter end, not knowing if death or deportation awaited them.

Irene Hanson, an American Presbyterian, is believed to be the last missionary to leave the province. After serving the people selflessly for more than 25 years, she was deported from China in 1951. Hanson later wrote:

War had been declared against the Church; a subtle, divisive guerrilla war that broke out in unexpected times and places; a war that was hidden by day and waged insidiously at night.

A Communist was appointed head of the Christian Church of China and began to speak for all groups, without giving any the right of dissent. He handed down edicts that forced a fearful obedience on church leaders and members alike. Anyone who dared to differ with his directives was branded as a "spy," or a "running dog of the Imperialists." Freedom of religion came to be defined as "Freedom to persecute."[12]

Hanson owned a pet parakeet, which she had trained to repeat a few phrases. Sensing she would need all the encouragement she could get, she taught the bird to say "You believe the Lord" in Chinese. The missionary gained strength from this strange source, and said: "Often when I returned from a Communist grilling, shaken and disheartened, he would bring back a smile by talking to me."

The day of reckoning finally arrived, and Hanson was hauled before a hate-filled Communist court. "Kill her!" they screamed. "Kill her! She is an American spy and doesn't deserve to live!"

Much false information had been spread by the Communists to discredit missionaries, but not so well known are the numerous accounts of how brave Chinese Christians risked their lives by taking a stand for truth and refusing to give false testimony when ordered to do so. A man named Ga Li was called to give evidence against Hanson. "Isn't it true that she used mission funds to pay for spying activities against the People's Republic of China?" Ga Li was asked.

> "It is not," he responded in a clear voice. "She has not used any mission funds except for the expenses of the church. Every cent of money spent has been accounted for . . . She is not a spy. She has not been working against China. She is a friend of our people and our nation. She does not deserve to be on trial today."[13]

The judge was infuriated, as Ga Li was the prosecution's chief witness against the missionary. Because he had stood up for the truth, the case against Hanson was thrown into disarray. She was sentenced to "eternal deportation," never to be afforded the privilege of setting foot in China again.

Before her departure, Hanson received a secret visit from an elder of a Shandong church, who had walked many miles from the countryside. He slipped in through the back door of the missionary's home and said he had an important message from God to share with her. "The four things I have to tell you are from God," he emphasized, as he counted them off on his fingers . . .

One, tell the people in America not to be too discouraged about the Chinese Church. Two, tell them their gifts and offerings have been accepted by God. Three, the Church in China will go through great persecution and a time of winnowing the chaff from the wheat. Four, the Church will come back in great revival.[14]

Rarely have more accurate words been prophesied in China. Irene Hanson was unceremoniously removed, but as she boarded the ship, her pet parakeet was released from its cage by friends. It flew straight toward a crowded apartment block, telling the people again and again, "You believe the Lord! You believe the Lord!"

A great leap backward

The 1950s had been a terrible decade of severe persecution for the Church in Shandong, but the situation was exacerbated further when Mao launched the disastrous "Great Leap Forward" in 1958. Rarely has an initiative been so misnamed, as millions of people starved to death and untold misery and suffering was inflicted on the population.

The idea behind Mao's campaign was to turn China rapidly from an agrarian society into a modern industrialized nation. Millions of people were forced to migrate to other regions, rendering manual labor as the government built massive water irrigation projects and other initiatives. Mao spoke of China's economy passing that of the United Kingdom and the United States within 15 years. Private farming was outlawed, and those who engaged in it were punished and labeled "counter-revolutionaries."

Instead of achieving its stated goals, the Great Leap Forward was an economic catastrophe for the country. Believing that steel production was a key to becoming a world economic power, Mao ordered the construction of backyard furnaces throughout the country. People were forced to hand over farm tools, pots, pans, doorknobs and any objects made of metal, with the intent that the country would benefit with millions of tons of steel to build their new utopian society. In reality, the quality of the steel produced was poor and unusable, and villages were left with unseemly blobs of twisted metal and unused furnaces.

Historians have looked back on the Great Leap Forward with contempt at the sheer stupidity of it. China had embarked on:

> one of the greatest failed experiments in human history. The Communists tried to abolish money and all private property . . . China plunged into a famine of staggering proportions—an estimated 30 million Chinese starved to death (some put the figure at 60 million).[15]

The social fabric of society was torn apart as an iron fist of fear and intimidation descended on the population. People were urged to report any suspicious activities among their own family members, and countless millions of couples were forced to divorce as the state asserted pre-eminence over people's personal lives.

Christians throughout Shandong went into survival mode during this dark time. Most church leaders were arrested and received long prison sentences, often of 20 years or more. Hundreds of pastors were killed or perished in the harsh prison labor camps.

Although the shepherds had been removed by the government, many Christians continued to meet discreetly in small groups of three or four. Often the believers walked into the forest or the hills to have their meetings, to lower the chance of detection and being reported to the authorities. The

Church throughout Shandong survived, however, as the Holy Spirit had already done a deep work in the hearts of countless thousands of disciples before the excesses of the 1950s and 1960s.

1960s

By 1966, Mao's China was lurching toward a precipice. He launched the Cultural Revolution, which resulted in the deaths of tens of millions of people and reshaped Chinese society more in ten years than had any other event in China's history. Customs and traditions that had taken millennia to foster were cast aside as the Red Guard swept throughout the length and breadth of the land. During the Cultural Revolution, "all visible churches in Shandong were closed, pastors imprisoned, and church buildings were used for Communist propaganda centers or supply houses. In the midst of this harsh persecution, however, God wonderfully multiplied His church."[1]

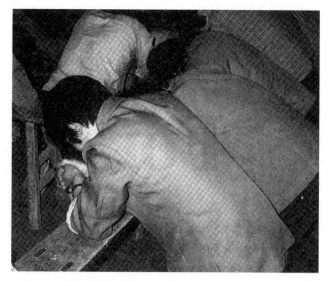

House church men praying on their knees

Many years later, a report shared how revival had broken out again in Shandong in 1965. By that time, all denominational churches had been disbanded, but the Holy Spirit visited believers in simple house church gatherings throughout the province. In the 1980s one Christian recalled the depth of spiritual life he found in the fellowships he visited in Shandong at the time:

I truly feel grateful to the Lord for His grace—for allowing a man of small faith to witness His mighty acts in person. What we human beings cannot do, God can do. The church is a beautiful testimony to this fact.

The revival here began in 1965. During the Cultural Revolution, many young people were moved by the Holy Spirit and rose up to preach the gospel. Some were arrested, others struggled against, and still others persecuted. But nevertheless, they did not forsake the faith; on the contrary, their faith became even stronger. These people today are the pillars of the Church.

Today there are no officially open churches here, but house churches are everywhere. In each of these house church meetings, there are maybe 20 to 30, 50 to 60, over 100 or sometimes even 200 people. The government knows about these meetings, but they do not bother them.

I saw how the brothers and sisters who preached came from all kinds of vocations and across other boundaries; there were workers, teachers, cobblers, and others. Among them were many young people with tremendous gifts of preaching.

One house church arranged for no more than six people to give their testimonies. After these six had spoken, there were many others who wanted to stand up and give their testimonies . . .

The county here has a population of around half a million. Those who believe in the Lord number 50,000–60,000, and among them Christian sisters are the majority.[2]

Pastor Tian

On a trip to China in 2001, the author had the privilege of meeting a house church leader from Shandong whose father, Pastor Tian,[3] had been gloriously martyred for Christ during the Cultural Revolution. Tears rolled down his cheeks as he recounted his father's experiences. Here is Pastor Tian's testimony in the words of his son:

> In 1967, in the coalmining city of Zibo in northern Shandong, my father was arrested for being a preacher of the gospel. The Red Guards beat him almost to death. He was covered in blood and many of his bones were broken. The tortures they gave him were indescribable. My skin stands up even today when I think about that day. The guards forced me and my son (his grandson) to witness the torture.
>
> After the beatings my dad's barely-alive body was placed on a trolley with wheels. My son and I were required to push him around the city streets so that people could see the terrible fate that would befall anyone who preaches the gospel. The mobs hurled insults and missiles at us as we struggled to protect my beloved father's body from the taunts and fury of the crowds. My dad, who had served the Lord for many years, was labelled a "counter revolutionary" and an "enemy of the state," but I knew that nobody loved China more than my father. He had wept in prayer many times for the salvation of the Mother Land.
>
> The guards forced us to enter a cemetery, where they had erected a platform to hold a mock trial. Hundreds of people gathered to watch. They propped my father up and told him he had one last chance to be forgiven of his crimes. If he would just renounce Christianity and his belief in Christ he would be set free. If not, the guards threatened, he would regret his decision. "We offer you this precious chance for life. Choose wisely," they snarled.
>
> After waiting for the crowd to fall silent, my father began to speak in a clear, loud voice. This was a miracle in itself because

he was in such terrible shape after the beatings he had endured. To the crowd of shocked onlookers and Red Guards, he boldly declared, "You can cut my head off, and you can spill my blood, but I will NEVER forsake Jesus Christ! He has been faithful and has blessed me for many years, and nothing you do can ever make me renounce my loving friend and Savior."

As soon as these words came out of my dad's mouth, a mob of enraged guards leapt onto the stage, thrashing him with their fists and steel-capped boots. They flung his body off the stage and continued to beat him as he lay in the mud. Many people in the crowd wept loudly but they could do nothing to stop the carnage.

My father was beaten to death in front of my eyes. His faith and courage left a deep impression on me, and I decided to be fully committed to the Lord Jesus Christ for the rest of my life. Many other Christians in the crowd were also strengthened by my father's example.

Because my dad was willing to endure to the end, great fruit has resulted. I still follow Christ, as does my son and my grandson. Three generations have followed the Lord, and we hope many more generations to come will do so as well![4]

Zhang Jiakun—a broken vessel

Born in Shandong Province in 1913, Zhang Jiakun was raised in a devout Christian family. As a teenager she committed to studying the Bible at school, and later felt led to work with a student ministry in Yantai.

In 1948, just before the advent of the People's Republic of China, Zhang moved to Shanghai and worked for the publications department of the Chinese Christian Evangelism Fellowship. She was a prolific writer and editor of Christian books and articles, and is best remembered for her devotional, *Living Water*, which is still popular among Chinese Christians

Zhang Jiakun kneeling beside her bed in the "tiny dark room" she was imprisoned in for 22 years

today. During the dark years, when all religious books were banned and those caught with them risked execution or imprisonment, many Christians hand-copied Zhang's devotional and passed it around to help encourage their fellow believers.

In 1956 the government shut down the ministry where Zhang worked and arrested all the staff. She was later charged with being a counter-revolutionary and was sentenced to prison in 1960. For much of her time she was incarcerated in a tiny damp room measuring 65 square feet (six square meters). She covered the moldy cement walls with newspapers and stored all her worldly possessions on a single bamboo shelf.

During those dark years, Zhang Jiakun clung tightly to Jesus Christ and gained an intimate relationship with her Savior. Finally in 1972, after 12 years of incarceration, Zhang wrote down some of her feelings. Her words reveal a lowly and broken vessel who, despite all her dreams for life having been snatched away, had instead found a great reward in Jesus Christ. In part, Zhang wrote:

In the past I was a very sentimental person, but I have lost my tenderness now. I have forsaken the world and the world has forsaken me. Because God is my greatest treasure, I always call on Him who gives me strength to be exalted in my body, whether in life or in death . . . I have promised Him that I will offer all I have without reservation . . .

He gave me a very small test, and I flunked. Even though I often fail, I have also been promoted to the next grade. When I reach the finish line, I will be like the others . . . It doesn't matter if one walks slowly, what matters is to not give up halfway through . . .

I do not deserve to get a prize. If I were to get the last seat in heaven, I would still be content. If there is also a prize for me, it should go to my brothers and sisters. They provide me with the necessities of life, and they lift me up in prayer; if a prize is to be given, it should go to them. I am a maidservant purchased by precious blood; that I love Him is a matter of course. I have nothing to boast about. When all my work is done, I will say, "I am an unworthy servant. I have only done my duty."

On my journey, I have many shortcomings and often fall short. If He had not used His precious blood to ransom me, how could I have paid the ransom on my own? The ransom for a life is costly, and no payment is ever enough. He delivered me from death. I have eternal life, and He has raised me from the dead and seated me with Him in the heavenly realms. When He appears, I will appear with Him in glory. I shall be free from the bondage of this body then, and I shall see Him face to face—Christ whom I love, the great and glorious King. I shall bow down at His feet and worship Him . . .

So, do not bless me. In this world, I do not want people's blessings. I would rather suffer with Him because I know that suffering helps me succeed! . . . I am already without parents, and have no children. I have been stripped of everything. I am by myself and I am old . . .

I have gone through a bit of suffering, so I think others should sympathize with me for my loneliness. Not only does no one sympathize with me but instead they bully me. My heart is a little bitter. Then I think, "How foolish am I! I am of no use to anyone so why do I want people's sympathy? . . . I still desire to live for Him."[5]

Finally in 1982—after 22 years—Zhang Jiakun was released from prison. Five years later, with the help of friends, she migrated to California, where she lived a peaceful but busy life until her death in 1993. It pleased God to use his maidservant again, and he allowed her to bring much glory to his name in the sunset of her life. During the seven years she spent in

Zhang Jiakun's passport photo taken before she left China for the first time

America, Zhang had seven more books published in Chinese, strengthening the faith of thousands of believers.

A letter from behind the curtain

After China sealed its borders off from the rest of the world, members of the global body of Christ waited patiently for any glimpses they could get into the state of the Church. Many foreign missionaries who were expelled from China publicly lamented that Christianity had been exterminated, saying that if the doors ever reopened the gospel would need to start again from scratch.

Insights into how the Church in Shandong was coping at the time were impossible to ascertain, although one source later estimated there were 70,000 Christians living throughout the province in 1965, meeting in 350 different churches.[6]

Rare snippets of information did filter out of Shandong from time to time. The waiting Christian world treated each word like unexpected news from a long-lost family member.

In 1968 a Hong Kong pastor received this letter from a Christian in China, which offered a slither of hope that all was not lost among Christians living behind Mao's Bamboo Curtain. The letter said:

As I am an expert in engineering, I held a high post and received a nice salary. I enjoyed my life, but now as a result of the Cultural Revolution I have lost my job and salary and everything. I am now working as a common laborer. However, I rejoice in that I have regained the full joy in Christ. I know there are other friends who have the same experience.[7]

1970s

The Chang family's godly heritage

The Chang family of Qingdao in eastern Shandong has a rich Christian heritage, which stretches back nearly a century and continues to the present day.

Its story began in the 1920s, when Mrs. Chang Aizhu was unable to have a child, which was considered a deep disgrace in Chinese society at the time. Doctors could not help her, so one day in her desperation she visited a church in Qingdao, where she spoke with a pastor named Tang. She begged him: "Please help me! I want to have a child! We have tried for many years

Chang Zihua in the 1930s

but I cannot conceive." Tang replied: "There's nothing I can do to help you, nor can any other person. There is only One who can intervene in your situation and grant you the desire of your heart—the Lord Jesus Christ." The childless woman immediately replied, "Please introduce me to this Jesus."

Around that same time, one of the first Korean missionaries to China, Pang Zhiyi, came to Qingdao and proclaimed the gospel. Mrs. Chang believed the message and was saved. Her husband, Chang Zihua, was a hard-hearted man who wanted nothing to do with the "Western religion."

After Mrs. Chang cried out to the Lord in prayer, he opened her womb and she conceived. She visited the doctor who had told her she could never have a baby, and shared the exciting news with him. "You're crazy!" he exclaimed. "This bump in your stomach isn't a baby. It's just a tumor!" She returned home disappointed.

Three months passed, and Mrs. Chang felt the baby move inside. She was certain of the pregnancy and returned to the doctor. He checked again and was shocked to discover she was indeed carrying a baby!

Seven months into the pregnancy, complications set in and the hospital told Chang Zihua that they needed to perform an emergency operation, and that either the mother or her baby would survive, but not both. He chose to save his wife, and the surgery proceeded. After Mrs. Chang's life was spared, however, her husband was astonished to hear the sounds of a crying baby coming from the operating theater! Miraculously, both mother and baby had survived. Chang Zihua knew the hand of the living God was involved. He knelt down on the floor, repented of his sins, and gave his life to the Lord Jesus Christ.

The Changs named their special son Enhui (signifying grace from the Lord). Born in 1927, the boy grew up at a difficult time in China's history, with war, famine and other disasters afflicting the lives of millions in Shandong. During those dark days, however, the Lord didn't forget the Chang family.

After giving birth to her miracle son in 1927, Mrs. Chang was told by her doctor to prepare for an early death, due to the toll the delivery had taken on her body. The woman of God, however, once again cried out to the Lord Jesus, begging him to give her ten more years to raise her son. She often prayed from Psalm 90: "Teach us to number our days aright, that we may gain a heart of wisdom."

Chang Zihua was a wealthy businessman, having made a fortune running a dye business for a British company. One day one of the British owners visited the Changs' home. Mrs. Chang, who had matured into a strong and committed disciple of Christ, fervently prayed in her room while her husband met with the foreign guest in the living room. The man was shocked when he overheard Mrs. Chang's prayers, and asked his host: "I didn't know your wife had learned to speak English! Where did she learn? I've never heard such perfect English spoken anywhere in China before." God had apparently performed another miracle, for Mrs. Chang had never studied a word of English.

When God was challenged

Meanwhile, Chang Zihua matured into a God-fearing man. He shared the gospel with his employees and friends but was often met with resistance and ridicule. Once, a man mocked his faith and told him it was foolish to believe in an invisible God. For weeks the weather had been heavily overcast and rainy, and he challenged Chang to prove his God was real. "Pray to your God and ask him to make the sun shine through," the man demanded. "If it happens I will believe in him too."

Chang was perplexed by this unexpected challenge. Not wanting to put God to the test or disgrace his name in front of unbelievers, he asked God to reveal his will on the matter. After a time of fervent prayer, Chang was convinced that the Holy Spirit had revealed God's will to him, and he told the man, "Tomorrow at noon the Lord Jesus Christ will cause the sun to shine and you will know that he is the true god."

News of the unique showdown quickly spread throughout the local community, as the rain continued to lash down that day and throughout the night.

The next morning dawned with torrential rain still pouring down from the sky. Dark clouds completely filled the horizon. Many unbelievers in the neighborhood gathered to see what the Christian would do when his faith was shown to be fraudulent. At eleven o'clock the Changs looked out of their window to see the countryside still being saturated by a downpour. At 11:30 nothing had changed, nor at five minutes before noon. It had rained continually for days.

A large grandfather clock stood against the wall in the Chang home. At 11:59 a.m. there was still no sign of the sun. The man who had issued the challenge stood poised, ready to mock. Just before noon the clock began to chime: "Dong . . . Dong . . . Dong . . ."

At the very moment of the last chime, at precisely twelve o'clock, the sky suddenly split open and rays of bright sunshine burst through the clouds, illuminating the drenched community. The locals were astonished, and acknowledged the Christian God was the one true God. A new respect was given to members of the Chang family, and their faith was admired.

Mrs. Chang continued to be a vibrant witness for the kingdom of God. She often visited the slums in Qingdao, which were packed with refugees who had fled there to escape the ravages of war, flood and famine.

One day, while ministering in one of the unhygienic squatter camps, Mrs. Chang contracted tuberculosis, from which she didn't recover. She had asked God to extend her life by ten years after giving birth to Chang Enhui in 1927, and she died in 1937, just after her son turned ten.

Thousands of impoverished slum-dwellers attended the funeral, having been touched by Mrs. Chang's love and grace. For many years she had displayed the glory of God in her life and lived up to her given name, Aizhu, which means "Beloved of God."

Chang Enhui—a witness to the People's Army

After the death of his wife, Chang Zihua remarried, but his second union did not carry the same measure of God's blessing as the first. He was unable to cope with raising Enhui, so the boy, who had given his life to Jesus at the age of 11, was sent to live in the Jesus Family compound at Mazhuang. He remained there for two years under the godly tutelage of the founder of the community, Jing Dianying, and the other leaders of the group.

Chang Enhui grew up and became a highly respected surgeon in the Chinese army. He never forgot his Christian heritage, and continued to serve his Savior in the midst of the Communist army until his retirement in 1988. Enhui often prayed discreetly for his sick patients, even risking his life to share Christ during the harsh years of Mao's Cultural Revolution from 1966 to 1976.

Chang Enhui became a key leader in the Shandong churches during this difficult period, tirelessly encouraging believers to follow God and not grow weary. He was greatly admired by all Christians. Not only did he have a tremendous testimony

Chang Enhui and his wife in 1988

of God's provision and grace, but he was never too proud to publicly confess his personal weaknesses and sins, and to share how God had helped him overcome.

On one occasion he tried to share the gospel with an army captain who was close to dying of cancer. The captain protested: "Stop! I'm tired of your foolish talk! I am a member of the Communist Party and I cannot believe in religion!"

The army captain's wife was more open to the truth, however, and she told Enhui: "If your God heals my husband we will all become Christians."

Chang Enhui visited another town for a few days, and when he returned to the hospital he was dismayed to find the captain had died. The man of God was saddened that the opportunity to win the man to Christ had passed.

A few weeks later Chang Enhui was summoned to the home of the former army captain. When he arrived, Chang found the widow, her children and their extended family waiting to see him. The widow explained:

> When my husband was about to die and was struggling to breathe, we were gathered around his bed preparing for his soul to depart this world. All of a sudden he sat upright, his eyes opened wide, and he declared, "I saw heaven! It's real!" He then closed his eyes and passed away. We all want to believe in Jesus. Please tell us how![1]

Chang Enhui, who was miraculously spared by the Lord at his birth in 1927, lived a full life serving God in Shandong Province until his death in 2001, at the age of 74.

1980s

A famine of God's word

The 1980s brought fresh hope to many Christians throughout China. Several years had passed since the end of the Cultural Revolution, and promises of greater liberties were being made not only to people of faith but to the country as a whole.

Despite three decades of persecution and having been cut off from the body of Christ around the world, the Church in Shandong had not only survived the dark times but had flourished in the crucible of testing. In the early 1980s, veteran missionary Leslie Lyall reported that the churches in Shandong were "experiencing tremendous growth, and cottage meetings

A precious handwritten Chinese Bible

have multiplied. In Jinan, the provincial capital, there are reported to be 20,000 believers. In the picturesque port city of Qingdao over 1,000 Christians attend Sunday worship, and in Yantai over 600."[1]

In 1985, one visitor to a church in eastern Shandong reported:

> The church has about sixty members . . . most of whom attended the Lord's Supper, when they knelt down in groups of five or six. The pastor blessed each one personally, giving a word of encouragement or exhortation before dispensing the bread and wine, which they drank from one cup. Many were weeping and openly confessing their sins before the Lord.
>
> The pastor of the church is over 70 years old and widely respected as a house church leader. He was arrested in the 1950s and imprisoned for about twenty years. The Christians here are short of Christian literature. However, they are afraid to receive material even posted within China. The leaders and some of the members have Bibles, but most of the young converts do not have the Scriptures. They are, however, happy to receive material hand-carried in.[2]

The Church in Shandong had grown throughout the 1970s despite severe hardship and persecution. Although the number of believers had mushroomed at the start of the 1980s, the body of Christ faced a crucial roadblock—the lack of Bibles.

Bibles had been banned throughout China for nearly three decades, and many believers who owned a copy of God's word during the Cultural Revolution had been afraid to reveal it, as being found with a Bible could result in their arrest and the grim possibility of many years in prison. As a result, Bibles were placed inside airtight canisters and buried in the ground, while others were skillfully concealed inside the wall panels or rafters of homes and barns.

One veteran missionary attended a registered church in Shandong in the early 1980s, when a lady sitting next to him reached into her bag and casually pulled out a huge old Chinese Bible with ragged edges. Surprised, Paul Kauffman, an American missionary who had founded Asian Outreach, turned to her and asked where she got it. "Oh, it was my mother's Bible," she replied.

The missionary asked if the Red Guards had searched her home. "Yes," the woman confirmed:

> but mother had hidden the Bible under the eaves of the house. See? The rats have eaten the edges of the leather binding, and my mother has gone on to be with the Lord, but I still have her Bible.[3]

Believers throughout Shandong yearned and prayed for a day when they could once again access God's word without fear of reprisal, but the acute shortage of Bibles resulted in hand-copied pages being circulated around the churches. Many Christians memorized a portion before swapping their page with someone who possessed another page or two of the precious Scriptures.

As more people desired to replace the spiritual void in their hearts by following Jesus Christ, the lack of Bibles slowed down the advance of God's kingdom, and threatened to derail it completely.

The turning point

The Chinese Church cried out to God for mercy, asking him to feed his starving children. In response, in the late 1970s a strongly built American missionary, known as Brother David, responded to a call from God to help courier Bibles into China from neighboring countries. He started by carrying just a few Bibles inside his bag, but the initiative grew until teams with a dozen or more travelers hauled hundreds of Bibles across the border from Hong Kong each day.

Although the Scriptures that Brother David and others managed to smuggle into China were a tremendous blessing to the recipients, the scale of the need ensured those Bibles were akin to trying to douse a blazing forest fire with a garden hose. David and his co-workers came up with a risky, Holy Spirit-inspired plan to deliver one million Bibles into China in a single day. This bold delivery, which came to be known as Project Pearl, was bitterly opposed by many other mission groups, who were concerned the plan was just too bold and brazen. Others appeared upset and envious that the huge project was discreetly implemented without their knowledge or participation.[4]

Inside China, however, the body of Christ cared little about the political maneuverings of the outside Christian world. Believers didn't particularly care how Bibles reached them.

Some of the one million Bibles on the barge that entered China in July 1981
Brother David

They were desperate for the Scriptures, and realized the future of Christianity in China depended on whether or not new babes in Christ would be able to access God's word.

After years of planning and one aborted attempt, Brother David and a group of dedicated missionaries finally launched out from Hong Kong aboard a tugboat in June 1981, pulling a barge containing one million Chinese Bibles. Realizing that if they were caught they faced possible execution or at least many years in prison, Brother David successfully led his crew in one of the most courageous Christian acts of the twentieth century.

With thousands of Chinese Christians waiting on a beach in Shantou, Guangdong Province, the missionaries unloaded their precious cargo before escaping to the Philippines as quickly as possible.

Although the Chinese authorities managed to confiscate about 10,000 Bibles after they realized what had taken place under their noses, the overwhelming majority of the one million Scriptures were successfully delivered and distributed to astonished church leaders the length and breadth of China.

In the aftermath of the Project Pearl delivery, reports of powerful heaven-sent revival came in from across China. Many Chinese believers told of the role the Bibles played in fanning the flames of revival. The audacious delivery was the turning point for the house church movement in China. One pastor later said:

> The delivery was the spark that set many house churches alight, as believers gained strength and faith from God's word. Looking back with the hindsight of years, I believe the timing of Project Pearl was God-ordained. In 1981 the harvest in China was ripe and the believers were desperate for God's word. In a sense, if we had done the delivery a few years later the impact might not have been quite as great.[5]

Among the hundreds of letters of appreciation received by Brother David and his ministry in the aftermath of the delivery were some from Shandong Province, where tens of thousands of Bibles had successfully reached the churches. One letter, signed by "The Church at Yanzhuang" (a town in southern Shandong), explained the impact the Bible delivery had on their church:

> Now we have Bibles and everyone can study the word of God. The flock that is hungry and thirsty can now feed on wholesome spiritual food, and drink from the pure spiritual fountain. Our lives are now flourishing like healthy trees in spring time. Many have believed in the Word of the Lord and have endured trials. Now we have learned to stand firm, discern true from false, and stand against the evil one and all of his attacks.
>
> The word of God really is a lamp unto our feet and a light unto our paths. It is our foundation and we will stand on it for ever. The flock is now making great progress in the pursuit of spiritual maturity. We know that prayer provides power, and realize how sweet it is to commune with the Lord early in the morning. Praise the Lord!
>
> We fully understand that the Bibles did not come to us easily. We know that for the suffering Church and the spiritual needs of the flock you did your best. Brothers and sisters, your labor is not in vain. Your love has blessed numerous congregations and has awakened many who were drunk in this world, saving a multitude of souls.
>
> We have learned from your example of selfless love and we share your desire to spread the gospel throughout the whole earth, so that the Church will be revived and bring much glory to the name of the Lord.
>
> Please pray for us often. All the brothers and sisters in our church greet you.
>
> Emmanuel,
> The Church at Yanzhuang.[6]

A missionary's surprise

After Deng Xiaoping assumed power in China in 1978, his new open-door policy brought swift economic reforms and ushered in a new era for the Church. After having been closed off from the rest of the world for three decades, foreign Christians were now able to travel into China, and astonishing reports emerged of revival in many areas where it was previously assumed the churches had been wiped out.

Paul Kauffman, the late founder of Asian Outreach, was born to missionary parents in Qingdao in 1920. After serving on the Tibetan border for years, Kauffman's father, Ivan, relocated to Shandong for his third term of missionary service. Not knowing a soul when he arrived in Qingdao, Ivan Kauffman was walking down a street when a stranger accosted him. His son later shared the story:

> "Pardon me, sir," said the man in Chinese, "aren't you the man who has come to teach us about the Holy Spirit?" Startled, my father asked, "What made you ask?"
>
> The man had been a believer for several years, but heard that a person could be filled with the Holy Spirit. Then, he was told, one would have supernatural power to witness for Christ. He earnestly began seeking God for the gift of the Spirit. One day God gave him a vision in which he saw the face of a Western man. The Lord told him the man was coming to teach him about the Holy Spirit. "You are the man I saw in the vision," he said to my father. What a wonderful confirmation of father's guidance in coming to Qingdao. The Holy Spirit had announced our arrival![7]

In the mid-1980s Paul Kauffman returned to the town of his birth after an absence of almost six decades. His father had been a greatly respected missionary in Qingdao, and the Kauffman Memorial Church was constructed in 1935 to honor his sacrificial service. It had been turned into a factory by the Communists in the 1950s, but was returned and restored as a place of worship in the more tolerant atmosphere of the mid-1980s.

As he caught a taxi to the old church, Paul Kauffman wondered if he would find any believers. He reported:

> Alighting from the car, we were quickly surrounded by believers on their way to the church. The building had been constructed to seat 300, but to our delight we found it was packed with 800 worshippers. People were crammed into every nook and corner. The four walls could hardly contain the worshippers who jammed every window and doorway. This was only the first service; there would be two more services, equally crowded, that morning . . .
>
> I sat on the crowded platform, tears rolling down my cheeks. It was just like the services I had attended as a boy during the great Shandong Revival. Nothing had been able to extinguish the fire of the Holy Spirit . . .
>
> Not many in that service knew my father who had died 55 years before. How thrilled father would have been to see the fruit his early efforts had borne.[8]

Revival comes to southern Shandong

In the spring of 1989, Pentecostal teaching flooded into southern Shandong after two house church preachers from Zhejiang traveled north into the province. They encountered many formal churches with a Presbyterian root, where most of the believers had never experienced the work of the Holy Spirit. Although large numbers had remained faithful to the word of God, the faith in many parts of Shandong had become dry and dusty, without much spiritual life or love.

When they heard that two visiting preachers were seeking to preach in their churches, many pastors in southern Shandong

A rural house church meeting in the 1980s

gathered together to discuss whether they should grant them permission. When asked what message they intended to share, the humble duo explained that revival from God had broken out throughout China, due to the power and presence of the Holy Spirit. They desired to share what God was doing and to encourage believers to receive God's Spirit. Suddenly a young man got to his feet and declared in a loud voice:

> "We need the filling of the Holy Spirit. I have desired this for a long time, but didn't have the courage to say so" . . . The words had hardly come out of his mouth when another man jumped to his feet and said in a loud voice, "In my heart I am so bored. The church is boring me to death. We must have a revival meeting!"[9]

Many churchgoers shared a similar desire for more of Jesus Christ. A meeting was organized and more than 100 thirsty preachers attended. The meetings started at six o'clock in the morning, and the two preachers from Zhejiang taught on the baptism of the Holy Spirit while testifying to what the living God was doing in various parts of the country. The Shandong church leaders listened attentively, but many had been warned over the years to be wary of Pentecostal teaching, so there was considerable resistance.

At the conclusion of the second day of meetings, the preachers prayed earnestly for a breakthrough. The next morning, during the intercession time, the brothers laid hands on a young 13-year-old girl. She suddenly stood up and cried out: "Lord, I ask you to have mercy on us!" As soon as the words left her lips:

> The meeting place was shaken and each and every one began to weep loudly, some of them beating their chests and confessing their sins. Many wept bitterly for the lukewarm, backslidden churches in southern Shandong . . . Ninety percent of them were filled with the Spirit, and began to fervently clap their hands and praise out loud. The whole meeting place was shaken as their shouts were like thunder . . .
>
> On the last day of the meetings the participants asked the two preachers to lay hands on them. As they did so, several people saw a dove hovering about their heads. One brother had been afflicted with arthritis for many years and was not able to move his hands. The preachers laid hands on him and he was immediately healed. Lifting his hands up high he began to dance and praise God.[10]

While many of the local pastors were greatly refreshed by the revival meetings, others grumbled against them, with one key elder angrily saying: "This is the work of evil spirits," as he stormed out of the room.

Most of the churches that were led by receptive pastors experienced strong growth in the following months. The work of evangelism expanded quickly, and "in several villages even the government officials believed. In one village, the believers grew in a few months to 80 percent of the population. Out of 600 people, 400 became Christians."[11]

On the other hand, the church led by the elder who had walked out of the meeting in disgust decreased from 90 to just 10 believers. Hungry Christians left his church and went to where the Holy Spirit was moving, as bees are automatically attracted to a honey pot.

In the next few years the Zhejiang churches sent many more evangelists and teachers to southern Shandong. During one meeting, a 22-year-old paralytic was carried to the front. He lived alone and his body and hair were filthy. Whenever he saw people all he would do is stare at them and laugh.

By that time the Shandong Christians were boldly ministering in the power of the Holy Spirit. They laid hands on the young man and asked God to deliver him from the grip of the devil in the name of Jesus. The next evening a clean young man walked into the meeting. Nobody recognized him as the same person who had been carried in the previous day.

Faced with the reality of hundreds of transformed lives that displayed the fruit and gifts of the Holy Spirit, the elder who had opposed the meetings repented with tears and he too was filled with God's Spirit. Revival finally also came to his church.

1990s

Cold reception for visiting preachers

Because of its deep ties to Western denominations during the long missionary era, the Church in Shandong gained a reputation for being conservative and resistant to change. This has been a blessing in some ways, as a healthy skepticism helped believers avoid much of the false teaching introduced both from overseas and from other parts of China in recent decades. A reporter who visited churches in Shandong in 1993 found that:

Young Chinese women intently studying the Bible during the 1990s

Many of them take a negative view of assistance from overseas believers, fearing that they will bring in harmful and divisive teachings. This past spring some of the leaders of the house church movement in the province convened a meeting in which they reaffirmed a policy of non-contact with overseas churches.[1]

When Brother Yun—who later became well known for his autobiography *The Heavenly Man*—visited Shandong in the 1990s, he and his co-workers were given a poor reception by a group of local believers, which was a typical experience for preachers from other provinces. The resistance against outside influence continues in various degrees to the present day. Preachers from Henan and other rural provinces tend to be looked down on by the more sophisticated and wealthy Shandong believers. Yun recalled:

> The key leader in Shandong prepared a meeting for seven days. On the afternoon of the sixth day, while Brother John was sharing, some of the Shandong believers started to find fault with our message. They quizzed us with some difficult questions about controversial verses in the book of Revelation . . . One old man, an elder of a church, and two other men stood up and exclaimed, "You teachers from Henan need to shut up! You're so young and inexperienced. You are dirt-poor and know nothing. How can you teach us when you don't even know the meaning of these Scriptures?"
>
> The three old men picked up their belongings and started to leave the meeting, and they commanded their church members to leave with them. I immediately followed them into the courtyard and prayed in a loud voice, "O Lord, thank you for my honorable brothers. Please help them not to be so angry because we are so ignorant of the Scriptures."
>
> Two of the disgruntled leaders laughed at me and called out, "Yun, take your soldiers back to where you belong. Roll up your flag and take it back to Henan."

213

I knew this incident was a disturbance from the devil. With sincere tears in my eyes I pleaded with them to return to the meeting so we could all pray and seek the Lord's will. Their hearts were touched and they quietly returned to their seats. I asked everyone in the meeting to kneel down and seek the Lord. The love of God was poured out on all of us and there was much wailing and many broken hearts . . .

Those three elders came forward and knelt down in front of the people. They bowed their heads and said, "Brother Yun, please forgive us for speaking such rude and insulting words." The whole congregation, when they saw the contrite hearts of the three elders, knelt down and prayed with many tears. They asked us to stay and teach for several more days in different places around Shandong.[2]

Growth and persecution in the house churches

Although visiting preachers may have received a mixed reception from some Shandong fellowships, the Holy Spirit continued to empower the messengers of the gospel, and the number of Christians grew exponentially during the 1990s.

A man named Huang and his wife placed their trust in Christ in 1988 after hearing the gospel via a shortwave radio broadcast. They gradually matured as believers, and found many people around them were also keen to know the truth. By the mid-1990s, the house group that met in the Huangs' apartment crammed into every available inch to hear the teaching of God's word. On Christmas Day in 1995, a total of 56 people repented of their sins and believed in Christ in the home meeting.[3]

In China, revival in the house churches is often followed by a season of persecution. In early 1996 the authorities cracked down on the Huangs' house church, but when the police sirens blazed into the neighborhood:

the congregation was not frightened at all. The arrested leaders stepped into the police cars with heads held high. As the cars drove off, the congregation sang aloud from the Bible. As soon as the cars went out of view, the believers went back inside and continued their meeting.

The house church had been targeted by the authorities three years earlier. Huang recalled:

> Last time, the sheep were intimidated and scattered. But now they have matured. We now look at persecution as a crowning glory, a blessing. The churches are more unified and our prayers more fervent. We believe that a larger revival follows persecution.[4]

The Jesus Hospital

After the Jesus Family was apparently destroyed by the Communists in the 1950s and its leaders died, most observers thought that all memory of the unique movement would soon be forgotten. The movement of the Holy Spirit had planted the gospel deep within the hearts of the Jesus Family members, however, and the movement survived throughout Shandong Province.

In Linqu County, the Ai De ("Love and Virtue") Hospital was established right across the street from a former chapel of the Jesus Family. By 1995 the facility boasted 36 doctors and nurses, many of whom were nationally admired for their skill. Most of the hospital staff had family roots in the Jesus Family. One article revealed that at the Ai De Hospital:

> All staff members, from the director down to the cleaning lady, receive the same salary of 80 Yuan, hardly more than pocket money. To make ends meet, they still till their family fields, mostly before the clinic opens at 8:00 a.m. and after it closes at 5:00 p.m.

Members of the Jesus Family taking Communion together in 1992

Due to the staff's modesty, fees are kept low. Patients come from far and wide. The seriously sick are pushed in on wooden wheelbarrows, a common mode of transport in China's remote areas. Since there is no medical insurance for poor peasants, many patients have a hard time settling their bills. In such cases payment is deferred, reduced or cancelled.

All staff members at the clinic are Christians. They begin each day with morning devotion at 5:30 a.m. and conclude with evening prayer at 7:30 p.m. Locals refer to it as the "Jesus Hospital." Doctors and nurses are used to giving personal witness and counseling their patients spiritually. In this way, countless patients have left the place more than just physically healed, and many have started a new life in Christ.[5]

Wu Xiuling

Throughout the 1990s, reports surfaced from China that mentioned the remnants of the Jesus Family, including the grim story of a woman named Wu Xiuling, who was martyred in Shandong in March 1995. She was just 36 years old.

Wu's troubles began in 1989, when a team of Public Security officers suddenly arrived at her home in Zhao village near Zaozhuang City, and placed her under arrest. At the police station she was told she was in trouble because she believed in Jesus and because she had preached from the book of Revelation—a part of the Bible particularly feared by the Chinese authorities.[6] Wu was allowed to go home after being repeatedly threatened.

Wu Xiuling's second arrest occurred in June 1993. A group of house church believers were meeting at a house in Weishan County, when suddenly a group of about 20 police officers arrived. They:

> used guns and electric clubs to force the Christians to get onto the police truck and took them to the county Public Security Bureau. With hands cuffed, Xiuling was shown to the public around the county on a police vehicle for several days. Then she was taken back to the police station and interrogated for three months, during which period she was beaten so severely that injuries covered her body. She was sentenced to three years in jail after being tortured and humiliated.[7]

Wu Xiuling and two other arrested sisters were sent to a prison labor camp at Zibo in central Shandong. The prison manufactured clothing, most of which was exported overseas. Every day Wu was given a strict work quota that had to be completed, otherwise she would be beaten and abused. The quota was beyond her capability, and after a while her body began to break down from the constant pressure and beatings.

One day Wu fainted, but the guards shook her back to consciousness and forced her to continue working even though she had a high fever. Her request for medical assistance was firmly rejected. Finally, in October 1994 the prison authorities could see that Wu Xiuling was near death. They sent her back home for treatment. After two months she showed few signs of improvement. The treatment was discontinued because of a lack of money and one report noted:

> Her bones were just under the skin, and her face was distorted. Her skinny hand became transparent and the bones could be seen. Her face did not show any trace of blood and her eyes had deeply sunk back. In early March 1995 Xiuling finally passed away at the age of 36.

Wu Xiuling's funeral was scheduled for March 6, but so many Christians wanted to attend that the police decided to block all the roads leading to the burial site, and the young martyr was buried without any witnesses. Wu had remained pure her whole life and constantly testified to the goodness of Jesus Christ. Much of her life had been spent in isolation and suffering, and even in death she was alone. She would not have minded, however, for she was already safe in the arms of her loving God.

Rapid growth brings spiritual concerns

As the twentieth century drew to a close, the Church in Shandong had come a long way. Impressive numerical growth was seen throughout the 1990s, and in many places both registered Three-Self churches and the independent house church fellowships were filled to overflowing with people.

Some parts of the province experienced more Christian influence than others. Just in Linyi Prefecture in southern Shandong, the Three-Self Patriotic Movement in 1994 reported between 100,000 and 250,000 church members.[8] Although data on the house church networks in Linyi was more difficult to obtain, one source said there were more than 170,000 Christians in just "four poor counties" within the prefecture.[9]

In Qingdao and surrounding parts of eastern Shandong, the churches had also greatly increased. By the end of the decade, Qingdao City had 50,000 registered believers meeting in 60 churches,[10] while in 1998 the official Amity News Service reported that 30,000 believers had been baptized in the city since 1980, "with a large unrecorded number of believers baptized before that date."[11] The house churches in Qingdao also experienced similar rates of rapid growth.

At Weihai, which overlooks the Yellow Sea at the northeast tip of the province, the government-approved Three-Self Church started with just 40 people in 1994. The Holy Spirit moved, however, and services were soon filled to overflowing. By the start of the new millennium more than 3,000 people attended the Christmas services at Weihai.

Similar accounts of growth were repeated from numerous counties and districts throughout Shandong in the 1990s. Province-wide, the Three-Self churches at the start of the decade had reported 307,000 members meeting in 2,464 registered churches.[12]

By 1997, however, official sources listed 900,000 Three-Self Christians in the province, meaning the registered churches had nearly tripled in size in seven years.[13]

Even those statistics are considered conservative, however, for the Three-Self churches typically only count baptized adult church members, and no children or teenagers are allowed to attend their meetings.

Because the illegal, unregistered house church networks had been forced to operate in the shadows, accurate estimates of their size in the 1990s are hard to ascertain, but with the registered churches reporting 900,000 members throughout Shandong, it can be reasonably estimated that the province contained at least two million house church believers at the same time.

Although by the late 1990s it appeared as if Christianity had blossomed spectacularly in Shandong and was on the verge of even greater growth, grave concerns were held by some China church watchers, who warned that the numeric growth of the Church had far outpaced the spiritual maturity of its members.

In keeping with the churches in many other provinces, a lack of trained pastors and the persistent shortage of Bibles combined to leave many churches without adequate leadership. Bible knowledge among believers was often superficial, causing missionary statesman Tony Lambert to repeat the lament of missionaries in Africa more than a century ago, who said, "The revival is a mile wide but only an inch deep."

Letters from Shandong

We conclude this chapter by reprinting a selection of letters that were received from Shandong by various Christian ministries during the 1990s. These precious communications reveal both the strengths and weaknesses of Christianity in Shandong, and provide insights into the daily lives and personal struggles of believers as they followed God. Their letters offer a fascinating snapshot of the ever-changing conditions experienced by the body of Christ at this time.

1990

I give thanks to God for the reference Bible and books I received. All the churches within a 200-mile radius are lacking in Bibles. Even if we received 5,000 Bibles, they still wouldn't meet the need of every believer. Because of the lack of Bibles, believers face the problem of understanding God's word.

Although we have about 40 young preachers called by God, we continue to carry a great burden . . . Many places only have three or four Bibles between all Christians, and there are some places where four or five people share a single Bible. The brothers and sisters are crying out to the Lord that He will meet their spiritual nourishment.[14]

1991

My efforts to find a Christian friend have been in vain. Nor have I been successful in borrowing a Bible. So far, I have only attended one Sunday service in secret. My mother feels that believing in Christ will bring me much trouble. Hence, I dare not share my faith with others. One day I told a friend that I no longer believed in God, and I experienced real conflict. I could neither sleep nor eat. My thoughts bothered me. I have tried so hard to stand up as a Christian without any support. No one, not even my parents, understands me.[15]

1992

I am a young farmer, aged just 22. Last summer I met a Christian friend who shared the gospel with me and invited me to attend their meetings. Every time I had to ride my bicycle twenty miles to reach the church, but I experienced the great power of the Lord. I have never experienced such a peaceful atmosphere. People help and support one another.

I have not been baptized yet, but from the first meeting I decided in my heart to become a Christian. According to our customs we have to bow before the idols during Chinese New

Year. I know that God is watching me, but I lack the courage not to bow to the idols, since I do not want to go against my parents and relatives.[16]

Although I do not quite understand the teachings of the Bible, I fully believe that all men have sinned and refuse to repent, especially in China with several thousand years of history! Our communities are full of exploitation and deceit. The light has dimmed and darkness is everywhere. I cannot see anything, but please believe me, I want to repent! Please pray for me and wish me success. How can I become a Christian? How should a Christian live, learn and work? What are his responsibilities?[17]

1993

One year after I came to the Lord I was afflicted with a disease. It has tortured me emotionally because appearance is very important to a girl. I have considered suicide, but am afraid of what others might say. Besides, committing suicide will disgrace God's holy name. Does the disease remain because I am not sincere? Or is it because I doubt the Lord's ability to heal? Should I give up using medication and rely totally on the Lord? I really don't know what to do. Due to family pressure, I seldom attend church services. I know very little about the Lord.[18]

Thanks be to God! For several years there has been an annual average increase of 200 people baptized in our church. Because our meeting place is small, we need to have two services on

Sunday mornings and one in the evening. We also have Bible studies on Monday, Wednesday and Friday evenings. We invite people to listen to gospel programs, so that more people may know our only true God, Jesus Christ![19]

We live in a village and have many chores to do. Going to church often becomes a formality and we receive no inspiration from reading the Bible. Our prayers lack power. It seems God is not listening to us. Often we feel weak and hopeless. We are poor in spirit and there are many reasons why we are not filled with the Spirit. First, we have no desire for growth. Second, we are spiritually dry without revival meetings. We only have one pastor in our county and he seldom visits the village churches. As a result we only have holy communion twice a year.[20]

In our county there is no official church organization, but we have established a house meeting. We have laid down three conditions, namely that there must be more than 30 believers, that a suitable meeting place is found, and that we are led by a voluntary worker. Hitherto we had to walk more than ten miles to worship together, and this has proved very difficult for elderly believers and those with children.[21]

1995

Five years ago, when I became a Christian, there were only elderly people in our church. Now God has added many young people, but the quality of our shepherds has not improved. This has led the sheep to go astray. Some days ago, several people came from Beijing. With Bibles in their hands, they taught many things such as 'The Holy Trinity is not mentioned in the Bible.' Some people stopped coming to services after listening to them, and some even went to be baptized again by them.[22]

I converted to Christ after listening to your broadcast. I regard you as my close friends and need your opinion on witchcraft. I previously believed in it and owned a mirror which could supposedly protect me from evil. My mother has one too. After conversion I broke mine, but my mother forbids me to throw hers away. A witch once advised me to renovate our bathroom. Should I change it back? I want my mother to believe in Christ, but she fears there will be accidents and attacks by demons. She heard that the daughter of a new convert accidentally died. This sister left Jesus as she thought God had failed to protect her family. I want to preach the gospel to them but I don't have the necessary weapon, i.e. the Bible.[23]

1996

My mother had to do all the household work. Because of her poor health she once asked me to help her. I was so selfish that I only thought of myself and I refused. Unfortunately, she died soon after. It was the biggest mistake of my life. I thought of committing suicide. I didn't do so because I had to take care of my aging father and the family. It was at this time that I came to know Jesus Christ. I repented and accepted Him as my Savior. From then on I possessed a new life and new hope. Glory to the Lord for His mercy and love![24]

This is law-enforcement year. The government is rigorously cracking down on criminals and exerting control over house church meetings. We were interrupted by the Public Security Bureau, who claimed that house church meetings are prohibited. They said all worship has to be conducted in open churches, or we will be fined, imprisoned, and treated as criminals. The churches in a neighboring county are being persecuted too. Many house churches have been forced to close down, so we just stay home and listen to gospel radio.[25]

1997

Quite a number of my classmates are religious. Some are Muslims, some Buddhists, but the most are Christians. The majority of the class claim to be atheists. Some even believe there is a God but just don't know who He is. I introduced Jesus Christ to them and thank God, some converted and now we have formed a prayer group. When we gather, we share and try to resolve spiritual and daily life difficulties.[26]

Our church has grown from seven to over 300 people. The local Religious Affairs Bureau tried to stop us meeting. Even when we attempted to register they still interfered. They put pressure on our landlord who had rented a barn for us to meet in, and we were driven out. They tried all sorts of tricks.

Then, on November 11, they mobilized 100 police officers to drive all the believers out and they locked and sealed our church. They posted a notice saying they would demolish the building, but the brothers and sisters were not afraid. They prayed with tears, testified, and sang hymns so that many passers-by and our neighbors came to support us, and some came to faith. After prayer, we church workers decided to take the road we had gone down before—meeting secretly in house churches.[27]

1998

I am 26 years old. My family is worried about my single status. They want me to get married as soon as possible and they even search for boyfriends for me. I have always preferred a believer to be my spiritual companion, and for a long time I have prayed to God for one. As a Christian I take marriage very seriously, since divorce is not allowed. Moreover, the Bible says, "Do not be yoked together with unbelievers." If I marry an unbeliever and he persecutes me, I will be responsible for my own suffering. If the marriage is prepared by God, He will look after me on all matters. Therefore I am unwilling to dive into something which would harm my faith and body.[28]

Four years ago we had a house church in our village and I found faith in Jesus Christ, who died on the cross for mankind. However, after a short while attendance at the church began to drop. Our minister had only one Bible and no commentary of any kind. His preaching style was very simple: just a few Bible passages and a song. Later he became ill and because his prayer for healing was not answered, he lost faith and the church was dissolved.[29]

I converted to Jesus Christ about two months ago. At first I didn't tell my husband because he's an atheist. I tried to share God's goodness with him but his response was very negative and he blasphemed God. Sometime later I felt I had to inform him of the changes in my life. He reacted angrily and tore my Bible to pieces. His family also oppose my faith. I pray God will forgive them.

Since my Bible was destroyed I have felt lost and sad. I am sorry that I was too weak to safeguard my Bible . . . Now I listen to your programs secretly at night and can't attend church services. Please tell me how to face my husband.[30]

I have believed in the Lord for less than a year. Since then, He has helped me change my attitude and thinking. Prior to my conversion I had a bad attitude and constantly yelled at people and even fought with them. At home I often quarreled with my parents, but since trusting in the Lord, His grace has helped me change all that. Now I am very happy inside.

I then suffered a serious back injury and could not work. Even walking was difficult. I spent a lot of money on treatment and went to many hospitals for medication, but there was no improvement. One night I heard that the Lord can heal. I did not believe in such things and asked some Christians if it was true. They told me, "If you truly believe in the Lord, He will heal you." Thinking I would try it out, I went to church. Each time they prayed for me my back would get better. Though I have not totally recovered, I don't need to take medication anymore and can do some work. It's all by the grace granted to me by our Lord Jesus Christ.[31]

1999

Here in Shenxian there are more than 30,000 Christians and 250 meeting places, both large and small. This is all by God's grace, but we have very few Christian workers. The Three-Self committee often persecutes believers on behalf of the government. In our county, if you want to study theology you have to be approved by the Three-Self officials. Up until now only four people have been allowed to study.[32]

After graduating from high school I was not able to study at university. The pain of not being able to reach my education goals was intense. I felt sorry for myself and cried all the time. I felt there was no hope for the future. I was depressed and angry and my self-confidence was totally crushed.

Thankfully, God did not forsake me. My mother is a Christian. When I felt hopeless, she shared the gospel of salvation and the mystery of the kingdom of heaven with me. At first I thought the gospel was nonsense owing to my atheist education. When I opened the Bible and read about how God created man from the dust I couldn't accept it. My mother then took me to church. As a grown man, at first I found sitting among senior folks rather absurd but I didn't quit. Later, I participated in singing hymns and studied God's word. Gradually I felt peace and joy. At last I mourned for my sins and repented. I am now a new creature in Christ.[33]

I turned to Jesus Christ in 1997. The first time I stepped into a church meeting I was deeply moved by the sermon. The light of the Holy Spirit shone on me and revealed my sins, and I could not stop weeping. I repented immediately and sought God's mercy.

In the past I was a timid and introverted person. My health was not strong and I easily grew tired. Thanks be to God for now He has changed my life! I have become a girl who is vibrant, cheerful, healthy, strong, and full of vigor and vitality. All these changes help me understand the great love of the Lord.[34]

2000s

—•◦•—

Revival fire continues to burn

Despite being persecuted and deprived of Bibles, the legal right to assemble and the ability to train leaders, Shandong's house churches began the new millennium in revival, and the fire of the Holy Spirit continued to burn brightly throughout the province well into the decade.

Sister Ding, a regional leader of the Fangcheng house church network, summarized how the extremely rapid church growth throughout Shandong in the 1990s continued into the 2000s:

Two eager women studying the Bible
Bibles pour la Chine

In 1992–3 we preached every day and saw hundreds of people come to the Lord. We were continually preaching and baptizing new believers. The hunger for the gospel was great! After one sermon in the morning we might have 500 new believers. Then after our afternoon meeting another 300 people might ask to be saved, followed by another 100 after the evening service. Therefore in a single day we would have 900 new believers to baptize! This was an amazing time. Churches sprung up everywhere.

By the end of the twentieth century in all of Shandong we had more than 4,000 churches. In Liaocheng City alone we have 500 churches. It all started when we sent just three co-workers from Fangcheng to Shandong! The new Christians were so innocent and hungry for the Lord that they considered every word we taught as if they were words from the Lord Himself. The ministry was marked with daily miracles. The blind saw and the lame walked. Generally speaking, the closer the area of Shandong was to Henan and Hebei, the stronger the house churches.[1]

Reports emerged from all over Shandong about how the gospel movement was spreading far too rapidly for anyone to control or even to count. Three female evangelists came to Shandong from Henan Province, and established 52 new house churches in just a ten-week period. The smallest church had 500 people, and several had over 1,000. Almost everyone in the churches was a new believer, and it was rare to find anyone who had believed in Jesus Christ for more than a few years.

One visitor to Shandong in the summer of 2002 was asked to teach at a house church Bible school. He reported:

These young students showed an unquenchable thirst for the Lord. They were so zealous for God's word that they set out to memorize chapter after chapter of the Scriptures . . . They were filled with the Spirit and began to weep. How soft and beautiful their spirits were. It is little wonder the Holy Spirit operated so powerfully there . . .

231

The training was held in a room packed with 150 people. The mid-summer heat permeated the room, making breathing a little difficult. Such conditions hardly affected the participants, however. During the worship time, they expressed their love for God. The atmosphere was filled with the presence of God like a fresh breeze ventilates a room. It was like wind in spring and rain in autumn.[2]

As the province fully opened to foreign investment and opportunities, many overseas Christians moved to Shandong. Whereas foreign believers had often been treated with suspicion during the 1980s and 1990s, the rapid changes to Chinese society meant that many barriers came down in the 2000s, with both positive and negative ramifications for the body of Christ.

One of the least desirable influences was the impact of Western "prosperity gospel" preaching that flooded into the province. While many of the older Christians saw the danger of a gospel that removes the need for self-denial and sacrifice, the message found fertile soil in the hearts of thousands of young believers, who had grown up in an era when a tsunami of materialism swept across China.

God's wrath stokes the flames

The spread of the gospel in some parts of Shandong at this time was assisted by manifestations of God's wrath. Government officials who reveled in persecuting Christians were suddenly struck down. Many people believed in Jesus as a result, for they knew the living God had intervened on behalf of his children by punishing the officials for their evil deeds.

In August 2002 a small group of female evangelists traveled to a village to share the gospel with idol worshippers. As they began to proclaim the gospel, a 30-year-old man approached the women and ordered them to stop preaching. The man flew into a demonic rage, blaspheming the name of Jesus and spewing forth filthy insults and curses against God's servants.

A crowd of onlookers gathered to observe the spectacle, and were amazed to see how calm the Christian women remained as they blessed and prayed for the man. After about 20 minutes he left the meeting, but a short time later, news came to the village that he had been knocked down and killed by a car. The villagers knew that God had poured out his wrath on the wicked man, and many repented of their sins and placed their trust in Jesus.

The Eastern Lightning cult

Like many other provinces of China, the Church in Shandong was blighted by wave after wave of attacks by cults during the 2000s, as Satan furiously lashed out and tried to stop the mighty revival that was sweeping multitudes of sinners into the kingdom of God. Members of these cults often don't bother trying to lure non-Christians to their sects, but they go straight to churches, hoping to deceive and convert new believers and those who are weak in their faith. A visitor to Shandong high-lighted some of the challenges facing the house churches in the province:

> The churches in Shandong have grown very quickly in the past ten years. Many people have become believers after being healed of sicknesses through prayer, and many young people are getting involved in God's work. Due to a lack of meeting places, the Shandong believers often hold worship meetings in the countryside, or in secluded mountains or forests . . . The government is not very effective in controlling the rural churches, which meet many times during the week without fear . . .
>
> The need for systematic training of Shandong's house church leaders is widespread and urgent. Many of the pastors are

uneducated women. They are very devout to the Lord and to the work of the ministry, even though they are also expected to do the housework and labor in the fields.

Most of them depend on gospel radio broadcasts for their biblical knowledge, but some are also trained by evangelists from neighboring Henan Province. Though illiterate and untrained in preaching, these leaders truly depend on the guidance and help of the Holy Spirit when ministering to the flock. It's not unusual for them to teach the congregation through spiritual songs, which are spontaneous melodies inspired by the Holy Spirit.[3]

Of the many active cults in Shandong in the past 30 years, the most widespread and dangerous is undoubtedly the Eastern Lightning. Thousands of Christians throughout China have been beaten, tortured or poisoned by this satanic group. A Shandong house church pastor recalled what happened when his churches were targeted by the cult:

> After the victims were tricked and brought somewhere else, the Eastern Lightning turned violent. Nearly all of their members carry a cudgel, which they use to hit the victim's vital parts, such as their four limbs or head, until they become unconscious. Then the believers were taken to a prearranged place where the Eastern Lightning indoctrinated them with the teachings of the cult. If the subject refused to accept the teachings, they turned to more violent methods.
>
> Friends told me of such cruel methods as cutting off victims' ears, breaking legs, and there was even one old sister who had her neck broken because she would not accept the teachings of the cult or their "lady Jesus." During this violent phase one of my father's colleagues was deceived into going with them, and acid was thrown at him. My aunt's neighbor was poisoned to death. These are accounts of which I am personally aware. The victims are always influential church members.[4]

Even secular newspapers in China have reported the crimes committed by the Eastern Lightning. One publication summarized the evil deeds of two cult members, Liu Shunting and Zhao Fating:

> They put people who opposed them or had any disagreement with them on a "blacklist," and took revenge on those people by attacking them one by one. For nearly two months the two of them, armed with daggers, steel bars, powdered lime and other equipment, lured their victims out of their villages on the pretext of praying for the relief of illness, and carried out eight separate ferocious criminal attacks, disfiguring their victims, breaking their legs, cutting off their ears, etc. They seriously injured nine people . . . Five of their victims had both legs broken, one had one leg broken, and two had their right ears cut off.[5]

Most people in Shandong paid little attention to the cult until a horrific incident occurred on May 28, 2014, at a McDonald's restaurant in Zhaoyuan City, when six Eastern Lightning members attacked and murdered a woman by continually stomping on her head in full view of the public. The brazen incident caused a public outcry. Although the attackers were arrested and two of them executed, the punishments did little to slow down the aggressive advance of the Eastern Lightning throughout Shandong and the rest of China.

The destructive influence of the Eastern Lightning has continued to wreak havoc throughout the churches of Shandong to the present time. The Chinese authorities don't appear to know how to deal with the cult, and have only attempted to prosecute members after they are caught committing criminal acts. The body of Christ has been required to wage intense spiritual warfare against the cult, in a bid to quell its demonic influence.

As the pervasive cult spread throughout Shandong, various mission organizations received letters from struggling believers in the province. The letters included three messages from Shandong church leaders who detailed their experiences with the Eastern Lightning. The first reported:

> Our church is constantly disturbed by the Eastern Lightning cult. They pretend to be church members and persistently preach a different gospel. Nevertheless, our brothers and sisters are strong in the faith and know the deeds of this evil sect. They often enter our homes and pretend to be new converts thirsting for the truth, but when we advise them to talk to our faithful pastors they always make some excuse to leave. In reality, they are afraid of the truth.[6]

Another pastor's letter told of a new convert in his church who was lured into the cult and began to spread its false teaching to others:

> There was a sister in our church who accepted Christ last year. After that she came into contact with the Eastern Lightning cult. Her whole personality changed. She abandoned her elderly father at home and stopped taking care of him. All she can think of is how to bring people into the cult. She shared her false teachings with our church co-workers and brings cult members to our service so they can hide among believers.[7]

Finally, a senior church leader in Shandong shared some of his personal experiences in dealing with the insidious Eastern Lightning:

About three years ago I was contacted by someone claiming to be from a fellowship in a neighboring province. They said they had heard I was an influential leader in Shandong and they wanted to gain a deeper understanding of the Bible. I sensed the Holy Spirit restraining me; but felt that I must help these people if they were really as sincere as they claimed. I invited them to meet me in a neighboring village, and at first they used many smooth words to try to convince me to join their 'special fellowship.'

Finally, they opened a bag that was full of 100 Yuan bills. It was the equivalent of thousands of US dollars. I was shocked when I realized they were trying to buy my influence. I grabbed the bag of money and threw it at the main spokesman, declaring, "I don't want your dirty money!" They were so dazed that they just let me go; but a few days later they returned and kidnapped me. Fortunately my sons and some brothers from the church found out where I was being held and successfully freed me. I believe the most important thing we can do to fight cults like the Eastern Lightning is to give people the Bible to help them realize what true Christianity is![8]

Fire and blood

As the decade of the 2000s continued, the dual characteristics of revival and persecution continued to run alongside each other in Shandong. The authorities were powerless to stop the advance of Christianity, and the wind of the Holy Spirit blew wherever it pleased.

In December 2007 a large group of 270 Christians were detained during a mass arrest in Heidi District of Linyi City, as the believers met together for leadership training. An eye-witness said that between 40 and 50 officers were mobilized from 12 different towns to conduct the large-scale raid. The Christians were handcuffed together and taken to the local police station for questioning. Most were fined and released, but the authorities identified 21 leaders of the group and charged the 17 men and 4 women with holding an "illegal religious gathering." Each of the church leaders was sentenced to between 15 months and 3 years in prison.

A similar raid in December 2008 resulted in 50 more house church arrests in Xiji town, Zaozhuang City. The motive for this mass arrest appears to have been financial, as each person was ordered to pay 2,500 Yuan (about $375) to secure his or her freedom.

A Christian woman named Zhang Hongmei was a member of a house church in Dong Miaodong village, near Pingdu City. Zhang was arrested by the police on October 29, 2003, and taken to the local station for questioning. Zhang was charged with "illegally carrying out religious activities," meaning she had been involved with an unregistered house fellowship that refused to come under the authority of the government-approved Three-Self Church.

That afternoon, Zhang's family relatives a call and were told to pay a bribe of 3,000 Yuan ($380) to secure her release. Being poor farmers, the family was unable to raise the money so at about seven o'clock in the evening Zhang's husband, Xu Fenghai, and her brother went to the Public Security office to plead for her release. They were shocked to see her chained up and so seriously beaten that she was unable to speak. Despite their frantic protests, the two men were forced to return home.

On the following afternoon, October 30, members of the Zhang family were summoned to the police station. They were told that Hongmei had died earlier that day. An autopsy revealed "several wounds to her face, hands and legs, along with serious internal bleeding."[9] News of Zhang's murder shocked and angered the whole community. The following day approximately 1,000 people marched on the city offices demanding an inquiry, but nothing was ever done.

The totally unnecessary nature of the 33-year-old Zhang Hongmei's death makes the incident even sadder. It seems the police did not really have any desire to persecute her, but had just wanted to extort money from the Christian community.

Bob Fu

Bob Fu (Chinese name: Fu Xiqiu) is a Shandong native, born in 1968 in unfashionable Gaomi County in the eastern part of the province. Although few Christians in Shandong have ever heard of Fu, outside his homeland he has come to be regarded as one of the most prominent, albeit controversial Chinese Christians of the past few decades.

Fu and his future wife Heidi were involved in the 1989 Tiananmen Square democracy protests. They left Beijing just days before the massacre, but Fu was so distraught over news of the government crackdown against the unarmed students that it plunged him into deep depression. He was interrogated for his role in the demonstrations, causing him to feel betrayed by his government and to abandon all hope in the Communist system.

Fu was raised in a non-Christian home, and he didn't hear the gospel until an English teacher gave him a book containing the testimony of the nineteenth-century Chinese pastor Xi Shengmo, who had been delivered from opium addiction after receiving Jesus Christ.

Fu repented of his sins and placed his trust in the Savior of the world. He later recalled:

> My heart felt like it was going to leap out of my chest . . .
> Suddenly I had become aware there was a supernatural power,

Bob and Heidi Fu and their children soon after they left China

and that knowledge had miraculously replaced the hatred and anger I'd previously harbored against so many people.[10]

Fu's vibrant new faith completely transformed his life, and by the time he graduated from Liaocheng University with a law degree in 1991, Bob and his wife Heidi had led 30 of their classmates to faith in Christ. Bob and Heidi moved to the outskirts of Beijing, where they were involved with the house church movement. They met many persecuted Christians who had no way of speaking out against the tyranny they were experiencing. This time helped cement Fu's desire to speak out boldly against injustice, and it set the course of his future ministry. He later fondly recalled:

> In 1993 I was given the job of teaching English at the Communist school, where they trained senior and middle level Party leaders. I also met Jonathan Chao, a well-known Chinese Church historian and scholar. He came to our school and secretly discipled twenty to thirty of us in a disused toilet block. One weekend, from Friday to Sunday, he taught all day and into each night on Chinese Church history. It was a blessed time, being trained in a toilet block right under the nose of the Communist Party.[11]

By the mid-1990s the Fus again found themselves on the government's radar, and both Bob and Heidi were imprisoned for their faith. After being released two months later, Heidi discovered she was pregnant and faced the likelihood of a forced abortion when the authorities found out. After Bob and Heidi were placed on a government blacklist, they hid for months in a remote area of Shandong. After much prayer they reached the painful decision to leave China. Through a string of divine interventions they ended up in Hong Kong, and finally received permission to travel to the United States just one day before Hong Kong was handed back to Mainland China in July 1997.

After settling into life in America, Bob Fu established a ministry, China Aid Association, which has strongly advocated for the rights of the oppressed in China to the present day. His adventure has led him to help thousands of persecuted Christians back in his homeland, and he has testified before the United Nations, the US Congress and various other political bodies. Fu also developed a warm relationship with President George W. Bush, and ended up moving his ministry to the Bush family's hometown of Midland, Texas.

Bob Fu's fearless exposure of injustice and his political connections deeply upset the Chinese government, which dispatched agents to harass him in the United States, and powerful computer viruses were sent to him from China, which wiped his hard-drives of numerous important documents.

Back in China, the authorities vented their fury on Fu's father, Fu Yubo—an elderly hunchback in his seventies who had only recently become a follower of Christ. In a bid to get at his absent son, government officials arrested and tortured the old man, even though he had recently suffered a stroke and was partially senile. Realizing his father was suffering because of his son's actions on the other side of the world placed a heavy burden on Bob. He said:

> I could hardly bear the strain. My dad had twice tried to come to America to see me, but each time the US Embassy in Beijing rejected his application for a tourist visa, saying he was unable to prove he had sufficient funds to sustain himself while in America. After the second denial something snapped inside my father. He lost hope and was depressed, believing all hope of seeing me again had gone.[12]

Realizing the Chinese government's inhuman treatment of his disabled father was a trap set in the hope it might cause him to return to his homeland, Bob wisely kept well clear of China's reach, but he concocted a daring plan to smuggle his tiny 70-pound (32 kg) father out of China to live with his family in America. The plan was successful, but unfortunately Fu's father was in the dusk of his life, and cancer claimed him just a few months later.

Although some parts of the body of Christ choose to shy away from people like Bob Fu because of their political connections, those who personally know him realize his actions are motivated not by politics but by a deep love for Jesus Christ and a God-given desire to help the Christian community in China. Fu explained:

Over the years the Lord has taught me to stand for the truth, regardless of the consequences. I will continue to advocate on behalf of my persecuted brothers and sisters in China. Although I am grateful for my life in the United States, and all the gracious hospitality we have received from the American people, I still long for the day when my family might be able to return to a different China, one where people are treated with dignity and where different ideas and beliefs are allowed to flourish.[13]

Although some Christians who believe religion and politics must never mix may feel uncomfortable with the pathway Bob Fu has been called to walk down, history may well regard this unassuming man as one of the most influential Shandong Christians of his generation.

Letters from Shandong

2000

My parents accepted Jesus Christ in the spring of 1998. Their lives were transformed and they passed the gospel of salvation to me and my sister. At school we are indoctrinated with Marxism and Darwinism, so I dare not disclose my Christian identity. I always commit trivial sins and only pray when I need help from God. I don't read the Bible even though I have time. How can I evangelize my classmates? I wrote to two of them but they replied that faith in God stems only from a psychological need.[14]

I am married and have a four-year-old son. I met Jesus Christ and accepted Him as Lord and Savior while visiting my mother. When I returned home I told my husband that I had attended a gospel meeting. He scolded me for my ignorance and stupidity and persuaded me to give up my belief. I refused his threats and decided to believe in Christ no matter what happens.[15]

In 1993 I received the grace of God's salvation after listening to your gospel program. I desired to be His ambassador to preach God's wondrous love to others. Owing to my timid personality and my inability to abstain from worldly matters, I backed away from God's great mission. My love for God and my fellow man grew cold. Thank the Lord that your message awakened my numb heart. He opened my eyes to realize that 1,300 million souls in this country are lost without a clue how to find God. Once again I enrolled as God's soldier and vowed to cut off all worldly concerns. I am willing to live for the Lord, to love Him, and to serve Him by evangelizing by His mighty grace.[16]

I am handicapped and formerly held extreme views of the world. I even wanted to kill myself, but everything changed after I met Jesus three years ago. A brother from a neighboring village led me to Christ. We often meet to discuss the Bible as we encourage one another. We are children of the Heavenly Father and are people of God, so I don't care what the world says about me. Like a lost lamb who has found his home, I feel warm and happy.[17]

2001

I went to a church meeting and when I heard the testimonies of the brothers and sisters I had a strange, inexpressible feeling. The leader gave me a Bible and a hymnbook. I began at Genesis and was enthralled by the teaching, and started attending church regularly. There are not many young people in our church so I found I could help the elderly learn to sing the hymns. If I miss a Sunday meeting they always inquire why I did not come.

I was baptized and became a lamb in Christ's flock. I praise God from the bottom of my heart that He has chosen me and saved me from sin. He has sent His Spirit to work in my heart. When I meet with difficulties or persecution my Lord always grants me the victory. Since my conversion my behavior has completely changed. At work I memorize and recite Bible verses and hymns and I don't feel tired at all. Work that used to take me four hours to complete I can now finish in an hour and a half![18]

More and more people are being converted—workers, peasants and students. Just a few days ago a group of police from the city rushed to a middle school in our small town, because many students are attending church. Rural churches are packed out on Sundays.[19]

2002

I am a brother who meets in a house church in Jinan City. Because I have been attending a Bible study class, the Public Security Bureau, State Security Service and the Religious Affairs

Bureau have all investigated me. I have stopped my Christian work and am quietly praying and reading the Bible at home. My Christian brothers and sisters have temporarily stopped having contact with me.[20]

2003

In 1993 my husband started his own business. I later discovered he loved someone else and it broke my heart. God saved me at the lowest point of my life. Although my husband has not yet repented, my heart is full of peace and joy. I previously worshipped idols, burned incense and spoke foul language, but Jesus had mercy on me and saved me by the cross. I was set free from the bondage of sin and became a child of God. I am so thankful for His great love. Now I am no longer a slave of sin. I believe in due time He will save my husband too because the Lord does not want anyone to perish.[21]

I have been diagnosed with high blood pressure, arteriosclerosis of the brain, and a shortage of blood circulation, but I am determined to carry on my service for the Lord because I am the only seminary graduate among 17,000 believers in our county. I am 74 years old in the flesh but am only a baby in the spirit. I will not lose heart even though my hair has turned gray. I have decided to complete this spiritual journey.[22]

2004

The Lord has led me to do children's Sunday school work. I have given myself entirely to the Lord, and wherever He leads, I will follow. It is more dangerous to do children's work than to work with adults. If arrested I will immediately be sentenced to jail. I believe God will revive Christian work among the youth of China. Even though I do not fully understand God's ultimate purposes for me, I have given myself to Him and will not look back.[23]

2006

I am 76—an old sister in Christ. In the spring of 1990 I visited Jinan City, where one of my daughter's neighbors asked if I had heard of Jesus the Savior. Awakened with a sense of guilt, I felt God call me . . . a sinner who had forsaken God for years. I confessed my sins to Him and repented. I am willing to turn my life to God and honor His Lordship. It is His blood that redeemed me. Both my daughter and I now believed in Jesus. How wonderful it was that God should seek me![24]

2010s

A time of consolidation

After more than 30 years of almost unhindered growth in Shandong, the house churches appeared to enter a new period in the 2010s. While evangelism still continued and many new people came to faith in Jesus Christ—especially in the rural areas of the province—the leaders of God's flock realized they also needed to concentrate on training in order to establish the millions of new believers in the faith.

A contemporary Christian worship service at an urban church
RCMI

Like countless other revivals throughout church history, the Shandong churches entered a period of consolidation, where they focused more on retaining the gains made during the 1980s, 1990s and 2000s. They realized it made no sense to win people to the Lord if there was no structure in place to keep them grounded in the faith.

Ironically, although the house churches in other parts of the country sometimes ridiculed the Shandong believers for their cautious and conservative ways, those traits that were considered weaknesses by outsiders proved to be great strengths. Because of their desire to keep heretical teaching and practices out of the Shandong churches, many pastors throughout the province had a solid base in their lives, enabling them to reach out and teach others how to handle the Scriptures correctly.

Although countless people continued to enter the kingdom of God, the Shandong revival showed signs it was beginning to slow down, especially in urban areas. As Chinese society lurched toward extreme consumerism, people's hearts were generally not as receptive to the gospel as in previous decades. It was not as though the fire was close to going out, however. Rather, instead of hundreds of thousands of people coming to faith each year in the house churches, now 'just' tens of thousands came.

The continuing famine of God's word

The need for Bibles among China's house churches was acute in China in the 1980s and 1990s, when thousands of Christians from around the globe traveled to Hong Kong and lovingly carried Bibles across the border into Mainland China. In the new millennium, however, many overseas believers were unaware that the need for Scriptures remained great in China, due to a variety of factors.

Although a certain number of Bibles were legally printed inside China each year by the government-approved Amity Press, those copies were only made available to members of the Three-Self Patriotic Movement. The house church networks, which constitute approximately two-thirds of Evangelical Christians in Shandong, have been left to pick up the crumbs that fall from the table of the registered Church.

The house church leaders throughout the country are convinced that the government, in collusion with the Three-Self Church, is deliberately seeking to strangle the spiritual life out of the unregistered house church movements by strictly controlling the supply of Bibles. This is yet another form of persecution, and it has left the millions of house church believers in Shandong vulnerable to spiritual immaturity and exposed to dangerous cults.

Many Three-Self Church affiliated Christians, however, have shown smug disdain for the struggles of the house church believers. A prevailing thought of some registered believers is that the house churches should swallow their pride and register with the government. Many house churches, however, are adamant they will never submit to an entity controlled by atheists, and they continue to stand their ground, even if it means they are unable to access God's word.

A small number of ministries helped the house churches print Bibles illegally inside China for a number of years, but the project carried great risk, and anyone caught printing or distributing an illegal Bible faced a minimum of three years in prison without trial. The need was so great, however, that many were willing to take that risk.

In the twenty-first century, Asia Harvest emerged as one ministry willing to go against the flow and print the word of God for the Chinese house churches. At the time of this book going to print, Asia Harvest had printed and distributed

875,942 full Chinese Bibles for the house church believers in Shandong. In response, the ministry received many touching letters from thankful Shandong church leaders, which provide insights into the massive scale of the problem. One letter, received from a regional church leader in 2011, said:

> You may have heard about recent drought in our area and how we are unlikely to have a winter wheat crop because the drought is so severe. What the news doesn't report is the great spiritual harvest we are reaping, as every day many souls come to the Lord throughout our province. We are even seeing God work through the drought as many farmers are now willing to hear the gospel since they have lost confidence in their own abilities. Now they understand how precious it is when God sends rain on the land, and they have repented of their sins.
>
> Because of the large number of new converts throughout Shandong, we currently need 589,812 Bibles just to provide one for each person in our fellowships. We ask God to pour out a special blessing on you for providing these precious Bibles to us.[1]

In the following years, Asia Harvest received more letters from other Shandong house church leaders, revealing the serious challenges facing believers in the province. In 2012 one senior church leader wrote:

> The house churches throughout Shandong have experienced great growth in recent years. One of the side effects of this growth is that we struggle to get enough Bibles to meet the need of new believers. We cannot thank you enough for providing Bibles to us. Our fellowships are growing stronger in faith and

knowledge as well as in number as a direct result of these precious gifts you provide. At this moment, we need 146,238 more Bibles so that each new believer will have their own copy. From the bottom of our hearts we say thank you and God bless you![2]

In 2013 an evangelist from a rural area of Shandong wrote:

When the gospel was first shared with us last December, we did not have any Bibles among us. We felt such a hunger to know more about the Truth that we had been searching for all our lives. The evangelist who preached to us did not have an extra Bible either, and he attempted to obtain Bibles for us that winter without success. When we cried out to the Lord with a burning desire to know him, we received a peace in our hearts that our Heavenly Father was going to provide, but we did not understand how. In May 2013 the Lord answered our prayers and every fellowship leader and evangelist among us received a Bible. We fell down on our faces before the Lord and wept with joy as we thanked him for providing the Bread of Life.

The people who brought the Bibles to us explained that they are provided by Christians around the world who care for us and who sacrificed their hard-earned money so we could have God's word. We are just peasants from the countryside, so we don't understand much about the world outside of China. Everything overseas seems so strange to us; but we now feel this strong connection to God's people around the world even though we haven't met them yet.

Now the Lord has given us a desire to tithe from our vegetables, rice, wheat, chickens and eggs that we take to the city market. We will use the proceeds to help provide the Scriptures to other Christians in China who do not yet have any. This is our way of passing on the most wonderful gift we have received in our lives. Although we don't know you by name, we thank you from the depths of our hearts for providing these Bibles to us. We believe that in heaven the Lord is going to reveal those of you who provided the word of God. We look forward to worshiping before the Lord with you! God's grace and peace be with you until then.[3]

As this book was being prepared for publication, two more letters were received from Shandong. The first emphasized the urgency of the situation in the province:

Thank you for the Bibles you delivered to us recently. These have been distributed and were received with many thanks to the Lord. They are the answer to our prayers. Although it's sometimes possible for believers in big cities to buy a Bible from the Three-Self church, our believers in farming areas have no such access, and most are so poor that they could never afford the price of a Bible even if they were able to obtain one. Please send more.

The second letter was written by a church elder in late 2016:

I first heard the gospel from a traveling evangelist many years ago. He was very sorry that he couldn't leave a Bible with us. He only had one personal copy. It was many years before I saw a Bible and heard the gospel again; but the message shared with me at that time had a huge impact and I often thought about it over the years. After much searching I repented of my sinful ways and now I serve the one true God.

In 2007 I received a Bible through your ministry. It consumed me and I read it many hours each day as I sought to know God's plan for my life. Nine years have passed, and now I am involved in helping to get Bibles to new believers in rural districts. It is such an honor and pleasure to serve God's children this way. I get to witness their tears of joy and gratitude when they hold God's word for the first time.[4]

Jesus in the boardroom

With China's growing wealth and emergence as a world power, in recent years a breed of Christians surfaced in Shandong that would have been almost impossible for previous generations of believers to imagine. Many wealthy business owners—some running billion-dollar companies—have risen to prominence in the "new China." The difference with some of these men and women, however, is that they are committed followers of Jesus Christ, and they see their companies as a vehicle provided by God for spreading the gospel.

One such Christian businessman is Wang Ruoxiong, the founder and chairman of the huge Chinese real estate company Tiantai Group. In 2015 the BBC examined this peculiar partnership between the corporate boardroom and Christianity. Wang made it clear where his company derived its motivation. The BBC reported:

Saying prayers with colleagues would feel a bit uncomfortable; too intimate an activity in the workplace for many people. Yet at Chinese real estate giant Tiantai Group . . . that is exactly what they do in the boardroom before making important decisions.

Three-quarters of the firm's eight-strong senior management team are Christians and founder and chairman Wang Ruoxiong, who himself became a Christian seven years ago, says that when the company has to make difficult decisions, it turns to the Bible for guidance. In fact, he goes as far as to say that it's not him but God running the firm.

"He controls everything. I am merely a housekeeper of Jesus, assisting him in taking care of the company," he says.[5]

Calm before the storm

The 2010s started relatively peacefully for the Church in Shandong and most other parts of China. Persecution appeared to be at its lowest ebb since the advent of Communism in 1949, although believers faced new difficulties as materialism and the love of money rose up like a massive two-headed god. The Lord Jesus Christ, however, preserved a remnant of those who love him with all their hearts, and the Shandong Church continued to grow every year, though not at the same rate as in previous decades.

Although persecution of Christians appeared to reduce in the first half of the 2010s, there were occasional reminders of the past. In January 2011, for example, the police raided a large Christian meeting of more than 1,000 people in Cangshan County in southern Shandong. Local Public Security officials burst into the church and forced the meeting to end, before they took the leaders into custody, including the speaker Lu Daihao, a well-known visiting evangelist from Taiwan.

In 2014 China shocked the world by announcing the closure of all prison labor camps—horrid places where tens of thousands of Christians were mercilessly tortured over the previous six decades.

The status quo resumes

In 2016 the Chinese president, Xi Jinping, demanded to meet privately with several of China's senior house church leaders.

Although the content of their discussions was kept strictly confidential, the results were soon clearly evident, as wave after wave of persecution against the house churches was launched throughout China.

In eastern Shandong's Qingdao City, the police visited a local house church leader and told him: "We know all about your various meetings. We have been instructed to close you down, but we will continue to let you meet if you give us all the weekly offerings you collect in your churches!"[6]

The house church leader rejected their attempted extortion, and the church broke into numerous smaller groups, allowing them to meet discreetly and without disturbance from the corrupt local authorities.

In September 2016, when the government announced new religious restrictions aimed at curbing the growth of Christianity, it seemed the more tolerant attitude prevailing in China had come to an abrupt end. Throughout the nation, house church leaders soon found themselves under tremendous pressure.

Many pastors and evangelists were arrested and interrogated, while others had their meetings shut down. Worse, some leaders went missing, having been bundled into vans or taken from their homes and sent to one of China's notorious secret 'black jails'—unofficial places where the government's perceived enemies are taken and tortured mercilessly. These jails are often located inside secure places like deserted junk yards or abandoned factories, where the wicked men and women of China's state security division feel free to do their worst to the children of God.

At the time of completing this book, one Shandong house church leader contacted us to say:

Things here are like in Mao's day! We never thought we would return to such a time. The younger generation of believers have never experienced severe persecution, and they are shaken. Please pray they will patiently endure, and their faith will be tested and found to be like pure gold.[7]

Another letter from Shandong presented a sobering summary of the conditions in the province at the end of 2016:

The new Communist leadership requires that all churches be controlled by the Communist Party. They must even display a national flag to show their loyalty. Some large churches have been asked to hand over the church offerings to the police. When the pastors refuse to do so, they are ordered by the police to disband their congregations. Some large house churches have been forced to restructure into many small cell groups. The crackdown has been spreading and there will be tough times ahead.

The government is once again trying to squeeze the life out of the Church. There are new laws prohibiting any religious activities without government approval—even holding Bible studies of more than ten people in homes. We need to conduct trainings with fewer participants.

One of our workers went so far as to say, "China has closed . . . the door is closed"—at least temporarily. What she means is that ministries operating in China are limiting what they are doing and trying to lower their profile.

Apparently, the government is using a new method to deal with people when they arrest them. Instead of beating them, they are drugging them with a mind-altering chemical that diminishes the person's mental capacity. Ministry is still possible, but we need to move with extreme caution.[8]

As you have read in the pages of this book, the history of the Church in Shandong has been blessed with powerful revivals, and from the ruins of ashes, floods, famines and wars arose a shining and pure bride of Christ. The living God, Jesus Christ, has gained much glory from his disciples in Shandong.

While the current Chinese rulers appear determined to repeat the mistakes of their predecessors by once again trying to hurt and destroy God's people, may we pray that the persecution will again result in revival and rapid growth in Shandong—the blessed Revival Province of China.

The future of the Church in Shandong

As we reach the end of our look at the wonderful things God has done in Shandong Province over the decades, one thing is clear: the Church of Jesus Christ has been established, and despite generations of battering and persecution, God has raised up a vibrant body from among the huge population of almost 100 million people.

The history of God's kingdom in Shandong has been a rich yet difficult one. The early Evangelical missionaries in the nineteenth century overcame overwhelming odds to plant the seed of the gospel in the province, and as the Church gradually passed from foreign to Chinese control, it matured and strengthened into a powerful body able to withstand decades of hardship.

Hundreds of Chinese Christians sacrificed their lives during the Boxer Rebellion of 1900, having learned how to endure when their faith was under fire from the extraordinary example of Lottie Moon and others like her who loved the people of Shandong even unto death.

The first half of the twentieth century brought many intense struggles, but the blessing of God was also seen as he sent servants like Marie Monsen of Norway, whose simple question, "Have you been born again?" searched the hearts of many believers and helped spark revival in Shandong during the 1920s and 1930s.

And what a revival it was! The Holy Spirit was poured out on hundreds of thousands of people throughout the province, and the Church, which had been small in number, suddenly burst into the open. The witness of the Jesus Family and other indigenous church movements added to the beautiful tapestry of the body of Christ in Shandong, and the purity of those true believers shone like a beacon for the world to see.

During the powerful revival of the 1930s, few Christians realized that God was quietly strengthening the Church ahead of its most excruciating trial of all, when Communism would bring persecution at unprecedented levels. The Church in Shandong effectively went underground for decades in order to survive the battering.

The rulers of China at the time arrogantly thought they had destroyed God's people, with Mao's wife even proclaiming that Christianity in China was dead and buried and had been confined to the history section of the museum.

What she and many other enemies of God didn't realize, however, was that Jesus Christ had declared:

> Very truly I tell you, unless a kernel of wheat falls to the ground and dies, it remains only a single seed. But if it dies, it produces many seeds. Anyone who loves their life will lose it, while anyone who hates their life in this world will keep it for eternal life. (John 12.24–25)

During much of the 1960s and 1970s, Christians in Shandong were hidden from view, but God had not forgotten them. Indeed, he had them exactly where he wanted, and in due course the seed sprang back to life and produced many more seeds.

Today, as the table on pages 268–72 reveals, we estimate there to be approximately 5.3 million professing Christians of all creeds in Shandong Province. Of these, about 2.9 million belong to unregistered house churches; 1.5 million attend government-approved Three-Self churches; while Catholics presently number around 800,000 in the province, distributed among both registered and unregistered congregations.

Although there is much to rejoice about as we reflect on the marvelous deeds God has performed in this blessed part of China, it is sobering to remember that today only about five percent of Shandong's population professes to be Christian. That leaves 95 out of 100 people yet to believe in Jesus Christ, while many have yet to hear the gospel in a way that would enable them to make an informed decision to accept or reject God's salvation.

Although there is a geographical divide within the Church in Shandong, with the southern regions of the province tending to be more Christian than the northern and eastern areas, the more pronounced divide is between Christians living in the cities and those in rural farming areas. The proportion of believers in Shandong is strongly tilted in favor of people living in rural regions, which is consistent with most other provinces in China.

This dichotomy between urban and rural Christians has created tension in some church movements, with those living in the cities tending to be more educated and sophisticated, while most rural believers lead hard lives and are trapped in poverty. In the past three decades a huge trend toward urbanization has been underway throughout China. Large numbers of rural Christians in Shandong have left farming areas in search of jobs in Jinan, Qingdao or one of the other major cities. Others have left the province altogether in search of a better standard of living.

While some of the migrated Christians have done well in their new environments and have shared the gospel with those they meet, many others have struggled, and the dislocation caused by being away from their spiritual support base, and exposure to the vices and temptations of city life have devastated countless lives. Many without a strong root in God's word have abandoned the faith.

In previous generations the churches in Shandong faced floods, famines, pestilences and wars. Today they are battling materialism and cults, and have struggles exacerbated by the lack of Bibles and a dire shortage of church leaders who are able to teach the word of God in a balanced and effective manner.

The Church in Shandong today, despite its long history of revival and amazing testimonies, is in need of continual pruning and awakening if the fruit of the harvest is to remain useful for God's kingdom.

May Shandong long continue to deserve its reputation as "China's Revival Province"!

Appendix

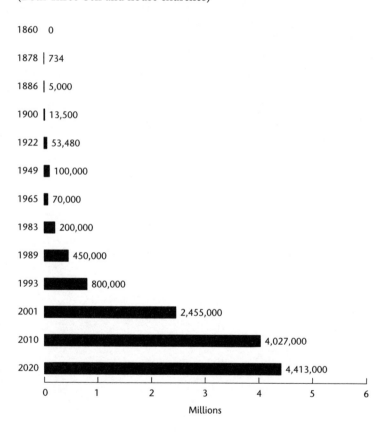

Evangelical Christians in Shandong (1860–2020)

(Both Three-Self and house churches)

1860 0

1878 734

1886 5,000

1900 13,500

1922 53,480

1949 100,000

1965 70,000

1983 200,000

1989 450,000

1993 800,000

2001 2,455,000

2010 4,027,000

2020 4,413,000

0   1   2   3   4   5   6

Millions

Appendix

Sources:

0	(1860)
734	(1878 – *China's Millions*, January 1879)
5,000	(1885 – *Chinese Recorder*, November 1885)
13,500	(1900 – *International Bulletin of Missionary Research*, April 1998)
53,480	(1922 – Stauffer, *The Christian Occupation of China*)
100,000	(1949 – *Global Chinese Ministries*, October 2003)
70,000	(1965 – *Global Chinese Ministries*, October 2003)*
200,000	(1983 – *Global Chinese Ministries*, October 2003)*
450,000	(1989 – *Shandong Yearbook*)*
800,000	(1993 – *Bridge*, October 1993)*
2,455,000	(2001 – Johnstone and Mandryk, *Operation World*)
4,027,000	(2010 – Mandryk, *Operation World*)
4,413,000	(2020 – Hattaway, The China Chronicles)

* These sources may only refer to registered church estimates. Three-Self figures typically only count adult baptized members.

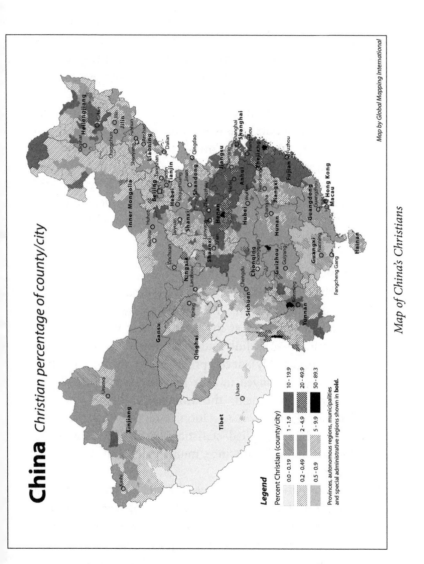

China *Christian percentage of county/city*

Legend

Percent Christian (county/city)

0.0 – 0.19	1 – 1.9
0.2 – 0.49	2 – 4.9
0.5 – 0.9	5 – 9.9
10 – 19.9	
20 – 49.9	
50 – 89.3	

Provinces, autonomous regions, municipalities
and special administrative regions shown in **bold**.

Map by Global Mapping International

Map of China's Christians

A survey of Christians in China

For centuries, people have been curious to know how many Christians live in China. When Marco Polo made his famous journey to the Orient 700 years ago, he revealed the existence of Nestorian churches and monasteries in various places, to the fascination of people back in Europe.

Since I started traveling to China in the 1980s, I have found that Christians around the world are still eager to know how many believers there are in China. Many people are aware that God has done a remarkable work in the world's most populated country, but little research has been done to put a figure on this phenomenon. In recent decades, wildly divergent estimates have been published, ranging from 20 million to 230 million Christians in China.

Methodology

In the table on pages 269–73, I provide estimates of the number of Christians in Shandong. Full tables of the other provinces of China can be found at the Asia Harvest website (see the 'The Church in China' link under the Resources tab at <www.asiaharvest.org>). My survey provides figures for Christians of every creed, arranged in four main categories: the Three-Self Patriotic Movement; the Evangelical house churches; the Catholic Patriotic Association; and the Catholic house churches. I have supplied statistics for all 2,370 cities and counties within every province, municipality and autonomous region of China.

The information was gathered from a wide variety of sources. More than 2,000 published sources have been noted in the tables published online, including a multitude of books, journals, magazine articles and reports that I spent years meticulously accumulating. I have also conducted hundreds of hours of interviews with key house church leaders responsible for their church networks throughout China.

Before entering data into the tables, I began with this assumption: that in any given place in China there are no Christians at all, until I have a figure from a documented source or can make an intelligent estimate based on information gathered from Chinese Christian leaders. In other words, I wanted to put aside all preconceptions and expectations, input all the information I had, and see what the totals came to.

A note about security

None of the information provided in these tables is new to the Chinese government. Beijing has already thoroughly researched the spread of Christianity throughout the country, as shown by high-ranking official Ye Xiaowen's 2006 announcement that there were then 130 million Christians in China. In December 2009, the national newspaper *China Daily* interviewed scholar Liu Peng who had spent years researching religion for the Chinese Academy of Social Sciences. Liu claimed the "house churches have at least 50 million followers nationwide." His figure at the time was consistent with my research.

After consulting various house church leaders in China, I was able to confirm that all of them were content that this information should be published, as long as the surveys focus on statistics and avoid specific information such as the names and locations of Christian leaders.

The Chinese Church in perspective

All discussion of how many Christians there are in China today should be tempered by the realization that more than 90 percent of the population face a Christless eternity. Hundreds of millions of individuals have yet to hear the gospel. Church leaders in China have told me how ashamed and burdened they feel that so many of their countrymen and women do not yet know Jesus Christ. This burden motivates them to do whatever it takes to preach the gospel among every ethnic group and in every city, town and village—to every individual—in China, and to do whatever necessary to see Christ exalted throughout the land.

May we humbly give thanks to the living God for the great things he has done in China. We are privileged to live in a remarkable time in human history, like in the days prophesied by the prophet Habakkuk:

> Look at the nations and watch—and be utterly amazed. For I am going to do something in your days that you would not believe, even if you were told. (Habakkuk 1.5)

Table of Christians in Shandong 山东

| Shandong 山东 | POPULATION | | | | | CHRISTIANS | | | | | | | |
| | | | | | | Evangelicals | | | Catholics | | | Total Christians | |
County or City	Census 2000	Census 2010	Growth		Estimate 2020	TSPM	House church	TOTAL Evangelicals	CPA	House church	TOTAL Catholics	TOTAL	Percent of 2020 Population
Binzhou Prefecture													
Bincheng District	600,883	682,717	81,834	13.62%	764,551	7,951	13,279	21,230	2,064	4,129	6,193	27,423	3.59
Boxing	462,815	487,116	24,301	5.25%	511,417	5,319	8,882	14,201	1,381	2,762	4,142	18,344	3.59
Huimin	604,751	602,491	-2,260	-0.37%	600,231	6,242	10,425	16,667	1,621	3,241	4,862	21,529	3.59
Wudi	423,113	418,687	-4,426	-1.05%	414,261	4,308	7,195	11,503	1,119	2,237	3,356	14,859	3.59
Yangxin	419,591	427,014	7,423	1.77%	434,437	4,518	7,545	12,063	1,173	2,346	3,519	15,582	3.59
Zhanhua	366,178	351,672	-14,506	-3.96%	337,166	3,507	5,856	9,362	910	1,821	2,731	12,093	3.59
Zouping	686,590	778,777	92,187	13.43%	870,964	9,058	15,127	24,185	2,352	4,703	7,055	31,240	3.59
	3,563,921	3,748,474	184,553	5.18%	3,933,027	40,903	68,309	109,212	10,619	21,238	31,858	141,070	3.59
Dezhou Prefecture													
Decheng District	552,445	679,535	127,090	23.01%	806,625	6,776	11,315	18,091	2,178	4,356	6,534	24,625	3.05
Leling City	615,833	652,415	36,582	5.94%	688,997	8,612	14,383	22,995	1,860	3,721	5,581	28,576	4.15
Lingxian	529,537	569,007	39,470	7.45%	608,477	5,111	8,536	13,647	1,643	3,286	4,929	18,576	3.05
Linyi	508,213	511,105	2,892	0.57%	513,997	4,318	7,210	11,528	1,388	2,776	4,163	15,691	3.05
Ningjin	432,880	449,891	17,011	3.93%	466,902	3,922	6,550	10,472	1,261	2,521	3,782	14,254	3.05
Pingyuan	439,701	442,948	3,247	0.74%	446,195	3,748	6,259	10,007	1,205	2,409	3,614	13,621	3.05
Qihe	593,341	602,042	8,701	1.47%	610,743	5,130	8,568	13,698	1,649	3,298	4,947	18,645	3.05
Qingyun	286,427	294,684	8,257	2.88%	302,941	2,545	4,250	6,794	818	1,636	2,454	9,248	3.05
Wucheng	361,179	376,063	14,884	4.12%	390,947	3,284	5,484	8,768	1,056	2,111	3,167	11,935	3.05
Xiajin	479,817	500,514	20,697	4.31%	521,211	4,378	7,312	11,690	1,407	2,815	4,222	15,912	3.05
Yucheng City	494,301	490,031	-4,270	-0.86%	485,761	5,878	9,816	15,693	1,312	2,623	3,935	19,628	4.04
	5,293,674	5,568,235	274,561	5.19%	5,842,796	53,702	89,682	143,384	15,776	31,551	47,327	190,710	3.26
Dongying Prefecture													
Dongying District	568,510	756,676	188,166	33.10%	944,842	7,370	12,308	19,677	2,551	5,102	7,653	27,330	2.89
Guangrao	472,841	507,523	34,682	7.33%	542,205	4,229	7,063	11,292	1,464	2,928	4,392	15,684	2.89
Hekou District	220,334	247,595	27,261	12.37%	274,856	2,144	3,580	5,724	742	1,484	2,226	7,950	2.89
Kenli	242,654	242,292	-362	-0.15%	241,930	1,887	3,151	5,038	653	1,306	1,960	6,998	2.89
Lijin	288,832	281,252	-7,580	-2.62%	273,672	2,135	3,565	5,699	739	1,478	2,217	7,916	2.89
	1,793,171	2,035,338	242,167	13.50%	2,277,505	17,765	29,667	47,431	6,149	12,299	18,448	65,879	2.89
Heze Prefecture													
Cao	1,335,422	1,365,675	30,253	2.27%	1,395,928	36,950	61,707	98,657	10,469	20,939	31,408	130,065	9.32
Chengwu	596,339	612,016	15,677	2.63%	627,693	16,615	27,747	44,362	1,695	3,390	5,084	49,446	7.88
Dingtao	563,352	565,793	2,441	0.43%	568,234	15,041	25,119	40,160	1,534	3,068	4,603	44,763	7.88
Dongming	691,206	711,080	19,874	2.88%	730,954	19,348	32,312	51,660	1,974	3,947	5,921	57,581	7.88
Juancheng	715,684	721,898	6,214	0.87%	728,112	19,273	32,186	51,459	1,966	3,932	5,898	57,357	7.88
Juye	839,438	860,581	21,143	2.52%	881,724	23,339	38,977	62,316	2,381	4,761	7,142	69,458	7.88
Mudan District	1,280,031	1,346,717	66,686	5.21%	1,413,403	37,413	62,479	99,892	3,816	7,632	11,449	111,341	7.88
Shan (Dan)	1,050,701	1,063,243	12,542	1.19%	1,075,785	28,476	47,555	76,031	2,905	5,809	8,714	84,745	7.88
Yuncheng	1,025,800	1,040,690	14,890	1.45%	1,055,580	27,941	46,662	74,603	2,850	5,700	8,550	83,153	7.88
	8,097,973	8,287,693	189,720	2.34%	8,477,413	224,397	374,743	599,140	29,589	59,179	88,768	687,909	8.11

| Shandong 山东 | POPULATION | | | | | CHRISTIANS | | | | | | | |
| | | | | | | Evangelicals | | | Catholics | | | Total Christians | |
County or City	Census 2000	Census 2010	Growth		Estimate 2020	TSPM	House church	TOTAL Evangelicals	CPA	House church	TOTAL Catholics	TOTAL	Percent of 2020 Population
Jinan Prefecture													
Changqing District	506,579	578,740	72,161	14.24%	650,901	8,201	41,007	49,208	1,757	3,515	5,272	54,480	8.37
Huaiyin District	396,846	476,811	79,965	20.15%	556,776	7,015	35,077	42,092	1,503	3,007	4,510	46,602	8.37
Jiyang	518,879	517,948	-931	-0.18%	517,017	6,514	32,572	39,086	1,396	2,792	4,188	43,274	8.37
Licheng District	878131	1124306	246,175	28.03%	1,370,481	17,268	86,340	103,608	3,700	7,401	11,101	114,709	8.37
Lixia District	582,520	754,136	171,616	29.46%	925,752	11,644	58,322	69,987	2,500	4,999	7,499	77,485	8.37
Pingyin	344,386	331,712	-12,674	-3.68%	319,038	4,010	20,099	24,119	989	1,978	2,967	27,086	8.49
Shanghe	574,789	564,125	-10,664	-1.86%	553,461	6,974	34,868	41,842	1,494	2,989	4,483	46,325	8.37
Shizhong District	572,141	713,581	141,440	24.72%	855,021	10,773	53,866	64,640	2,309	4,617	6,926	71,565	8.37
Tianqiao District	570,296	688,415	118,119	20.71%	806,534	10,132	50,812	60,974	2,178	4,355	6,533	67,507	8.37
Zhangqiu City	977,324	1,064,210	86,886	8.89%	1,151,096	13,253	73,440	86,793	3,108	6,216	9,324	96,117	8.35
	5,921,891	6,813,984	892,093	15.06%	7,706,077	95,945	486,404	582,349	20,934	41,868	62,802	645,151	8.37
Jining Prefecture													
Jiaxiang	761,086	818,188	57,102	7.50%	875,290	11,204	18,710	29,914	2,363	4,727	7,090	37,004	4.23
Jinxiang	602,555	625,262	22,707	3.77%	647,969	8,294	13,851	22,145	1,750	3,499	5,249	27,394	4.23
Liangshan	675,392	730,652	55,260	8.18%	785,912	10,060	16,800	26,859	2,122	4,244	6,366	33,225	4.23
Qufu City	625,313	640,498	15,185	2.43%	655,683	9,704	16,206	25,910	1,770	3,541	5,311	31,221	4.76
Rencheng District	1,050,522	1,241,012	190,490	18.13%	1,431,502	21,186	35,381	56,567	3,865	7,730	11,595	68,162	4.76
Sishui	552,028	536,087	-15,941	-2.89%	520,146	6,558	11,119	17,777	1,404	2,809	4,213	21,990	4.23
Weishan	645,728	633,357	-12,371	-1.92%	620,986	7,949	13,274	21,223	1,677	3,353	5,030	26,253	4.23
Wenshang	702,095	684,617	-17,478	-2.49%	667,139	8,539	14,261	22,800	1,801	3,603	5,404	28,204	4.23
Yanzhou District	598,387	618,394	20,007	3.34%	638,401	6,767	11,301	18,068	1,724	3,447	5,171	23,239	3.64
Yutai	426,172	437,146	10,974	2.58%	448,120	5,736	9,579	15,315	1,210	2,420	3,630	18,945	4.23
Zoucheng City	1,101,003	1,116,692	15,689	1.42%	1,132,381	12,456	20,802	33,258	3,057	6,115	9,172	42,430	3.75
	7,740,281	8,081,905	341,624	4.41%	8,423,529	108,553	181,283	289,836	22,744	45,487	68,231	358,066	4.25
Laiwu Prefecture													
Gangcheng District	234,891	308,994	74,103	31.55%	383,097	4,214	7,037	11,252	1,034	2,069	3,103	14,355	3.75
Laicheng District	998,634	989,535	-9,099	-0.91%	980,436	10,785	18,011	28,795	2,647	5,294	7,942	36,737	3.75
	1,233,525	1,298,529	65,004	5.27%	1,363,533	14,999	25,048	40,047	3,682	7,363	11,045	51,092	3.75
Liaocheng Prefecture													
Chiping District	546,125	520,016	-26,109	-4.78%	493,907	5,482	9,156	14,638	1,334	2,667	4,001	18,639	3.77
Dongchang District	950,319	1,229,768	279,449	29.41%	1,509,217	15,752	27,976	44,729	4,075	8,150	12,225	56,953	3.77
Dong'e	413,735	352,630	-61,105	-14.77%	291,525	3,236	5,404	8,640	787	1,574	2,361	11,001	3.77
Gaotang	456,464	473,422	16,958	3.72%	490,380	5,443	9,090	14,533	1,324	2,648	3,972	18,505	3.77
Guanxian	707,137	764,864	57,727	8.16%	822,591	9,131	15,248	24,379	2,221	4,442	6,663	31,042	3.77
Linqing City	694,247	719,611	25,364	3.65%	744,975	20,636	34,462	55,098	2,011	4,023	6,034	61,132	8.21
Shenxian	921,225	958,827	37,602	4.08%	996,429	11,060	22,121	33,181	2,690	5,381	8,071	41,252	4.14
Yanggu	722,863	770,725	47,862	6.62%	818,587	9,086	15,174	24,260	2,210	4,420	6,631	30,891	3.77
	5,412,115	5,789,863	377,748	6.98%	6,167,611	80,827	138,631	219,458	16,653	33,305	49,958	269,416	4.37

Shandong 山东

County or City	POPULATION					Evangelicals			Catholics			Total Christians	
	Census 2000	Census 2010	Growth		Estimate 2020	TSPM	House church	TOTAL Evangelicals	CPA	House church	TOTAL Catholics	TOTAL	Percent of 2020 Population
Linyi Prefecture													
Feixian	904,696	923,475	18,779	2.08%	942,254	22,614	37,766	60,380	2,544	5,088	7,632	68,012	7.22
Hedong District	587,897	633,522	45,625	7.76%	679,147	16,300	27,220	43,520	1,834	3,667	5,501	49,021	7.22
Junan	964,591	886,376	-78,215	-8.11%	808,161	20,042	33,471	53,513	2,182	4,364	6,546	60,059	7.43
Lanlin (Cangshan)	1,128,161	1,161,932	33,771	2.99%	1,195,703	29,653	49,521	79,175	3,228	6,457	9,685	88,860	7.43
Lanshan District	938,159	1,159,181	221,022	23.56%	1,380,203	34,229	57,162	91,392	3,727	7,453	11,180	102,571	7.43
Linshu	597,850	617,081	19,231	3.22%	636,312	15,781	26,353	42,134	1,718	3,436	5,154	47,288	7.43
Luozhuang District	412,454	510,945	98,491	23.88%	609,436	15,114	25,240	40,354	1,645	3,291	4,936	45,291	7.43
Mengyin	535,070	489,537	-45,533	-8.51%	444,004	11,011	18,389	29,400	1,199	2,398	3,596	32,997	7.43
Pingyi	974,213	900,167	-74,046	-7.60%	826,121	20,488	34,215	54,702	2,231	4,461	6,692	61,394	7.43
Tancheng	972,268	936,166	-36,102	-3.71%	900,064	22,322	37,277	59,599	2,430	4,860	7,291	66,889	7.43
Yinan	869,535	822,727	-46,808	-5.38%	775,919	19,243	32,135	51,378	2,095	4,190	6,285	57,663	7.43
Yishui	1,057,758	998,331	-59,427	-5.62%	938,904	23,285	38,886	62,170	2,535	5,070	7,605	69,776	7.43
	9,942,652	10,039,440	96,788	0.97%	10,136,228	250,081	417,636	667,717	27,368	54,736	82,103	749,821	7.40
Qingdao Prefecture													
Chengyang District	494,007	737,209	243,202	49.23%	980,411	19,804	33,073	52,877	2,647	5,294	7,941	60,819	6.20
Huangdao District	1,066,176	1,392,554	326,378	30.61%	1,718,932	34,722	57,986	92,709	4,641	9,282	13,923	106,632	6.20
Jiaozhou City	783,478	843,054	59,576	7.60%	902,630	9,297	15,526	24,823	2,437	4,874	7,311	32,135	3.56
Jimo City	1,111,202	1,177,201	65,999	5.94%	1,243,200	13,800	23,045	36,845	3,357	6,713	10,070	46,915	3.77
Laixi City	728,796	750,225	21,429	2.94%	771,654	8,874	14,820	23,694	2,083	4,167	6,250	29,944	3.88
Laoshan District	254,625	379,469	124,844	49.03%	504,313	5,800	9,685	15,485	1,362	2,723	4,085	19,570	3.88
Licang District	352,801	512,389	159,588	45.23%	671,977	7,728	12,905	20,633	1,814	3,629	5,443	26,076	3.88
Pingdu City	1,321,975	1,357,424	35,449	2.68%	1,392,873	25,907	43,265	69,173	3,761	7,522	11,282	80,455	5.78
Shibei District	933,602	1,020,715	87,113	9.33%	1,107,828	12,740	21,276	34,016	2,991	5,982	8,973	42,989	3.88
Shinan District	447,532	544,847	97,315	21.74%	642,162	7,385	12,333	19,718	1,734	3,468	5,202	24,919	3.88
	7,494,194	8,715,087	1,220,893	16.29%	9,935,980	146,057	243,915	389,972	26,827	53,654	80,481	470,454	4.73
Rizhao Prefecture													
Donggang District	920,511	920,511	0	0.00%	920,511	18,502	30,899	49,401	2,485	4,971	7,456	56,857	6.18
Juxian	1,034,519	995,552	-38,967	-3.77%	956,585	19,227	32,110	51,337	2,583	5,166	7,748	59,085	6.18
Lanshan District	400,067	400,067	0	0.00%	400,067	8,041	13,429	21,470	1,080	2,160	3,241	24,711	6.18
Wulian	503,219	484,883	-18,336	-3.64%	466,547	9,378	15,661	25,038	1,260	2,519	3,779	28,817	6.18
	2,685,928	2,801,013	-57,303	-2.13%	2,743,710	55,149	92,098	147,247	7,408	14,816	22,224	169,471	6.18
Tai'an Prefecture													
Daiyue District	922,491	975,380	52,889	5.73%	1,028,269	9,152	15,283	24,435	2,776	5,553	8,329	32,764	3.19
Dongping	725,877	741,566	15,689	2.16%	757,255	6,740	11,255	17,995	2,045	4,089	6,134	24,128	3.19
Feicheng City	948,602	946,627	-1,975	-0.21%	944,652	10,391	17,353	27,744	2,551	5,101	7,652	35,396	3.75
Ningyang	777,546	754,647	-22,899	-2.95%	731,748	6,513	10,876	17,389	1,976	3,951	5,927	23,316	3.19
Taishan District	615,720	760,045	144,325	23.44%	904,370	8,049	13,442	21,491	2,442	4,884	7,325	28,816	3.19
Xintai City	1,344,395	1,315,942	-28,453	-2.12%	1,287,489	14,549	24,296	38,845	3,476	6,952	10,429	49,273	3.83
	5,334,631	5,494,207	159,576	2.99%	5,653,783	55,392	92,505	147,898	15,265	30,530	45,796	193,693	3.43

| Shandong 山东 | POPULATION | | | | CHRISTIANS | | | | | | | | |
| | | | | | Evangelicals | | | Catholics | | | Total Christians | | |
County or City	Census 2000	Census 2010	Growth	Estimate 2020	TSPM	House church	TOTAL Evangelicals	CPA	House church	TOTAL Catholics	TOTAL	Percent of 2020 Population
Weifang Prefecture												
Anqiu	1,096,782	926,894	-169,888	-15.49%	9,160	15,297	24,457	2,044	4,088	6,132	30,588	4.04
Changle	593,009	615,910	22,901	3.86%	18,526	30,938	49,463	1,725	3,450	5,174	54,638	8.55
Changyi City	683,182	603,482	-79,700	-11.67%	6,181	10,322	16,502	1,414	2,828	4,243	20,745	3.96
Fangzi District	256,590	512,161	255,571	99.60%	22,264	37,181	59,445	2,073	4,146	6,219	65,664	8.55
Gaomi City	842,403	895,582	53,179	6.31%	10,816	18,063	28,878	2,562	5,123	7,685	36,563	3.85
Hanting District	355,945	424,106	68,161	19.15%	14,276	23,840	38,116	1,329	2,658	3,987	42,104	8.55
Kuiwen District	384,576	692,643	308,067	80.11%	29,217	48,464	77,485	2,702	5,404	8,106	85,591	8.55
Linqu	869,470	834,314	-35,156	-4.04%	23,176	38,703	61,879	2,158	4,315	6,473	68,352	8.55
Qingzhou City	894,468	940,355	45,887	5.13%	17,950	29,976	47,925	2,663	5,326	7,989	55,914	5.67
Shouguang City	1,081,991	1,139,454	57,463	5.31%	13,765	22,987	36,751	3,232	6,463	9,695	46,446	3.88
Weicheng District	383,189	415,118	31,929	8.33%	12,964	21,650	34,615	1,207	2,414	3,621	38,236	3.55
Zhucheng City	1,053,695	1,086,222	32,527	3.09%	18,012	30,080	48,092	3,021	6,041	9,062	57,154	5.11
	8,495,300	9,086,241	590,941	6.96%	196,108	327,501	523,609	26,128	52,257	78,385	601,994	5.22
Weihai Prefecture												
Huancui District	609,219	844,310	235,091	38.59%	14,788	24,696	39,483	2,914	5,829	8,743	48,227	4.47
Rongcheng City	732,147	714,355	-17,792	-2.43%	9,543	15,937	25,480	1,881	3,761	5,642	31,122	4.47
Rushan City	580,326	572,481	-7,845	-1.35%	6,493	10,844	17,337	1,525	3,049	4,574	21,911	3.88
Wendeng District	675,061	673,625	-1,436	-0.21%	6,991	11,675	18,665	1,815	3,630	5,445	24,110	3.59
	2,596,753	2,804,771	208,018	8.01%	37,815	63,151	100,965	8,135	16,269	24,404	125,369	4.16
Yantai Prefecture												
Changdao	52,890	44,025	-8,865	-16.76%	302	505	807	95	190	285	1,092	3.11
Fushan District	355,803	600,468	244,665	68.76%	7,268	12,138	19,406	2,282	4,564	6,846	26,252	3.11
Haiyang City	654,594	638,729	-15,865	-2.42%	7,724	12,898	20,622	1,682	3,363	5,045	25,667	4.12
Laishan District	181,963	329,304	147,341	80.97%	4,099	6,846	10,945	1,287	2,574	3,861	14,806	3.11
Laiyang City	897,681	878,591	-19,090	-2.13%	9,884	16,507	26,391	2,321	4,641	6,962	33,353	3.88
Laizhou City	889,361	883,896	-5,465	-0.61%	9,751	16,283	26,034	2,372	4,744	7,115	33,149	3.77
Longkou City	671,335	688,255	16,920	2.52%	6,911	11,541	18,452	1,904	3,808	5,712	24,164	3.43
Muping District	498,999	467,907	-31,092	-6.23%	3,757	6,274	10,030	1,179	2,359	3,538	13,568	3.11
Penglai City	500,408	451,109	-49,299	-9.85%	2,009	3,355	5,364	1,085	2,170	3,255	8,619	2.15
Qixia City	651,357	589,620	-61,737	-9.48%	6,229	10,402	16,631	1,425	2,851	4,276	20,907	3.96
Zhaoyuan City	593,705	566,244	-27,461	-4.63%	5,765	9,628	15,392	1,455	2,909	4,364	19,757	3.67
Zhifu District	687,639	830,054	142,415	20.71%	8,363	13,967	22,330	2,626	5,251	7,877	30,207	3.11
	6,635,735	6,968,202	332,467	5.01%	72,062	120,343	192,405	19,712	39,424	59,135	251,540	3.45

| Shandong 山东 | POPULATION | | | | CHRISTIANS | | | | | | Total Christians | |
| | | | | | Evangelicals | | | Catholics | | | | |
County or City	Census 2000	Census 2010	Growth	Estimate 2020	TSPM	House church	TOTAL Evangelicals	CPA	House church	TOTAL Catholics	TOTAL	Percent of 2020 Population
Zaozhuang Prefecture												
Shanting District	443,983	464,804	20,821	4.69%	485,625	5,488	9,164	14,652	1,311	2,622	3,934	18,585	3.83
Shizhong District	482,444	535,515	53,071	11.00%	588,586	6,651	11,107	17,758	1,589	3,178	4,768	22,526	3.83
Tai'erzhuang District	276,340	279,474	3,134	1.13%	282,608	3,193	5,333	8,527	763	1,526	2,289	10,816	3.83
Tengzhou City	1,548,817	1,603,659	54,842	3.54%	1,658,501	18,741	31,298	50,039	4,478	8,956	13,434	63,472	3.83
Xuecheng District	454,051	481,450	27,399	6.03%	508,849	5,750	9,602	15,352	1,374	2,748	4,122	19,474	3.83
Yicheng District	339,980	364,238	24,258	7.14%	388,496	4,390	7,331	11,721	1,049	2,098	3,147	14,868	3.83
	3,545,615	3,729,140	183,525	5.18%	3,912,665	44,213	73,836	118,049	10,564	21,128	31,693	149,742	3.83
Zibo Prefecture												
Boshan District	473,653	463,013	-10,640	-2.25%	452,373	3,302	5,515	8,817	1,221	2,443	3,664	12,481	2.76
Gaoqing	351,348	347,867	-3,481	-0.99%	344,386	2,514	4,198	6,712	930	1,860	2,790	9,502	2.76
Huantai	474,908	504,011	29,103	6.13%	533,114	3,892	6,499	10,391	1,439	2,879	4,318	14,709	2.76
Linzi District	607,189	642,831	35,642	5.87%	678,473	4,953	8,271	13,224	1,832	3,664	5,496	18,720	2.76
Yiyuan	540,695	549,491	8,796	1.63%	558,287	4,075	6,806	10,882	1,507	3,015	4,522	15,404	2.76
Zhangdian District	712,290	929,242	216,952	30.46%	1,146,194	8,367	13,973	22,340	3,095	6,189	9,284	31,625	2.76
Zhoucun District	327,169	362,294	35,125	10.74%	397,419	2,901	4,845	7,746	1,073	2,146	3,219	10,965	2.76
Zichuan District	697,178	731,848	34,670	4.97%	766,518	5,596	9,345	14,940	2,070	4,139	6,209	21,149	2.76
	4,184,430	4,530,597	346,167	8.27%	4,876,764	35,600	59,453	95,053	13,167	26,335	39,502	134,555	2.76
Totals	89,971,789	95,792,719	5,820,930	6.47%	101,613,649	1,529,569	2,884,204	4,413,773	280,719	561,439	842,158	5,255,931	5.17

Notes

The China Chronicles overview

1 R. Wardlaw Thompson, *Griffith John: The Story of Fifty Years in China* (London: The Religious Tract Society, 1908), p. 65.

Introduction

1 Paul Hattaway, *China's Unreached Cities*, Vol. 2 (Chiang Mai, Thailand: Asia Harvest, 2003), p. 72.

2 Norman H. Cliff, "Building the Protestant Church in Shandong, China," *International Journal of Missionary Research* (April 1998), p. 62.

3 Marco Polo, *The Travels of Marco Polo: The Complete Yule-Cordier Edition*, Vol. 2 (New York: Dover Publications, 1903), p. 154.

4 Leo J. Moser, *The Chinese Mosaic: The Peoples and Provinces of China* (Boulder, CO: Westview Press, 1985), p. 58.

5 Moser, *The Chinese Mosaic*, p. 59.

6 There were 100,000 Protestants in Shandong in 1949, according to *Global Chinese Ministries* (October 2003).

1860s

1 John J. Heeren, *On the Shantung Front: A History of the Shantung Mission of the Presbyterian Church* (New York: The Board of Foreign Missions of the Presbyterian Church in the United States of America, 1940), p. 36.

2 Heeren, *On the Shantung Front*, p. 39.

3 William Robson, *Griffith John: Founder of the Hankow Mission, Central China* (New York: Fleming Revell, 1890), p. 48.

4 Robson, *Griffith John*, p. 49.

5 Nicolas Standaert, *Handbook of Christianity in China, Volume One: 635–1800* (Leiden: Brill, 2001), p. 385.

6 *Chinese Recorder and Missionary Journal* (May 1880), p. 194.

7 Norman H. Cliff, "Building the Protestant Church in Shandong, China," *International Journal of Missionary Research* (April 1998), p. 63.

8 Winston Crawley, *Partners Across the Pacific: China and Southern Baptists, Into the Second Century* (Nashville, TN: Broadman Press, 1986), p. 49.

9 Norman Howard Cliff, "A History of the Protestant Movement in Shandong Province, China, 1859–1951" (PhD thesis, Univesity of Buckingham, 1994), p. 39.

10 G. Thompson Brown, *Earthen Vessels and Transcendent Power: American Presbyterians in China, 1837–1952* (Maryknoll, NY: Orbis Books, 1997), p. 54.

11 Brown, *Earthen Vessels and Transcendent Power*, p. 55.

12 Brown, *Earthen Vessels and Transcendent Power*, p. 56.

13 "The Late Emeute at Chi-Mi," *Chinese Recorder and Missionary Journal* (September 1874), p. 270.

14 "The Late Emeute at Chi-Mi," pp. 270–1.

15 Brown, *Earthen Vessels and Transcendent Power*, p. 78.

16 Daniel W. Fisher, *Calvin Wilson Mateer, Forty-Five Years a Missionary in Shantung, China* (Philadelphia, PA: Westminster Press, 1911), p. 121.

17 Fisher, *Calvin Wilson Mateer*, p. 121.

18 Fisher, *Calvin Wilson Mateer*, pp. 131–2.

19 Fisher, *Calvin Wilson Mateer*, pp. 317–18.

20 W. P. Bentley, *Illustrious Chinese Christians: Biographical Sketches* (Cincinnati, OH: The Standard Publishing Company, 1906), p. 183.

21 Bentley, *Illustrious Chinese Christians*, p. 184.

22 Bentley, *Illustrious Chinese Christians*, p. 188.

23 Bentley, *Illustrious Chinese Christians*, pp. 188–9.

24 Rev. J. Innocent, "In Memoriam, Rev. W. Nelthorpe Hall," *Chinese Recorder and Missionary Journal* (December 1878), p. 463.

1870s

1 John J. Heeren, *On the Shantung Front: A History of the Shantung Mission of the Presbyterian Church* (New York: The Board of Foreign Missions of the Presbyterian Church in the United States of America, 1940), p. 59.

2 *Missionary Record of the United Presbyterian Church* (January 1876).

3 "Statistics of the Shantung Protestant Missions," *Chinese Recorder and Missionary Journal* (September 1877), p. 380.

4 "Statistics of the Shantung Protestant Missions," pp. 380–1.

5 *China's Millions* (July 1888).

6 Norman H. Cliff, "Building the Protestant Church in Shandong, China," *International Journal of Missionary Research* (April 1998), p. 64.

7 Heeren, *On the Shantung Front*, p. 71.

8 American Presbyterian Mission, *The China Mission Hand-Book* (Shanghai: American Presbyterian Mission Press, 1879), p. 42.

9 Pat Barr, *To China with Love: The Lives and Times of Protestant*

Missionaries in China 1860–1900 (London: Secker & Warburg, 1972), pp. 44–5.

10 Timothy Richard, *Forty-Five Years in China: Reminiscences by Timothy Richard* (New York: Frederick A. Stokes, 1916), p. 157.

11 *China's Millions* (January 1879), p. 8.

12 "Christian Movement in the Province of Shantung," *Chinese Recorder and Missionary Journal* (August 1878), p. 282.

13 John L. Nevius, "Mission Work in Central Shantung," *Chinese Recorder and Missionary Journal* (October 1880), p. 357.

14 Hunter Corbett, "Shantung Presbytery," *Chinese Recorder and Missionary Journal* (January 1880), pp. 72–3.

1880s and 1890s

1 Hunter Corbett, "The Work of Protestant Missions in the Province of Shantung," *Chinese Recorder and Missionary Journal* (April 1881), p. 87.

2 Bertram Wolferstan, *The Catholic Church in China from 1860 to 1907* (London: Sands & Co., 1909), p. 451.

3 *Chinese Recorder and Missionary Journal* (November 1885), p. 434.

4 Miss Fosbery, "The Story of a Chinese Boy," *China's Millions* (March 1886), pp. 34–5.

5 Mr. Judd, "Baptisms at Ning-Hai, Shan-tung," *China's Millions* (September 1888), p. 114.

6 Mrs. Judd, "To the Poor the Gospel Is Preached," *China's Millions* (May 1889), p. 62.

7 Pat Barr, *To China with Love: The Lives and Times of Protestant Missionaries in China 1860–1900* (London: Secker & Warburg, 1972), p. 93.

8 Barr, *To China with Love*, p. 43.

9 Norman Howard Cliff, "A History of the Protestant Movement in Shandong Province, China, 1859–1951" (PhD thesis, University of Buckingham, 1994), pp. 204–5.

10 A. G. Jones, "The Poverty of Shantung, Its Causes and Treatment," *Chinese Recorder* (Vol. 25, No. 4, 1894), pp. 182–3.

11 *Chinese Recorder and Missionary Journal* (May 1891), p. 234.

12 *Chinese Recorder and Missionary Journal* (December 1890), pp. 578–9.

13 *Chinese Recorder and Missionary Journal* (November 1892), p. 542.

14 Norman H. Cliff, "Building the Protestant Church in Shandong, China," *International Journal of Missionary Research* (April 1998), p. 64.

The Boxer Rebellion

1 "Introducing the Jesus Family," *Bridge* (July–August 1992), p. 8.
2 Mrs. A. H. Mateer, *Siege Days: Personal Experiences of American Women and Children During the Peking Siege* (New York: Fleming H. Revell, 1903), p. 23.
3 Harold Irwin Cleveland, *Massacres of Christians by Heathen Chinese and Horrors of the Boxers* (New Haven, CT: Butler & Alger, 1900), p. 538.
4 Cleveland, *Massacres of Christians*, p. 539.
5 Cleveland, *Massacres of Christians*, p. 539.
6 Cleveland, *Massacres of Christians*, p. 539.
7 Isaac C. Ketler, *The Tragedy of Paotingfu: An Authentic Story of the Lives, Services, and Sacrifices of the Presbyterian, Congregational and China Inland Missionaries Who Suffered Martyrdom at Paotingfu, China, June 30th and July 1, 1900* (New York: Fleming H. Revell, 1902), p. 325.
8 Norman Howard Cliff, "A History of the Protestant Movement in Shandong Province, China, 1859–1951" (PhD thesis, University of Buckingham, 1994), pp. 210–11.
9 Cited in Cliff, "A History of the Protestant Movement in Shandong Province," p. 211.
10 Cliff, "A History of the Protestant Movement in Shandong Province," p. 134.
11 Luella Miner, *China's Book of Martyrs: A Record of Heroic Martyrdoms and Marvelous Deliverances of Chinese Christians During the Summer of 1900* (Philadelphia, PA: Westminster Press, 1903), pp. 165–6.
12 Miner, *China's Book of Martyrs*, p. 162.
13 James and Marti Hefley, *China! Christian Martyrs of the 20th Century* (Milford, MI: Mott Media, 1978), p. 32.
14 Miner, *China's Book of Martyrs*, p. 188.
15 Charlotte E. Hawes, *New Thrills in Old China* (New York: George H. Doran Company, 1913), p. 105.
16 See table in Cliff, "A History of the Protestant Movement in Shandong Province," p. 222.

1900s

1 *China's Millions* (September 1902), p. 124.
2 Louisa Vaughan, *Answered or Unanswered? Miracles of Faith in China* (Philadelphia, PA: Christian Life Publishing Fund, 1920), p. 1.
3 Vaughan, *Answered or Unanswered*, p. 4.
4 Vaughan, *Answered or Unanswered*, pp. 49–50.

5 Vaughan, *Answered or Unanswered*, pp. 54–5.

6 Vaughan, *Answered or Unanswered*, p. 7.

7 Vaughan, *Answered or Unanswered*, p. 42.

8 Vaughan, *Answered or Unanswered*, p. 45.

9 "The Blessing at Weihsien," *China's Millions* (January 1909), p. 6.

10 J. Edwin Orr, *Evangelical Awakenings in Eastern Asia* (Minneapolis, MN: Bethany House Publishers, 1975), p. 35.

11 T. N. Thompson, "Shantung," *Chinese Recorder and Missionary Journal* (June 1906), pp. 348–9.

12 T. N. Thompson, "The Revival Still Continued," *Chinese Recorder and Missionary Journal* (November 1906), pp. 646–7.

13 Jonathan Goforth, *By My Spirit* (Minneapolis, MN: Bethany House Publishers, 1942), p. 106.

14 "Mr. Goforth's Meetings at Tsingchowfu, Shantung," *Chinese Recorder and Missionary Journal* (April 1914), pp. 254–6.

15 H. W. Luke, "The Revival in Weihsien College," *Chinese Recorder and Missionary Journal* (August 1909), p. 474.

16 Goforth, *By My Spirit*, p. 107.

17 Goforth, *By My Spirit*, p. 107.

18 Goforth, *By My Spirit*, pp. 109–10.

19 Goforth, *By My Spirit*, p. 118.

20 Goforth, *By My Spirit*, p. 118.

21 Goforth, *By My Spirit*, p. 119.

Lottie Moon

1 Catherine B. Allen, *The New Lottie Moon Story* (Nashville, TN: Broadman Press, 1980), p. 84.

2 Ruth A. Tucker, *From Jerusalem to Irian Jaya: A Biographical History of Christian Missions* (Grand Rapids, MI: Zondervan, 1983), p. 237.

3 Janet and Geoff Bende, *Lottie Moon: Giving Her All for China* (Seattle, WA: YWAM Publishing, 2015), p. 129.

4 Tucker, *From Jerusalem to Irian Jaya*, pp. 235–6.

5 Tucker, *From Jerusalem to Irian Jaya*, p. 235.

6 Bende, *Lottie Moon*, p. 80.

7 Irwin T. Hyatt, *Our Ordered Lives Confess: Three Nineteenth-Century American Missionaries in East Shantung* (Cambridge, MA: Harvard University Press, 1976), pp. 49–50.

8 Hyatt, *Our Ordered Lives Confess*, p. 4.

9 Hyatt, *Our Ordered Lives Confess*, p. 45.

10 Bende, *Lottie Moon*, p. 136.

11 Bende, *Lottie Moon*, p. 138.
12 Tucker, *From Jerusalem to Irian Jaya*, p. 236.
13 John Woodbridge (ed.), *More Than Conquerors: Portraits of Believers from All Walks of Life* (Chicago: Moody Press, 1992), p. 60.
14 Bende, *Lottie Moon*, p. 139.
15 Bende, *Lottie Moon*, p. 148.
16 Allen, *The New Lottie Moon Story*, p. 287.
17 William R. Estep, *Whole Gospel Whole World: The Foreign Mission Board of the Southern Baptist Convention 1845–1995* (Nashville, TN: Broadman & Holman, 1994), p. 150.
18 Mary K. Crawford, *The Shantung Revival* (Shanghai: The China Baptist Publication Society, 1933), p. 35.

1910s

1 T. W. Ayers, "In Memoriam—A Great Missionary Fallen," *Chinese Recorder and Missionary Journal* (February 1912), p. 105.
2 Ayers, "In Memoriam," p. 104.
3 Charles Ernest Scott, *Answered Prayer in China: Some Prayer-Experiences of Present-Day Chinese Christians* (Philadelphia, PA: Sunday School Times Company, 1923), p. 127.
4 Scott, *Answered Prayer in China*, p. 127.
5 Scott, *Answered Prayer in China*, p. 131.
6 Scott, *Answered Prayer in China*, p. 134.
7 Mrs. Botham, "Of Such Is the Kingdom of Heaven," *China's Millions* (March 1914), p. 46.
8 Scott, *Answered Prayer in China*, pp. 203–5.

1920s

1 *China's Millions* (November 1905).
2 Milton T. Stauffer (ed.), *The Christian Occupation of China* (Shanghai: China Continuation Committee, 1922), p. 204.
3 Stauffer, *The Christian Occupation of China*, p. 202.
4 Gustav Carlberg, *China in Revival* (Rock Island, IL: Augustana Book Concern, 1936), p. 21.
5 Charles Ernest Scott, *Answered Prayer in China: Some Prayer-Experiences of Present-Day Chinese Christians* (Philadelphia, PA: Sunday School Times Company, 1923), p. 54.
6 Scott, *Answered Prayer in China*, pp. 57–64.

7 Valerie Griffiths, *Not Less Than Everything: The Courageous Women Who Carried the Christian Gospel to China* (Oxford: Monarch Books, 2004), p. 263.

8 Bertha Smith, *Go Home and Tell: How Answered Prayer Undergirded an Adventurous Witness in China* (Nashville, TN: Broadman Press, 1965), p. 39.

9 Griffiths, *Not Less Than Everything*, p. 258.

10 J. Edwin Orr, *Evangelical Awakenings in Eastern Asia* (Minneapolis, MN: Bethany House Publishers, 1975), p. 70.

11 Norman H. Cliff, "Building the Protestant Church in Shandong, China," *International Journal of Missionary Research* (April 1998), p. 67.

12 Paul Stephen Dykstra, *Triumphs of His Grace in Shantung, China* (Los Angeles: Angelus Temple, 1936), pp. 12–13.

13 Dykstra, *Triumphs of His Grace in Shantung*, pp. 12–13.

14 Dykstra, *Triumphs of His Grace in Shantung*, p. 16.

15 C. L. Culpepper, *The Shantung Revival* (Dallas, TX: Evangelism Division, Baptist General Convention of Texas, n.d.), p. 46.

16 Culpepper, *The Shantung Revival*, pp. 46–7.

17 Dykstra, *Triumphs of His Grace in Shantung*, p. 35.

Marie Monsen

1 C. L. Culpepper, *The Shantung Revival* (Dallas, TX: Evangelism Division, Baptist General Convention of Texas, n.d.), p. 19.

2 Culpepper, *The Shantung Revival*, p. 19.

3 Valerie Griffiths, *Not Less Than Everything: The Courageous Women Who Carried the Christian Gospel to China* (Oxford: Monarch Books, 2004), p. 261.

4 Culpepper, *The Shantung Revival*, p. 23.

5 F. Strauss, H. D. Hayward and M. Monsen, *We Are Escaped* (London: China Inland Mission, 1931).

6 Gustav Carlberg, *China in Revival* (Rock Island, IL: Augustana Book Concern, 1936), p. 77.

7 Carlberg, *China in Revival*, p. 78.

8 Carlberg, *China in Revival*, p. 80.

9 Carlberg, *China in Revival*, p. 82.

10 Carlberg, *China in Revival*, p. 120.

11 Griffiths, *Not Less Than Everything*, p. 257.

1930s

1 C. L. Culpepper, *The Shantung Revival* (Dallas, TX: Evangelism Division, Baptist General Convention of Texas, n.d.), p. 62.

2 Gustav Carlberg, *China in Revival* (Rock Island, IL: Augustana Book Concern, 1936), pp. 120–1.

3 Eloise Glass Cauthen, *Higher Ground: Biography of Wiley B. Glass, Missionary to China* (Nashville, TN: Broadman Press, 1978), p. 152.

4 Culpepper, *The Shantung Revival*, p. 27.

5 Culpepper, *The Shantung Revival*, pp. 63–4.

6 Culpepper, *The Shantung Revival*, p. 65.

7 Mary K. Crawford, *The Shantung Revival* (Shanghai: The China Baptist Publication Society, 1933), pp. 79–80.

8 Crawford, *The Shantung Revival*, pp. 88–9.

9 Crawford, *The Shantung Revival*, pp. 41–2.

10 Culpepper, *The Shantung Revival*, p. 73.

11 Crawford, *The Shantung Revival*, p. 57.

12 Culpepper, *The Shantung Revival*, p. 66.

13 Culpepper, *The Shantung Revival*, pp. 31–3.

14 Culpepper, *The Shantung Revival*, pp. 33–4.

15 Crawford, *The Shantung Revival*, pp. 35–6.

16 Culpepper, *The Shantung Revival*, p. 42.

17 Culpepper, *The Shantung Revival*, p. 43.

18 Crawford, *The Shantung Revival*, pp. 26–7.

19 Culpepper, *The Shantung Revival*, p. 44.

20 Culpepper, *The Shantung Revival*, p. 45.

21 Culpepper, *The Shantung Revival*, p. 45.

22 Carlberg, *China in Revival*, pp. 123–4.

23 Culpepper, *The Shantung Revival*, pp. 35–6.

24 Culpepper, *The Shantung Revival*, p. 40.

25 Paul Stephen Dykstra, *Triumphs of His Grace in Shantung, China* (Los Angeles: Angelus Temple, 1936), p. 34.

26 Culpepper, *The Shantung Revival*, p. 63.

27 Norman H. Cliff, *Fierce the Conflict: The Moving Stories of How Eight Chinese Christians Suffered for Jesus Christ and Remained Faithful* (Dundas, Canada: Joshua Press, 2001), p. 156.

The Evangelistic Bands

1 Mary K. Crawford, *The Shantung Revival* (Shanghai: The China Baptist Publication Society, 1933), p. 31.
2 Andrew Gih, *Launch Out into the Deep* (London: Marshall, Morgan & Scott, 1938), p. 43.
3 Gih, *Launch Out into the Deep*, p. 44.
4 J. Edwin Orr, *Evangelical Awakenings in Eastern Asia* (Minneapolis, MN: Bethany House Publishers, 1975), p. 70.
5 Leslie T. Lyall, *A Biography of John Sung: Flame for God in the Far East* (London: China Inland Mission, 1954), p. 107.
6 Angus Kinnear, *Against the Tide: The Story of Watchman Nee* (Wheaton, IL: Tyndale House, 1987), p. 146.
7 Lyall, *A Biography of John Sung*, p. 68.
8 Lyall, *A Biography of John Sung*, p. 70.
9 Lyall, *A Biography of John Sung*, p. 150.
10 Paul Stephen Dykstra, *Triumphs of His Grace in Shantung, China* (Los Angeles: Angelus Temple, 1936), p. 33.
11 Dykstra, *Triumphs of His Grace in Shantung*, p. 20.

1940s

1 H. R. Williamson, *British Baptists in China, 1845–1952* (London: Carey Kingsgate Press, 1957), p. 158.
2 L. C. Osborn, *The China Story: The Church of the Nazarene in China, South China, and Taiwan* (Kansas City, MO: Nazarene Publishing House, 1969), p. 25.
3 Osborn, *The China Story*, p. 27.
4 John Woodbridge (ed.), *More Than Conquerors: Portraits of Believers from All Walks of Life* (Chicago: Moody Press, 1992), p. 223.
5 Woodbridge, *More Than Conquerors*, p. 223.
6 Norman Cliff, *Prisoners of the Samurai: Japanese Civilian Camps in China, 1941–1945* (Rainham, Essex: Courtyard Publishers, 1998), p. 81.
7 "Eric Liddell Memorialized in Weifang," *China News and Church Report* (June 1991).

The Jesus Family

1 D. Vaughan Rees, *The 'Jesus Family' in Communist China: A Modern Miracle of New Testament Christianity* (Exeter: Paternoster Press, 1959), p. 37.

2 Rees, *The 'Jesus Family' in Communist China*, p. 39.
3 Norman Howard Cliff, "A History of the Protestant Movement in Shandong Province, China, 1859–1951" (PhD thesis, University of Buckingham, 1994), pp. 67–9.
4 Paul E. Kauffman, *Confucius, Mao and Christ* (Hong Kong: Asian Outreach, 1975), p. 95.
5 "Introducing the Jesus Family," *Bridge* (July–August 1992), p. 11.
6 Gustav Carlberg, *China in Revival* (Rock Island, IL: Augustana Book Concern, 1936), p. 236.
7 Kauffman, *Confucius, Mao and Christ*, p. 95.
8 "The Taste of the Jesus Family," *Tangent* (April 21, 1951).
9 *Tianfeng* (March 23, 1953).
10 Cliff, "A History of the Protestant Movement in Shandong Province," p. 66.
11 Cliff, "A History of the Protestant Movement in Shandong Province," p. 70.
12 "More About the Jesus Family," *Bridge* (July–August 1993), p. 11.
13 "More About the Jesus Family," p. 11.
14 *China Prayer Letter* (No. 83, July 1987).
15 "Tracing the Jesus Family," *Amity News Service* (March 1995).
16 *Pray for China* (January–February 1994).
17 *China Study Journal* (Vol. 16, No. 3, December 2001), pp. 21–2.
18 Eugene Bach, *Back to Jerusalem: The 30 Day Devotional* (Lumberton, MS: Back to Jerusalem), p. 147.
19 Bach, *Back to Jerusalem*, pp. 147–8.

1950s

1 Norman Howard Cliff, *Fierce the Conflict: The Moving Stories of How Eight Chinese Christians Suffered for Jesus Christ and Remained Faithful* (Dundas, Canada: Joshua Press, 2001), p. 153.
2 Cliff, *Fierce the Conflict*, p. 158.
3 D. Vaughan Rees, *The 'Jesus Family' in Communist China: A Modern Miracle of New Testament Christianity* (Exeter: Paternoster Press, 1959), pp. 72–3.
4 Rees, *The 'Jesus Family' in Communist China*, p. 73.
5 Rees, *The 'Jesus Family' in Communist China*, p. 85.
6 This testimony was told to the author by a senior house church leader, March 2002.
7 Also known as the Northwest Evangelistic Band.

8 Guang, "God's Messengers in Xinjiang," *Bridge* (October–November 1988), p. 16.

9 Paul Hattaway, *Back to Jerusalem: God's Call to the Chinese Church to Complete the Great Commission* (Carlisle: Piquant, 2003), p. 49.

10 Guang, "God's Messengers in Xinjiang," p. 17.

11 Guang, "God's Messengers in Xinjiang," p. 18.

12 Irene Hanson, *The Wheelbarrow and the Comrade* (Chicago: Moody Press, 1973), p. 160.

13 Hanson, *The Wheelbarrow and the Comrade*, pp. 179–80.

14 Hanson, *The Wheelbarrow and the Comrade*, p. 169.

15 Caroline Liou et al., *China* (Hawthorn, Australia: Lonely Planet Publications, 2000, 7th edn), p. 40.

1960s

1 Jonathan Chao (ed.), *The China Mission Handbook: A Portrait of China and Its Church* (Hong Kong: Chinese Church Research Center, 1989), p. 125.

2 Jonathan Chao, *Wise as Serpents, Harmless as Doves* (Pasadena, CA: William Carey Library, 1988), pp. 114–15.

3 Name has been changed for security reasons.

4 Personal interview with Pastor Tian's son, September 2001; published in Hattaway, *China's Unreached Cities*, Vol. 2 (Chiang Mai, Thailand: Asia Harvest, 2003), pp. 52–3; and *The Commission* (June 2002), p. 29.

5 Zhang Jiakun, "I Flunked" (Love China Ministries International: unpublished translation of Zhang's article written from prison in 1972).

6 *Global Chinese Ministries* (October 2003).

7 Leslie T. Lyall, *Red Sky at Night: Communism Confronts Christianity in China* (London: Hodder & Stoughton, 1969), p. 43.

1970s

1 Personal communication with the Chang family, September 2016.

1980s

1 Leslie T. Lyall, *God Reigns in China* (London: Hodder & Stoughton, 1985), p. 175.

2 *Pray for China* (March–April 1985).

3 Paul E. Kauffman, *Piecing Together the China Puzzle* (Hong Kong: Asian Outreach, 1987), p. 152.

4 For a gripping account of how this Bible delivery succeeded, see Brother David with Paul Hattaway, *Project Pearl: The One Million Smuggled Bibles that Changed China* (Oxford: Monarch Books, 2007).

5 Brother David, *Project Pearl*, p. 263.

6 Letter to Open Doors, July 1981.

7 *Asian Report* (Vol. 12, No. 2, March–April 1990).

8 *Asian Report* (Vol. 12, No. 2, March–April 1990).

9 Danyun, *Lilies Amongst Thorns* (Tonbridge, Kent: Sovereign World Books, 1981), p. 319.

10 Danyun, *Lilies Amongst Thorns*, p. 320.

11 Danyun, *Lilies Amongst Thorns*, p. 321.

1990s

1 *China Prayer Letter and Ministry Report* (No. 130, September–October 1993).

2 Brother Yun with Paul Hattaway, *The Heavenly Man: The Remarkable True Story of Chinese Christian Brother Yun* (London: Monarch Books, 2002), pp. 227–9.

3 *Asian Report* (Vol. 29, No. 4, May 1996).

4 *Asian Report* (Vol. 29, No. 4, May 1996).

5 "Tracing the Jesus Family," *Amity News Service* (March 1995).

6 Pastors with the government-sanctioned Three-Self Church in China are generally not permitted to preach from the book of Revelation.

7 From a report on The Committee for the Investigation of Persecution of Religion in China website: <www.china21.org>.

8 *Bridge* (August 1994).

9 *China News and Church Report* (June 16, 1995).

10 UCAN (April 24, 2000).

11 Amity News Service (January 1998).

12 *Global Chinese Ministries* (October 2003).

13 Amity News Service (September 1997).

14 Far East Broadcasting, January 1990.

15 Far East Broadcasting, November 1991.

16 Far East Broadcasting, June 1992.

17 Far East Broadcasting, December 1992.

18 Far East Broadcasting, March 1993.

19 Far East Broadcasting, May 1993.

20 Far East Broadcasting, July 1993.

21 *Tianfeng* (August 1993).
22 Far East Broadcasting, March 1995.
23 Far East Broadcasting, March 1995.
24 Far East Broadcasting, January 1996.
25 Far East Broadcasting, August 1996.
26 Far East Broadcasting, February 1997.
27 *Compass Direct* (December 1997).
28 Far East Broadcasting, March 1998.
29 Far East Broadcasting, June 1998.
30 Far East Broadcasting, October 1998.
31 Trans World Radio, November 1998.
32 *Lift Up Our Holy Hands* (January 1999).
33 Far East Broadcasting, July 1999.
34 Far East Broadcasting, November 1999.

2000s

1 Personal interview with Sister Ding, March 2001.
2 *The Challenge of China* (Issue 1, 2002).
3 *China Prayer Letter and Ministry Report* (No. 130, September–October 1993).
4 Chinese Christian Church of Saipan, "China's Cult of Satan Lightning of the East" (Saipan, Guam: September 2000).
5 *China Study Journal* (April 2001).
6 Far East Broadcasting, July 2002.
7 *Lift Up Our Holy Hands* (August 2002).
8 Letters from a Shandong house church leader to Asia Harvest, 2013.
9 "House-Church Christian Dies in Custody," *Christianity Today* (February 2004).
10 Bob Fu with Nancy French, *God's Double Agent: The True Story of a Christian's Fight for Freedom* (Grand Rapids, MI: Baker Books, 2013), p. 110.
11 Personal interview with Bob Fu, April 2002.
12 Personal interview with Bob Fu, April 2002.
13 Personal interview with Bob Fu, April 2002.
14 Far East Broadcasting, May 2000.
15 Far East Broadcasting, June 2000.
16 Far East Broadcasting, September 2000.
17 Far East Broadcasting, December 2000.
18 Overseas Missionary Fellowship, February 2001.
19 *Compass Direct* (May 2001).

20 *Compass Direct* (June 2002).
21 Far East Broadcasting, February 2003.
22 Far East Broadcasting, September 2003.
23 *Compass Direct* (December 2004).
24 *Antioch Missions* (July 2006).

2010s

1 Letter from a senior Shandong house church leader to Asia Harvest, 2011.
2 Letter from a senior Shandong house church leader to Asia Harvest, 2012.
3 Letter from an evangelist in Shandong to Asia Harvest, 2013.
4 Letters from Shandong house church leaders to Asia Harvest, 2016.
5 Katie Hope, "Firm Faith: The Company Bosses Who Pray," BBC News (July 6, 2015).
6 Personal communication with a Shandong house church leader, September 2016.
7 Personal communication from a Shandong house church leader, September 2016.
8 Personal communication from a Shandong house church leader, November 2016.

Selected bibliography

Allen, Catherine B., *The New Lottie Moon Story* (Nashville, TN: Broadman Press, 1980).

American Presbyterian Mission, *The China Mission Hand-Book* (Shanghai: American Presbyterian Mission Press, 1879).

Barr, Pat, *To China with Love: The Lives and Times of Protestant Missionaries in China 1860–1900* (London: Secker & Warburg, 1972).

Bende, Janet and Geoff, *Lottie Moon: Giving Her All for China* (Seattle, WA: YWAM Publishing, 2015).

Bentley, W. P., *Illustrious Chinese Christians: Biographical Sketches* (Cincinnati, OH: The Standard Publishing Company, 1906).

Brown, G. Thompson, *Earthen Vessels and Transcendent Power: American Presbyterians in China, 1837–1952* (Maryknoll, NY: Orbis Books, 1997).

Burt, E. W., *Fifty Years in China: The Story of the Baptist Mission in Shantung, Shansi and Shensi, 1875–1925* (London: Carey Press, 1925).

Carlberg, Gustav, *China in Revival* (Rock Island, IL: Augustana Book Concern, 1936).

Cauthen, Baker J., *Advance: A History of Southern Baptist Foreign Missions* (Nashville, TN: Broadman Press, 1970).

Cauthen, Eloise Glass, *Higher Ground: Biography of Wiley B. Glass, Missionary to China* (Nashville, TN: Broadman Press, 1978).

Chao, Jonathan, *Wise as Serpents, Harmless as Doves* (Pasadena, CA: William Carey Library, 1988).

Cleveland, Harold Irwin, *Massacres of Christians by Heathen Chinese and Horrors of the Boxers* (New Haven, CT: Butler & Alger, 1900).

Cliff, Norman Howard, *Fierce the Conflict: The Moving Stories of How Eight Chinese Christians Suffered for Jesus Christ and Remained Faithful* (Dundas, Canada: Joshua Press, 2001).

——, "A History of the Protestant Movement in Shandong Province, China, 1859–1951" (PhD thesis, University of Buckingham, 1994).

——, *Prisoners of the Samurai: Japanese Civilian Camps in China, 1941–1945* (Rainham, Essex: Courtyard Publishers, 1998).

Corbett, Hunter; W. F. Seymour et al., *A Record of American Presbyterian Mission Work in Shantung Province, 1861–1913* (Shanghai: American Presbyterian Mission Press, 1913).

Craighead, James R. E., *Hunter Corbett, Fifty-Six Years Missionary to China* (New York: Revell Press, 1921).

Crawford, Mary K., *The Shantung Revival* (Shanghai: The China Baptist Publication Society, 1933).

Crawley, Winston, *Partners Across the Pacific: China and Southern Baptists, Into the Second Century* (Nashville, TN: Broadman Press, 1986).

Culpepper, C. L., *The Shantung Revival* (Dallas, TX: Evangelism Division, Baptist General Convention of Texas, n.d.).

Danyun, *Lilies Amongst Thorns* (Tonbridge, Kent: Sovereign World Books, 1981).

David, Brother; with Paul Hattaway, *Project Pearl: The One Million Smuggled Bibles that Changed China* (Oxford: Monarch Books, 2007).

Dykstra, Paul Stephen, *Triumphs of His Grace in Shantung, China* (Los Angeles: Angelus Temple, 1936).

Estep, William R., *Whole Gospel Whole World: The Foreign Mission Board of the Southern Baptist Convention 1845–1995* (Nashville, TN: Broadman & Holman, 1994).

Fisher, Daniel W., *Calvin Wilson Mateer, Forty-Five Years a Missionary in Shantung, China* (Philadelphia, PA: Westminster Press, 1911).

Foster, L. S., *Fifty Years in China: An Eventful Memoir of Tarleton Perry Crawford* (Nashville, TN: Bayless-Pullen, 1909).

Fu, Bob; with Nancy French, *God's Double Agent: The True Story of a Christian's Fight for Freedom* (Grand Rapids, MI: Baker Books, 2013).

Gih, Andrew, *Launch Out into the Deep* (London: Marshall, Morgan & Scott, 1938).

Glover, Rev. Richard and Rev. B. Reeve, *Timothy Richard, DD: China Missionary, Statesman and Reformer* (London: S. W. Partridge & Co., 1911).

Goforth, Jonathan, *By My Spirit* (Minneapolis, MN: Bethany House Publishers, 1942).

Griffiths, Valerie, *Not Less Than Everything: The Courageous Women Who Carried the Christian Gospel to China* (Oxford: Monarch Books, 2004).

Hanson, Irene, *The Wheelbarrow and the Comrade* (Chicago: Moody Press, 1973).

Hattaway, Paul, *Back to Jerusalem: God's Call to the Chinese Church to Complete the Great Commission* (Carlisle: Piquant, 2003).

——, *China's Unreached Cities*, Vol. 2 (Chiang Mai, Thailand: Asia Harvest, 2003).

Heeren, John J., *On the Shantung Front: A History of the Shantung Mission of the Presbyterian Church* (New York: The Board of Foreign Missions of the Presbyterian Church in the United States of America, 1940).

Hefley, James and Marti, *China! Christian Martyrs of the 20th Century* (Milford, MI: Mott Media, 1978).

Hyatt, Irwin T., *Our Ordered Lives Confess: Three Nineteenth-Century American Missionaries in East Shantung* (Cambridge, MA: Harvard University Press, 1976).

Johnson, Eunice V., *Timothy Richard's Vision: Education and Reform in China, 1880–1910* (Eugene, OR: Pickwick Publications, 2014).

Kauffman, Paul E., *Confucius, Mao and Christ* (Hong Kong: Asian Outreach, 1975).

——, *Piecing Together the China Puzzle* (Hong Kong: Asian Outreach, 1987).

Lawrence, Una Roberts, *Lottie Moon* (Nashville, TN: The Sunday School Board of the Southern Baptist Convention, 1927).

Lyall, Leslie T., *A Biography of John Sung: Flame for God in the Far East* (London: China Inland Mission, 1954).

——, *God Reigns in China* (London: Hodder & Stoughton, 1985).

——, *Red Sky at Night: Communism Confronts Christianity in China* (London: Hodder & Stoughton, 1969).

Martin, S. G., *Chefoo School, 1881–1951* (Braunton, Devon: Merlin Books, 1990).

Miner, Luella, *China's Book of Martyrs: A Record of Heroic Martyrdoms and Marvelous Deliverances of Chinese Christians During the Summer of 1900* (Philadelphia, PA: Westminster Press, 1903).

Monsen, Marie, *The Awakening: Revival in China, a Work of the Holy Spirit 1927–1937* (London: China Inland Mission, 1961).

——, *A Present Help* (London: China Inland Mission, 1960).

Monsen, M. et al., *We Are Escaped* (London: China Inland Mission, 1931).

Moser, Leo J., *The Chinese Mosaic: The Peoples and Provinces of China* (Boulder, CO: Westview Press, 1985).

Mungello, D. E., *The Spirit and the Flesh in Shandong, 1650–1785* (Lanham, MD: Rowman & Littlefield, 2001).

Orr, J. Edwin, *Evangelical Awakenings in Eastern Asia* (Minneapolis, MN: Bethany House Publishers, 1975).

Osborn, L. C., *The China Story: The Church of the Nazarene in China, South China, and Taiwan* (Kansas City, MO: Nazarene Publishing House, 1969).

Owens, Donald, *The Church Behind the Bamboo Curtain: The Story of the Church Inside Red China* (Kansas City, MO: Nazarene Publishing House, 1973).

Price Evans, E. W., *Timothy Richard: A Narrative of Christian Enterprise and Statesmanship in China* (London: S. W. Partridge & Co., 1912).

Selected bibliography

Rees, D. Vaughan, *The 'Jesus Family' in Communist China: A Modern Miracle of New Testament Christianity* (Exeter: Paternoster Press, 1959).

Richard, Timothy, *Forty-Five Years in China: Reminiscences by Timothy Richard* (New York: Frederick A. Stokes, 1916).

Scott, Charles Ernest, *Answered Prayer in China: Some Prayer-Experiences of Present-Day Chinese Christians* (Philadelphia, PA: Sunday School Times Company, 1923).

Smith, Bertha, *Go Home and Tell: How Answered Prayer Undergirded an Adventurous Witness in China* (Nashville, TN: Broadman Press, 1965).

Stauffer, Milton T. (ed.), *The Christian Occupation of China* (Shanghai: China Continuation Committee, 1922).

Thomson, D. P., *Eric H. Liddell: Athlete and Missionary* (Crieff, Scotland: Research Unit, 1971).

Tucker, Ruth A., *From Jerusalem to Irian Jaya: A Biographical History of Christian Missions* (Grand Rapids, MI: Zondervan, 1983).

Vaughan, Louisa, *Answered or Unanswered? Miracles of Faith in China* (Philadelphia, PA: Christian Life Publishing Fund, 1920).

Williamson, H. R., *British Baptists in China, 1845–1952* (London: Carey Kingsgate Press, 1957).

Woodbridge, John (ed.), *More Than Conquerors: Portraits of Believers from All Walks of Life* (Chicago: Moody Press, 1992).

Wright, M. E., *The Missionary Work of the Southern Baptist Convention* (Philadelphia, PA: American Baptist Publication Society, 1902).

Yun, Brother; with Paul Hattaway, *The Heavenly Man: The Remarkable True Story of Chinese Christian Brother Yun* (London: Monarch Books, 2002).

Contact details

————•◦•————

Paul Hattaway is the founder and director of Asia Harvest, a non-denominational ministry that serves the Church in Asia through various strategic initiatives, including Bible printing and supporting Asian missionaries who share the gospel among unreached peoples.

The author can be reached by email at <**paul@asiaharvest. org**>, or by writing to him via any of the addresses listed below.

For more than 30 years Asia Harvest has served the Church in Asia through strategic projects that equip the local churches. At the time of going to print, Asia Harvest has successfully distributed more than 875,000 Bibles to house church Christians in Shandong Province, in addition to supporting many evangelists and providing aid to hundreds of persecuted church leaders and their families.

If you would like to receive the free Asia Harvest newsletter or to order other volumes in The China Chronicles series or Paul's other books, please visit <**www.asiaharvest.org**> or write to the address below nearest you:

Asia Harvest USA and Canada
353 Jonestown Rd #320
Winston-Salem, NC 27104
USA

Asia Harvest Australia
36 Nelson Street
Stepney, SA 5069
Australia

Asia Harvest New Zealand
PO Box 1757
Queenstown, 9348
New Zealand

Asia Harvest UK and Ireland
c/o AsiaLink
PO Box 891
Preston PR4 9AB
United Kingdom

Asia Harvest Europe
c/o Stiftung SALZ
Tailfinger Str. 28
71083 Herrenberg
Germany